C·

# Goodbye Buenos Aires

ANDREW GRAHAM-YOOLL

ELAND
London

First published in Spanish by Daniel Divinsky, at Ediciones de la Flor, Buenos Aires, 1997.

First English edition published by John Lucas at Shoestring Press, Nottingham, England, in 1999.

This edition first published by Eland Publishing Ltd, 61 Exmouth Market, London EC1R 4QL in 2011

ISBN 978 1 906011 70 3

Cover photograph: *Calle Florida* by Horacio Coppola © Courtesy of Jorge Mara – La Ruche Gallery

*In memory of Douglas Noel Graham-Yooll and of
Ines Louise Tovar and with thanks to my sister,
Joanne Graham-Yooll*

# Contents

'I don't see much difference between an autobiography and a novel.'

Christopher Isherwood to Michael Davie
From *Christopher Isherwood Diaries: Volume One (1939-1960)*,
ed. Katherine Bucknell (Methuen, London 1996)

# *Introduction: 1918-1928*

THIS IS A STORY I wanted to tell you. It is my father's story, mostly; it is written as he told it to me, in some ways. This is how his times were and the way I think they should be told. By this means he will survive me. Thus together we can make up for his early death.

My father's is the story of Argentina, of the end of Empire; an empire built by small countries to make a strong nation and by men who knew that hard work left no time to make money but only made rich men richer.

All the characters in these pages are real, distorted by memory, influenced by imagined recollections. All the situations are true, yet none of them need to be believed. This might cause some confusion. For what we understand is not true we call fiction, and what we do not believe we call fantasy. Such rules are clear. To alter them could give rise to mistaken impressions. This record has to be so.

This is a novel which claims to be the truth, sometimes.

The starting time is in a golden age of English influence in Argentina. It is English. It is not Scottish or Welsh, or anything else, because English is what people in Argentina called it. The *ingleses* were superior. That age is in part memory alone. Hence the events are recreated with a dash of whim by which many people recalled that they were part of events. Many thought that they were actors with a role to play.

My father was one of those many. The English, Scots and Welsh, and the US citizens, and the Canadians and Australians too, of that period at the start of the twentieth century in South America had much in their favour. It was enough for a man, and especially for a woman, to speak English to feel better than the others. England was at the centre of the world. That time of rich memory and impoverished reality also had the possibility of adventure in places remote from conventional society.

People dreamed of a chance of success without too much work, of the titillation of moderate danger, and yet they seemed fully aware of an approaching apocalypse leading to a future crash. For 'Anglo-Argentina', an expatriate state in which people were constantly escaping from the surrounding reality, and for the literary genre named *Southamericana*, that era, of commercial success, personal escapades and English-speaking pre-eminence, began in 1918. The period was intense and short.

That time began at the end of the First World War. On 2 October 1918, *The Times* printed a report from its Buenos Aires correspondent that showed just how 'European' Argentina wanted to feel:

Argentine joy at Allied victory. Buenos Aires, July 25: When brought into contact with the everyday life of Buenos Aires, it is difficult to believe that one is breathing a neutral atmosphere. Allied flags are everywhere; practically the entire Press rejoices with open enthusiasm at the news of Allied victory, and the Fourteenth of July was marked by a gigantic procession, which passed along profusely beflagged streets... When the news first arrived here of the dramatic turn of fortune on the Marne and the rolling back of the Hun forces, I was walking down the Calle Florida, the principal street of Buenos Aires. Newspaper boys were shouting the latest developments with enthusiasm...

European immigration and farming exports had made Buenos Aires one of the great cities of the world in under three decades. It was an attractive destination for expatriation. Think of a Europe blacked-out by war, sickness and poverty, trying to put behind it the enormous grief of long and bloody battles. Then imagine a Buenos Aires of bright lights twinkling, with the magic of wealth and new opportunities, without grief.

As recently as the end of the nineteenth century Buenos Aires had been a small town. The guide books had still been able to inventory facilities available in the urban centre that was to become a capital.

George Newnes's 1895 book, *From London Bridge to Charing Cross Via Yokohama and Chicago*, described the city as a large village. He listed four Protestant and twenty-five Catholic churches, eighty-three streets, twenty markets, fifty-five clubs, fifteen hotels, 322 schools and a fire brigade of seven companies. Helpfully, Newnes wrote:

In all parts of the city, and more especially in the vicinity of the Boca, there are numerous 'conventillos' or common lodging houses in which human beings are crowded together in a manner unknown in the worst slums of London. Some of these dreadful rookeries contain as many as 150 to 200 apartments... The air was deafened by the hiss and creak and rattle of machinery, trains, and lumbering vehicles; the hooting of tram horns, the shrill whistle of the police, the hum of myriads of insects, the incessant lurking of villainous dogs, and above all the peculiar, metallic, ear-splitting chirp of the tree frogs... The appearance of the city is monotonous and dismal, the majority of the streets being only forty feet wide, with high houses, and each bloc, or 'manzana', covering an area of about four acres.

But the gleam of something better was there. 'Very cosmopolitan are the crowds on the streets of pleasure-loving Buenos Ayres. Most people are dressed in European fashion, but large numbers of Basques and Italians wear their national costumes: moreover, the poorer classes of Argentine women still wear their picturesque mantilla,' wrote Newnes.

By the end of the First World War, Buenos Aires had nothing of the small town and was growing rapidly, in a haphazard way. J.A. Hammerton, author of *The Argentine Through English Eyes*, wrote in the Argentina chapter of *Peoples of All Nations*, a twelve-volume cyclopedia published in 1923:

> There is no romantic element in the character of the Argentine today. The vision of opportunities to make money in large quantities, and in a few years without much labour, took hold of him as soon as the development of the Republic by foreign capital began to bear fruit. He thinks about money all his time, he talks about it most of the time, he spends it lavishly, both in Buenos Aires and in Paris, and he is always planning how to get more...

This aspect of Argentina, Argentines, Argentineans, whatever, would never change. This was the country that the Prince of Wales, later Edward VIII, and then the Duke of Windsor, found on arrival in 1925. For the British and North Americans, corporations and individuals, in Argentina the decade was developing into one of comfort and success, of money, lots. Business had little difficulty in its operations.

President Alvear liked the English and tried to accommodate their wishes. The threat from an organized trades union movement had been eliminated after a decade of growth in labour strength. A strike in 1920 at the British-owned tanine producers, *The Forestal Land, Timber and Railways Company* in Santa Fe, had been crushed by the army. The defeat of a strike at the port of Buenos Aires, in May and June 1921, put an end to years of union progress. And the powerful railway unions had also been demolished. In Patagonia, a strike organised by expatriate European anarchists at British-owned sheep farms had been ended by the army, with the execution of the ring-leaders who fell riddled with bullets into the graves they had dug.

English and Scottish emigrants, travelling on their own, were favoured by a post-war fall in European immigration to Argentina. This made jobs easy to find for the loner with something of an education. Argentina's interests in foreign commerce made employment with export traders attractive and easily available.

The visit to Argentina by the Prince of Wales had been preceded, in August 1924, by that of the heir to the crown of Italy, Umberto di Savoia, who had been met at the port by over one hundred thousand of his homesick countrymen. He wanted his photograph taken with the tango singer and actor, Carlos Gardel. Everybody wanted their photograph taken with Gardel. He was a popular hero, known in all the capitals of Latin America, in New York, Paris and Madrid. So Gardel posed shaking hands with King Alphonse XIII of Spain, with the writers Ramón del Valle-Inclán and José Ortega y Gasset, with the French entertainer Maurice Chevalier, and with many more.

Even the Prince of Wales admitted that he would like to meet Gardel.

Buenos Aires and its stars had that kind of effect on visitors. The Maharaja of Kapurtala travelled to Buenos Aires wondering what the fuss was about and wanted to meet Carlos Gardel.

The city by the great brown river was an attraction to the wealthy and adventurous from all over the world, and the locals were flattered by such attention.

Ralph Deakin, correspondent of *The Times*, in his report on the Prince's tour in Africa and South America, and in his book *Southward Ho!* (1925), described great scenes of welcome. There was the city, three weeks sailing from Tilbury and two from New York, feeling far away, delighted to have European visitors, at once trying to lavishly care for and defraud those who made the long voyage south.

Ear-splitting shouts of '*Viva el Príncipe de Gales!*' broke out. The Prince's coach, one of the rarely used state landaus drawn by four magnificent black horses in gilded harness, was bombarded with roses, daffodils and lilies, which came hurtling down mercilessly shower after shower from women and girls leaning over the parapet of the Immigration Building. The carriage entered streets where millions who had waited impatiently almost exploded with enthusiasm... Progress through Florida, the Bond Street of the capital, was at a good deal less than walking pace. The party had just reached the state rooms at Government House when a mass of young men penetrated the hall below and had to be forcibly ejected.

From *Casa Basualdo* (the Ortiz Basualdo family base known as the Palace Andrew) in Buenos Aires, the Prince of Wales wrote to his *'Darling Mama'*, on 17 August 1925. He said that his stop in Montevideo had been more enjoyable, and quieter.

Thank you so much for 2 very sweet letters received in Monte-Video & will you please thank Papa for his & all the nice things he says about S. Africa which I appreciate very much. My 3 days in the capital of Uruguay went off all right tho, it was a comic turn we had some grand laughs – But they gave me a fine & I think genuine welcome & I did my best. I'm picking up a little Spanish and tango as well so as not to feel too much of a stranger in this continent of S. America! And neither are very difficult.

Of course this is a far bigger fence – the Argentine (than Uruguay) where we landed from 'Curlew' this afternoon sleeping the night on bd – to come up the Plate from Montevideo. You'll remember the President, Alvear – he came to London in 1923 – and seems a friendly man, tho I've seen but little of him as yet, only on an official drive thru this gt city, tho I had a fine welcome here.

The mail goes to-morrow so it's a rush but I wanted you to have a few lines from here even if I can't tell you much about this place yet. There's a big official dinner to-night – a full dress uniform stunt – and I'll have to read a speech. All of this week is mostly official but I hope it'll be better after that both in B.A. and way out in *estancias* in the country. I'm so tired of all these official stunts and stale too. You can understand that and you are too after this hectic summer you've had in England.

This is a wonderful city, some very fine buildings, and it's all lit up to-night. But there were huge crowds in the street – all making a lot of noise and throwing flowers – so one couldn't look around much. The Alstons, our minister and his wife, are v. nice. I was over at the Legation for tea this evening and met their staff and other Englishmen and their wives. But I must stop now and put my full dress uniform on. Bless you darling Mama. I'm very well but fed up with all these official stunts...

The prince's second letter from Buenos Aires on 24 August, addressed to his father from the *Estancia Huetel*, on the Southern Railway, revealed a man exhausted by the hospitality. He had come to Argentina after a gruelling four-month tour of Africa. Protocol and Royalty demanded tours, and public understanding of the significance of such visits.

I've had a frightful official week in Buenos Aires. The worst of my life, I believe, and it's a relief to get out to 'el campo' for a couple of days.

President Alvear and his wife are both v. nice and human but he has overdone the stunting and entertaining and we were all of us thru yesterday, tho feel better to-day after the first real night's sleep we've had! These Argentines are queer people – v. Latin in their touchiness and excitability but also human and cheery tho with quite a heavy veneer of pompousness. Their official and ceremonial stunts are v. ostentatious, but absolutely lacking in organization and time means nothing to them. Two or three days of it would have been interesting but a whole week has been too much. However I hope and believe there'll be a let up from now onwards and I'm doing two days stunting for the British Community in B.A. this week...

I've spoken in Spanish three times, just a few sentences and am picking up a little of the language. The wealth in B.A. is amazing, and the cost of living there is 40 per cent more than in New York. But I'm v. glad I've been able to come here despite having to go thru with last week and hope I'll enjoy the remaining month a bit – More private and peaceful days in B.A. and then seeing some estancias.

Still it's some consolation to feel that it's all been quite a success and these Argentines certainly are very enthusiastic and demonstrative in their welcomes everywhere. I've been absolutely mobbed at most of the stunts and I've had the wind-up for the safety of the people involved in the crowds. Alston has been wonderful and helped us thru marvellously. He and his wife are charming and I escape to the Legation often. He's coming around with me everywhere thank goodness...

There were between thirty and forty thousand British subjects in and around Buenos Aires and they had to be entertained. The North Americans were estimated at a little over one thousand, and they came along too. Keeping them happy was no easy matter. On 28 August, for example, the Prince was required at St Andrew's Scots School, founded in 1838, at 10 o'clock, within an hour he had to be at the British Hospital, on that site since 1887. Lunch with the British Chamber of Commerce at the restaurant in the Retiro terminal of the Central Argentine Railway was at 12.30. And then there was polo at Hurlingham Club at 2.30pm. Oh, and a banquet in the evening, poor Prince.

> In Latin America society begins its evening festivities at a late hour and finds it easy to turn night into day. The Prince drove to the State banquet at Government House at nine o'clock through thoroughfares as brightly lighted as at the hour of his arrival. The whole length of Avenida de Mayo was bridged with portals of electric light suspended above the sidewalks by invisible wires, the Prince's motto and feathers alternating with the Federal coat of arms and the English word, 'Welcome,'

wrote Ralph Deakin in *Southward Ho!*

Along the railway, which is British controlled and mainly British-owned, the settlements waited and waved, and at Temperley a large community of English residents hailed the train... 'There does not exist,' said Dr Cantilo, the Governor (of Buenos Aires), 'any expression of culture or progress in the province which, directly or indirectly, does not owe its growth and prosperity to your country...'

The Prince's third and last letter from Buenos Aires, sent to his mother on 1 September 1925, was written on the notepaper of the Argentine Navigation Company (Nicolás Mihanovich) Ltd.

> I'm sorry I've not written you in so long but these...! Argentine officials have given me a frightful program and no chance at all, with the result that I've been absolutely dead beat. You have to see the way they run an official visit before you can have any idea what it's like. '*Qué lástima!*' as they say in Spanish 'cos I'm interested in Argentina as I am in any new country and its people but I absolutely cannot compete with it all and be natural and cheerful when they won't treat me like a human being, which they don't seem to be able to do. But I won't bore you with details now... But how can one see estancias or

anything when one is surrounded by absolutely hundreds of officials – police – newspaper men (most of the police are newspapermen) and masses of stray and casual hangers-on who are using us (staff and self) to have a good time and eat and drink as much as possible at the expense of the Argentine government. And crowd out the special trains too.

I can laugh now but 'entre nous' I was as near a mental crash on Saturday night when I left Buenos Aires as doesn't matter. I felt so crushed by it all when I expected a little freedom and to be peaceful here. So much so that the Admiral and White suggested cutting out Chile.

I thought it over a few hours and then felt better and have decided to go thru with it. I really do feel better now although it's been a ghastly 2 days in a train going up to Mercedes (Provincia de Corrientes) and Colón (Provincia de Entre Rios) to see Liebig's estancias and 'frigorifico' or meat packing plant. I would have been interested without the crowd and have learnt something of it all despite everything. But it's a great relief to be on board this ship taking us back to B.A. down the Río Uruguay, where I can any way sleep which I couldn't do much in the train. We go to the Nelson's estancia at San Marcos for 2 days before we leave for Chile. I spent 3 days stunting for the British Community in B.A. last week before this trip...

The year 1928 was a good one in which to say goodbye to Scotland and take refuge in Argentina. In South America life looked more lenient than in the old world. In Argentina the British could enjoy the wealth of their fathers and grandfathers, their trade protected and encouraged by the mighty power of their faraway island and their responsibilities were few. Their idea and innovations were also reduced in number. But that was not noticed amid the great riches. In Buenos Aires, in spite of the distance, people tried to emulate some of the desperate search for a good time that occupied an impoverished Europe. The difference was that Argentines had few of the difficulties of the post war. In Europe history was being written with anxiety and refused to be ignored. Events raced into being, grandly, or perhaps quietly, but never furtively, to the breathless rhythm of Maurice Ravel's *Bolero*, which was published in 1928. The Opus Dei was started in Spain, Trotsky went to Siberia, Bertoldt Brecht published *The Threepenny Opera*, Aldous Huxley published *Point Counterpoint*; Andre Malraux's *The Conquistadors*, Federico García Lorca's *Romancero Gitano* and D.H. Lawrence's *Lady Chatterley's Lover* all went into print in that year.

The writers of Europe produced the papers that would punctuate the passage of a special decade in the century.

In Argentina history did not matter, there wasn't any, the country was not old enough to have a history.

'South America' was a vast region of cheer, tragedy and excitement, in large portions. It said so in *The Times*, in every report from the continent. The *Manguera samba* school was started in 1928.

Also in Brazil, Colonel Fawcett vanished. In a report dated in New York, on 11 October, *The Times* quoted commander George Dyott saying that he was convinced that Colonel P.H. Fawcett, the British explorer, his son John and Mr Raleigh Rimmel, of Los Angeles, missing since May 1925, were dead. 'He had found traces of their camps and trails, but rumours among the Indians indicated that the party had perished,' along the Xingú river.

Meanwhile, the Spanish were 'following with interest the progress of the flight of the *Graff Zeppelin*, because it depends on the result of the flight whether the airship service from Seville to Buenos Aires will be opened next spring or be postponed again.' A man named Jorge Luis Borges, aged 27, published a study of Argentina's Spanish, *The Language of the Argentines*. Nobody seemed to understand it very well but readers said that was because Borges was educated in Switzerland. To the embarrassment of the English-speaking community another local writer, Benito Edgardo Lynch (1880-1951), a descendant of Irishmen resident in Buenos Aires since the eighteenth century but identified by Anglo-Argentines as one of their own, published *El ingles de los güesos* (a play on words which translates as 'the Englishman of the bones', a thin man, but also an archaeologist). In the story, an old professor goes to work in a place uninhabited but for a family living in an isolated hut. There is an adolescent daughter whose wordless relationship with the visitor ends in tragedy. People thought that was bad for the English image: the old man and the young girl. The title soon entered the language as a cliché to describe an imaginary prototype of a tall, shy, eccentric Englishman.

In Buenos Aires, on 13 October 1928, Dr Hipólito Yrigoyen began his second term in office as President, amid forebodings of failure. Argentina's exports had totalled £200 million, the peak of prosperity of the golden years.

# PART I
## 1928-1934

# Chapter 1

DOUGLAS NOEL, so named for being born on Christmas Eve at Heatherlie House, in Leith, in the Royal Republic of Scotland, landed at Buenos Aires on Saturday, 13 October 1928, with one cabin trunk.

There was no other baggage to follow. Disembarkation took all day because Immigration authorities were searching the passengers' list for anarchists and prostitutes, the officials said, causing deep distress to the English and other European wives who were brusquely questioned.

As he came down the gangway of the Royal Mail Ship *Highland Rover*, Douglas thought of himself as a courageous figure whose past was in ashes, burned out of mind. Only memories could be kept and they weighed no more than he was prepared to carry. Those were the thoughts of a young man of twenty-one arriving in the new world, determined to leave the old one behind.

He was alone. His mother had promised to send a telegram to a lawyer who was eminent, to meet Douglas at the dock. Nobody showed up to welcome, let alone assist him. Douglas learned later that the acquaintance lived in Rio de Janeiro. But 'Buenos Aires, capital of Brazil' was a mistake that was common in Europe.

It was early Spring, the weather was beginning to warm. At times the sun over the River Plate faded into a cloud.

Guided by the ship's purser, he took a room at the Phoenix Hotel, on San Martín street, at the corner of Córdoba avenue. He liked the symbolism of the fresh start. He collapsed quite early into a deep sleep. The initial hours in the new country were a blank.

On Sunday, the purser took him to early Communion at St John's Anglican cathedral, then on a boring tour of port bars used by ships' crews from all over the world and by the local shipping agents. There were dozens of bars, with women stripping right through the day, from after early Communion to long after midnight Mass.

In the evening of his first day in the city he decided to go on a stroll to glimpse the people he had heard talked about. He stopped near the corner of the hotel. A few men in Sunday afternoon suits and wide rim felt hats chatted quietly on each corner. They glanced up and down the street, waiting for some event, anything, not disturbed but reflecting the slightly uneasy peace that is a feature of Sunday afternoons. The men looked like players off stage waiting for their cue to walk on. Before arrival Douglas had imagined the city populated by elegant men and very rich women who dressed in Paris. They did not leap into sight now. Buenos Aires, in his readings, was the gayest city in South America, but he found the streets without laughter. In a conciliatory mood, he told them, speaking to himself, that he too disliked the tail-end of Sundays.

The wheels of a tram ground the tracks noisily up the avenue from the port terminal, but there was little other traffic on the cobblestone street. Tomorrow, when the week started in earnest, he would find the city he had read about. He quietly screamed his excitement at the novelty and uncertainty and then mumbled a reminder that he was terrified of the future. He felt the joy of expectation and the restrained laughter made him shiver and sense a giddy lightness.

Alone, without any ideas better than his own, he looked at himself in a store window and saw that his cream gabardine suit had made him into a reasonably smart figure. Then he walked into the bar on the corner. There were two large billiard tables in a space well removed from the counter. A large blue fly chose his nose for scrutiny and circled it like a speedy bird of prey.

'*Inglés?*' asked a man with an apron around his waist.

'Yes, er, no, Scots...' Douglas replied, in an early assertion of identity in his new home. He had enough Spanish to enable such a defence.

'All the same,' the barman said. 'All from 'Inglaterra',' he laughed. 'Here is "Mac", a gentleman *inglés* from the railway.' The introduction was commercially friendly, but the response from 'Mac' was limited to a nod, hardly a grunt. Mac needed somebody with whom to play billiards.

He was a middle-aged expatriate, thin, with a bulging belt, whose nearly white hair exaggerated his years. Mac's economical introduction revealed a troubled bachelor so timid he did not raise his voice for fear of offending his own ears. They played three games, with long intervals for conversation. Mac, all the time fighting to break with the silence of the shy, spoke rapidly, his teeth clenched, expressing himself in the manner of the veteran resident. He ridiculed the newcomer for choosing this, of all places, for his future. He gave advice on the certainty that the 'lately-landed', as he called Douglas, would fall victim to one of the Chilean pickpockets on the pavement. If they did not finish him off, the country would. This land was corrupt; the soil so rich that everybody thought life was easy. A man could be destroyed by apathy and self-indulgence, envy and fantasy; all these states were easy traps for a person with no devotion to hard work.

Douglas listened, trying to shape a smile of contempt, without success. Mac warned that those who arrived without a return passage would never go back. Implicit in his remark were the unsaid words, '... like me.' Mac took rooms at the Phoenix Hotel whenever he was in town from work at the Rosario Junction, on the Central Argentine Railway, three hours north of Buenos Aires. The Phoenix was the trusted 'English' hotel; the closest he could get to England outside of the railways, he joked.

One of the drunks that are part of dusk on Sundays entered the bar, shouting his support for a cause known only to inebriates. He waved a knife which had a hard, vicious little blade that sliced bread on weekdays. Mac described him as a regular at the bar, one who had been sacked from a South Dock meat-packing company within weeks of it opening. The man had threatened Mac recently for no better reason than that he was an *Inglés de mierda*.

Mac recalled and retold the incident then took fright at his own tale and, without a word, hid behind the curtain that covered the passage to the toilet. There he held his breath against the stench from the loo and tried to control his own asthmatic wheeze which might betray the hiding place. The drunk said 'Hah', in a manner that could only have meant he had sighted the place to relieve himself. But in a sequel never properly described, the drunk dived at the curtain and plunged his knife through the cloth into Mac's small paunch.

There was no complaint, no exclamation of pain. The only sound was that of a rush of air, as if Mac had been deflated, then a thwup when the blade was pulled out. Mac emerged from behind the curtain holding what looked like most of his intestines in his hands. Over the billiard tables, with the lethargy of evening, floated the deep penetrating smell of long suffered constipation, caused by too many hard spirits and not enough wine. The blue fly which had first met the 'lately-landed' Scot at the door of the bar swooped on the contents of Mac's hands and then flew to Douglas with a report of filth that only flies can find attractive. From that day on, every time a 'blue-bottle' fly came close to his nose, Douglas would remember Mac's bowels.

The record of what happened next has been pruned, polished and improved over the years, but the truth told by Douglas was that he panicked. He spun the billiard cue round as only a man with fifth form and much truancy at Edinburgh Academy could have learned and with the tip in his hand he swung the pole. The grip hit the knifeman's forehead with the force of a lamppost racing towards a drunk. The bar's proprietor said for years after that the blood flowed as copiously as at the defloration of a farmer's fattest daughter. He said he knew. In Douglas's memory the spurt of blood reminded him of the bidet he had been sprayed by in his hotel room on discovery of the appliance that afternoon.

The bar owner filled a bucket of cold water and threw it over the bloodied floor. Stained sawdust floated on a pink tide onto the tiled pavement. Outside, somebody shouted '*Sangre!*' The barman cleaned the polished wood frame of the billiards table and checked the baize for stains. Then he turned to the injured.

'*Inglés!*' he shouted.

'Scot!' Douglas retorted. But he shook with shock and shivered all over. He lit a cigarette.

Mac grunted and sat down, then fainted onto the floor, fussed over by the owner who cleaned the blood off the chair. Douglas was speechless: he did not know the man, he knew nobody. He was frozen as much by fear as by the frustration of his ignorance as to where to run. He looked at the collapsed body of the drunk, his head in a pool of blood which the owner could not contain even with a floor mop and the evening newspaper. People were coming in from the darkening street. Where had they all been? A little earlier the avenue had been empty. A tram stopped and out ran the conductor and most of the passengers for a look into the bar. The owner pointed to the *Inglés*, and people muttered admiration for the youngster who had floored two men without creasing or staining his smart suit. That was style! Somebody patted his shoulder and the bar's proprietor pushed the admirer away, warning Douglas to look after his pockets. Somebody shouted '*Policía!*' and the onlookers crowded at the door to keep the law out, but no police arrived. Douglas fetched Mac's coat from a peg on the wall and searched the pockets, hearing the bar owner repeatedly say, '*Hospital Británico...*'

Carefully folded inside Mac's pocketbook were two pieces of paper that Douglas unfolded, in search of an address. One was called a 'Seaside song', nine couplets about drinking probably picked up from an organ grinder's parrot on some cold promenade and now kept as a souvenir of the good times that were possible in another land called 'home':

The horse and mule live thirty years
And nothing know of wine and beers.
The goat and sheep at twenty die,
And never tasted Scotch or Rye.
The cow drinks water by the ton
And at eighteen is mostly done.
The dog at fifteen cashes in
Without the aid of rum or gin.
The cat in milk and water soaks
And then in twelve short years it croaks.
The modest sober bone dry hen
Lays eggs for nogs then dies at ten.
All animals are strictly dry
They sinless live and swiftly die.
But sinful-ginful-rum-soaked men
Survive for threescore years and ten.
And some of us, the mighty few,
Stay pickled till we're ninety-two.

The other was a newspaper cutting. Douglas was aghast as he saw that it was the same news item that he carried in his own pocket. Trembling, no longer with a thought for the unconscious man, he opened Mac's piece of newspaper.

*The Times*, Tuesday, 18 December 1894. Death of Mr R. L. Stevenson.
Apia, Dec. Mr Robert Louis Stevenson, the well-known novelist, has died suddenly of apoplexy. He was buried at the summit of Pala Mountain, 1,300 ft. above sea-level. At the time of his death Mr Stevenson had half completed a new novel. - Reuter.

Sydney, Dec. 17. Advices just received from Samoa announce the death of Robert Louis Balfour Stevenson, the novelist. He had been in much better health lately... As for his native Edinburgh, much as he admired it he wisely avoided what he has denounced as the vilest climate in the world... We regret Mr Stevenson selfishly as well as sincerely, because in the crowd of successful and rising writers there is no one left who can even approximately fill his place...

This was Mac's testimony of expatriation. A piece of newspaper over thirty years old. Douglas wondered if the cuttings were in wide circulation, here, where the new world was the end of the world. 'You'll never go back,' Mac had said. Douglas took from his pocket his own copy of the obituary, cut from *The Scotsman*, given to him by a friend after a farewell supper in Edinburgh. 'The epitome of exile, take this as a warning that you must try to come back,' his friend had said when presenting the cutting from *The Scotsman*. Douglas quickly placed it in Mac's coat and pocketed the one from *The Times*. He was sure that in this part of the world, *The Times* carried more weight than *The Scotsman* – even if the presentation by his old school chum, on the pavement in front of 17 Heriot Row, in Edinburgh, carried strong personal memories. Douglas recited the words to himself in a whisper.

> For we are very lucky with
> a lamp before the door,
> And Leerie stops to light it as
> he lights so many more
> And O! Before you hurry by with
> ladder and with light
> O Leerie, see a little child and
> nod to him good night.

The shouting around him was loud. He recognised the words *Inglés* and *Hospital Británico*. He came out of his daze when he heard *asesino* spat across the billiard table. At that sound, the bar owner grabbed him by the elbow and rushed him on hands and knees through a small door behind the counter and into a patio that connected with the rear of the Phoenix Hotel. 'Wait,' the man signalled with hands together and two index fingers pointing at the floor tiles. Douglas spent his second night in Buenos Aires in that patio, surrounded by crates of empty wine and beer bottles, under an open sky. Two packets of cigarettes kept him company for a short time. He heard the police in loud conversation with the bar owner, but only recognised the words *Inglés* and *accidente*. Entering through another door, police searched the patio. But their prey was hidden in a chamber of bottle crates.

Douglas later heard the night porter at the Phoenix Hotel speaking loudly to police in the light well between buildings, denying any knowledge of the new guest – probably under threat of physical injury from the bar owner, a man of considerable girth and not much hair, who wanted to protect his patrons, especially the English ones. During Mac's introductory monologue Douglas had been told that it was important to Argentines to be able to say that they had 'English' friends.

Grunting from the effort, the owner crawled into the patio where Douglas sat on an empty crate in sweat soaked clothes, his body chilled by the night air. The man said Mac was comfortable at the British Hospital. There was no news of the drunk who might be dead, which was fine, the proprietor said. If he was dead there would be no witnesses and the case would be closed quickly. Each word was shouted, and accompanied by side-long glances at nowhere. The night and the possible police presence imposed caution. But comfort, reassurance, were the main aim of the speech, which was formulated slowly, lips framing the words, with the apparent conviction that volume facilitated comprehension. When Douglas said '*Qué?*' the same words were repeated, even more loudly, caution abandoned. Douglas began to tremble, shaking with feverish convulsions. He was assured that another *inglés*, one of Mac's bosses on the Central Argentine Railway, would arrive with daybreak to sort out everything.

The police gave up their search; the two buildings fell quiet. The proprietor gave Douglas an unknown drink so strong that he bent double from the blaze in his bowels. But the shivering stopped. The owner smiled.

Douglas wondered if he should be amused too. He had good reason for disliking Sundays.

So began the long residence of Douglas Noel, Scot, in the Argentine Republic.

# Chapter 2

A YOUNG WORKS ENGINEER, who introduced himself only as Nicholas, had been ordered by the Central Argentine Railway to get Douglas out of Buenos Aires. It was not concern for Mac's rescuer, but for the possibility of scandal. With little courtesy or even much interest in the details of the incident, Douglas was removed from the hotel. He was told to pack a light bag and send instructions later for transfer of his trunk. The car that came to fetch him was a very new Ford Tin-Lizzie – which Douglas was told by the engineer was a rare privilege because he was too junior, but management thought the emergency called for rushed treatment.

Douglas did not say goodbye to the bar owner. The engineer dismissed the idea as unimportant. Douglas muttered to his escort, 'I'm coming back.' The other youth said nothing.

The railway chauffeur drove them to the sidings alongside a huge shed. Douglas shouldered his canvas bag and was led to what seemed to be a special train carriage.

If only the 'Academicals' in Edinburgh could see him now.

A waiter in uniform helped him up the steps. Through double doors and a guard's position, he entered a sitting room. Deep dark leather armchairs sat as forbidding as might their occupants in the carpeted chamber. There were racing prints and pictures of the great railway engines of Britain on the panelled walls. The Argentine Republic's coat of arms hung above the *quebracho* wood mantelpiece over a grate with a polished brass fireguard.

Nicholas went ahead through a dining room that looked larger than the one at Heatherlie House, to a row of four cabins almost the size of his first class accommodation on the *Highland Rover*, which Douglas now missed just as a child would long for his home. His host pointed to one of the smaller rooms, where the bed was made.

'Digs, until tomorrow,' Nicholas told the shaken Douglas, who was becoming increasingly distressed by the events of the first two days that threatened to mark the end of the start of his future. 'Let me explain,' said the young engineer. 'You are on the managing director's train, which is sometimes used by the President of the Republic, although the president now has a great fear of moving on anything but his own two feet. I am the second of three junior assistants, not a secretary, mind, in the office of the managing director. I have been ordered to help you out of B.A. quietly, to Córdoba. There, somebody will offer you a temporary job. You and I are on the managing director's train because it is a convenient way of smuggling you up country in great secrecy. You may not like to see it this way, but this is a secret operation.'

Nicholas spoke slowly, carefully shaping each word. 'As if I were a lunatic,' Douglas thought.

'And personally I find all this great fun,' Nicholas continued without a trace of amusement. 'But there is also the matter of getting this coach to Córdoba for maintenance. Not really, you understand, but as the managing director does not like President Yrigoyen, he is damned if he is going to let him use this coach. So your accident was well timed, in a way ... I mean... Pedro, brandy...'

The elderly waiter, who had suffered ignominy all his life to reach the admired position of the managing director's coach valet, was in no doubt about whom he took orders from: 'Brandy is not for juniors or troublemakers...' Pedro replied in Spanish. News travelled fast on the British-owned railways. 'Oh, *ginebra* then?' Nicholas pleaded. The waiter agreed; managers drank the better class of spirits imported from Britain. Pedro could serve the local Dutch Gin because nobody checked the stocks.

Douglas looked at his pocket watch. It was 7.30 a.m. He was out of cigarettes and asked Nicholas for one. Pedro had no objection to going to buy him a packet from a nearby bar.

They spent the day in sidings, in the shed. By 10 a.m. not even Twinings tea could counter their *ginebra* haze and Douglas went to sleep, drowsy from alcohol and the tension of a sleepless night. At some time, while he slept, he thought he heard Nicholas speaking on a telephone: trains with telephones were also a novelty.

Both sobered in time for a late lunch. By then an order from a personnel manager anxious to have a say had improved Pedro's service. A starched cloth was put on the dining room table, which was made of a vast teak surface with no joints visible. The turned legs plunged down to the carpeted floor. It was difficult to associate trains with such palatial luxury.

Nicholas had spent some of his early school years in India – at a minor public school for the Indian civil service – which prompted him now to express such un-English thoughts as 'my food is my music' and to show an interest in the neo-colonial influence of England in Argentina. Nicholas said the country was a colony.

At dusk, the coach was drawn out of sidings and hooked onto the night train, 28 cars in all, including freight and passenger carriages. 'Eleven hours to Córdoba,' Nicholas said, as he looked out at the dark end of the platform. They were served brandy and soda, supplied by the night waiter who said he ranked as a station-master in the railway hierarchy when he was at home in the Córdoba hills. Out of his overnight bag the man produced a cap with a label *Gefe*, instead of *Jefe*. The misspelled hat band, imported from *Inglaterra*, was a source of pride in spite of the mistake.

'Pity you'll have to leave. There's not much hope for you after this,' Nicholas said. 'After all, nobody will give you a job now. Tell me how it happened. If you had stayed, you would see what a wonderful place this is. Mind you, we get all sorts. His nibs has to deal with many of them; almost like a government minister. The British railways in Argentina are really more important than the Legation, you know, in some ways. I read the old man's letters. Some are quite dotty: women who say their husbands went to India, or Australia, and promised to send for them but have vanished without trace, and they wondered if the bounder bolted to the Argentine. Well, they're right, in a way... Buenos Aires is further from Tilbury than Peking – only 130 miles more, but I looked it up. It makes us seem so far away from everywhere.

'God, I hope this country never stops being ours. They like us so much here. With a little luck we could be here for another two hundred years.'

As Nicholas spoke, Douglas wondered why he had to leave. He had come all this way to start a new life because his brother's illness and sisters' education before him had drained much of the money his father had left. He could not go home. There was no place for him and he was not wanted. The family liked him now, because he was not there and they only had to write him an occasional letter.

The train, moving north of Buenos Aires, gathered speed. His host led him to a framed pen-drawing on the wall. It showed the carriage they were in. There was a beautiful country house in the background. 'I have seen letters about the time President Roca went to that *estancia*, the *El Dorado*.' Nicholas proceeded to recite the account of a day in June 1902 when President Roca, two railway directors and Sir Thomas Holdich, the British minister, had visited the huge farm and luxurious home, guests at an opulent lunch with shooting in the afternoon. Ten carriages from the *estancia* had met the retinue of thirty people at Pinto station, in Buenos Aires province. Nicholas described the ostentation and excess, the female dresses and cloaks and the presidential flirting with three English women. Nicholas had not been born then, but he had read the correspondence and had heard the anecdotes. The detail he supplied was that of a man taken by the occasion and the gossip. The outings, courtesy of the British railways, were a symbol of the power and the wealth of the company and the country.

'This is a good life,' Nicholas said above the sound of the train, which had the smoothest running carriages Douglas had ever ridden in. His host's praise for the country seemed genuine though a little forced and Douglas wondered if the plaudits were heaped only to distress him. Nicholas was a snooper into the privacy of others. Knowledge of the intimate writings of people in the company made him feel strong. He had memorised the letters of appointment in the railway hierarchy; correspondence with government ministers had no secrets for him, and there were even the personal missives of wives to their men on the railways. At this he raised one corner of his mouth in leering conspiracy, but said nothing. The sampling from the managing director's files was intended to demonstrate the wonders of the railway and of the land it had colonised through the second half of the nineteenth century.

'India isn't everything – and I should know. You can't trust them, for a start... My father was a doctor in India... couldn't wait to get back to Bournemouth. My mother was born in New York and she hated India even more. In South America people are Europeans, not like us, but like Europeans, you know. Foreign but tolerable.

'This is not as shocking as India. We made India an empire for the likes of companies and armies. Argentina offers more chance for the man alone. You should see the lineage they have here. The Newbery family, the man who has been flying Argentina's new aeroplanes, is descended from Lady Hamilton. Well, that's what they say. It sounds true. And all their heroes came to England for help. Even the roughest, like a chap called Martín Güemes. He led roving bands against the Spaniards in the north. He is descended from the Wemyss family of Fife. A British minister here was Lionel Sackville West, grandfather of that woman who has been in the papers these days. I mention that in case you read the Personal notices. Anyway, he was one of the founders of the Tigre Boat Club – which you really should see.'

Nicholas rattled on, above the sound of the wheels on the tracks. Douglas had been warned on the Royal Mail ship during the voyage that Britain kept its eccentrics at home, but exported its cranks to the colonies or to the overseas companies.

The waiter announced that supper would be served in thirty minutes and both men went to wash and freshen up. Douglas had little to change into and decided to preserve what was still clean. He got out of his clothes, shook them, and put them on again.

The beef steak on his plate kept to the promise that this was the land of red meat, in plenty. He thought it would have been better placed on a tray.

They were given breakfast on the train. His host's last courtesy, more for his own satisfaction than that of his guest, was to show him the Jesuit buildings of Córdoba from the comfort of an open, horse-drawn carriage. Douglas was then taken to the timber yard next to the main station and shown into a dormitory for the junior English staff. He was not expected to bunk down with the native labour – and was told that he would be employed there for a week. He had to work for his accommodation. Then he would be fetched, taken by train south to Rosario and put on a grain ship for Brazil.

His attempted protests were rejected: 'Look laddie,' the grizzly under-manager snarled. 'You're seeing the country courtesy of the Central Argentine Railway, not even paying for a ticket. Nobody's told me what happened and I don't want to know. But it sounds like something dirty. You can't complain. And while you're in my charge you won't; you'll do as you're told.'

Douglas was up at dawn the next day, drinking *maté* – which tasted bitter – for breakfast with an English trainee and two local foremen. His first shift was the supervision of the removal of a stack of very long narrow planks to a shed nearby. Each stack, and there were several, eventually for use in the construction business, was enormous. Some were partly overgrown by grass.

The first disaster of that morning, the collapse of a man in a state of shock or seizure, made Douglas decide to leave Córdoba before lunch. He was not waiting for another incident.

The man, a timber yard *peón* in his late forties, perhaps, announced that he was going to the other side of a stack of planks for his morning bowel movement. After a few minutes there was a groan and the man collapsed. Douglas' limited Spanish delayed his acquaintance with the facts. The man had crouched and had relieved himself. Just then somebody, having misunderstood an order about which stack was to be moved into shelter, had removed the plank on which the man had deposited the product of his pushing. When the *peón* had turned to survey his morning's deposition he had found nothing and his heart had stopped. A steaming turd, meanwhile, had been transported across the yard into the shed on the end of a long plank.

Douglas heard the under-manager talking to one of his staff and learned that a truck was leaving for Misiones, one day's drive northeast, on a monthly run to pick up contraband cigarettes from Brazilian smugglers who delivered cheaper English Capstans than those bought through Buenos Aires. Douglas studied a torn map of Argentina on the shed wall and was satisfied that this seemed far enough from pursuers and protectors.

Misiones was the province of the great Iguazú falls which had been described at a lecture in London by one Frank Chevallier-Boutell, reporting on his travels in November 1904 and after. Now Douglas would see if the falls existed. In Edinburgh he had been told that the photographs shown at the talk had been forged to make them more impressive. They looked too big to be real.

Misiones 'sticks to you for the rest of your life' the truck driver warned Douglas. The red earth changed the colour of everything, from the light and the air, to the colour of men's skin. People who stayed too long later dared not go back to the city, for they were no longer white men and women, but different.

'Get out, don't stay,' the driver said as he put him down outside a small hotel which belched a smell of dampness.

On the ship sailing out from England, a woman passenger had described to Douglas a writer who dwelt in Misiones, a man with a huge, dark and wicked looking beard, who wrote horror stories like Edgar Allan Poe. She had never read any of them. She was, she said, more interested in the man's complicated life. He was Uruguayan-born, called Horacio Quiroga. Her husband, a land colonization agent, had said that Quiroga, a science and photography buff, was a teacher who supplemented his income by writing short stories for a Buenos Aires newspaper, that he did some farming and fruit packing in a failed search for a suburban idyll in the wilderness. Quiroga, a widower with two children, had fled the province chased by two Italian brothers because he had failed to keep his promise to marry their youngest sister. He had lived with her, but when he had tired of her she was forced out of his home; he put a snake between her bed sheets.

In Posadas, the provincial capital, Douglas was tracked down by Italian relatives of the Italian brothers of the girl Quiroga had dishonoured. The relatives thought he would understand their need for revenge because he was also 'from the Europes'. Douglas silently thanked Quiroga for leaving, for one more incident could, with the growing heat, scar his own nerves for ever.

Douglas was asked if he was as clever a Scot as the one who had been there 'just the other day'. The recent visitor had helped find an edible weed, named 'Good Henry', which was used as an alternative to spinach and was the only leaf that survived the swarms of locusts. Enquiries after the kind Scot revealed that Marcel Hardy of Edinburgh, lecturer in botany and geography at Dundee University up to 1905 and Fellow of the Royal Geographical Society between 1911 and 1914, had left the region over a decade before. He had first been in Mexico to try to make a fortune in coffee, but abandoned that when his house burned down. In 1911 Hardy had moved to Paraguay, farmed on the shores of lake Ipacaraí, played host to the President at his farm near San Bernardino and taken the first photographs of the Itaipú falls for the Royal Geographical Society. The locusts had struck three years in a row. Vast formations twenty miles long and over a mile wide had darkened the sky and made night out of day. They had eaten all that was in their path from the ground up, even the trousers on the clothes line, and they were most partial to starched shirts. Men and women went mad as they watched the invading cloud. Marcel Hardy had left with his daughters wondering why the locusts rejected only the spinach substitute, and why the swarms always flew north; ants always marched south.

The absence of a sense of time took years to come to terms with. People in Misiones talked in 1928 about 'the war' as if it had been yesterday. The conflict they referred to was that of the Triple Alliance, Argentina, Brazil and Uruguay, against Paraguay, between 1865 and 1870. For his benefit, and in the hope of securing his attention and perhaps some of his money, older men told Douglas they remembered the fleeting visit of Sir Richard Burton, on his return from the battlefields in September 1868.

Douglas had been more interested in the work of the South American Missionary Society. His mother had instructed him that way. She had thought that abandoning Edinburgh for South America would leave her youngest son bereft of all spiritual guidance and easy prey for the hated Catholics.

But his interest in the godly goings on of the SAMS was vanishing rapidly. At a mission outpost in Misiones he was told about the Society's good servant for thirty years up to 1921, the 'pacifier of the Indians' in the north of Argentina and Paraguay, a Scottish missionary named Wilfred Barbrooke-Grubb. But although the Bible had been around here for four and a half centuries, it seemed totally out of place, speaking as it did of remote deserts, which here in the jungle were not easily imagined.

He spent a month in Misiones, playing the part of the man he was: a youngster determined to find something uncertain before he was required to act responsibly. He showed interest in the purchase of land, in clearing the forest, in Horacio Quiroga's bankrupt *maté* plantation and orange-packing shed. But in the end all he bought, from a Paraguayan smuggler, was a .22 'long' Smith & Wesson pistol which hung lightly but handsomely from his belt, with the tip of the barrel just showing below his gabardine jacket. The suit had become lightweight from so many washings in cheap rooming houses and in lodgings with families, and had been coloured a lightish brown by the dust in the air.

He returned to Buenos Aires on the boat from Corrientes, scheduled to take six days of gentle cruising down the Paraná river.

The boat ran aground in front of a grey cluster of small buildings named Goya, still in Corrientes province. The planters, paymasters, gamblers and growers who had urgent business waiting left the ship and continued by road or on smaller craft to the next town south. For Douglas the journey took twelve days, attended by waiters who now had the time to give good service to the reduced passage.

The forecast said the water would not rise until there was rain in the north and that was not near. To escape the growing summer heat that made his cabin a furnace, he went ashore at Goya, which aspired to be a town in the future, and took a room at a hotel not far from the landing, to be near the ship when it came free. The surrounding countryside was bare apart from recent efforts to grow citrus. He went for long walks on the river bank, looking at the birds and insects, all the time feeling as if he were a windmill, with arms flailing against the mosquitoes. He tried to entice small monkeys from the *camalotes* of water lilies and rushes that floated by, populated by snakes constantly challenged by the birds of prey that flew overhead. Douglas began to feel at ease with the country. He wondered what awaited him in Buenos Aires, about employment and times ahead, and if he might have trouble with the police. He would seek advice, though he did not know from whom and he wanted to avoid lawyers. He still had some cash, what he had brought ashore on arrival and what Nicholas, for all his faults, had pressed into his hand in Córdoba. 'His nibs sent this... Keep you out of mischief. Do be careful.' The boy had almost sounded as if he cared.

Here in the heat, among the reeds, taking supper alone at a bar near the hotel and improving his Spanish by reading old newspapers, he thought he was comfortable. The contrast of the flat waterlogged land, where a distant horizon was always visible, with his memory of Scotland where he seldom saw the sky, began to play on the way he looked at things. At times he found it difficult to know where he was. In his dreams he came across a deserted plain that extended towards green distant hills. But he could not get closer to the rise in the land because the flats stretched ahead, putting the highlands ever further away.

A woman offered herself furtively in the bar. He rejected her. He knew he was getting too drunk when he started singing a rugby song which came to him from his schooldays.

In the hotel he heard a row in a room down the passage. A man was abusing a woman, shouting at her with urgency that bordered on violence. A woman screamed several times.

The scream was piercing pain put into sound.

Then it stopped abruptly. It became a continuous groan when Douglas opened the blinds and shouted into the enclosed patio, 'Less noise, *carajo*,' an order he had been taught in Misiones.

He was woken by a soft knock on the door.

Forgetting the new pistol which he had bought for such circumstances, he grabbed a shoe by the toe and raised it above his head. That too he had been taught in Misiones. There was no better defence than the heel of a shoe delivered with force on a person's nose. It had a stunning effect.

A woman, the one who had offered herself in the bar, stood there sobbing. One cheek streamed blood from a huge gash that ran from the edge of one eye to the corner of her mouth. Douglas retched. She stumbled into the room without invitation. The cause of the screams was clear. She had been 'marked' with a blade, probably for trying to leave her man. She would now be his or nobody's.

Douglas dressed as she demanded and escorted her to the *Sala*, the first aid centre next to the town doctor's house. She was sewn by a nurse so wide she had trouble bringing her hands together to put the thread through the needle. Douglas was made to pay for the repair and he did so without protest.

The injured girl, for she now looked no more than fifteen, spent the night on the floor at the foot of his bed.

She remained there for the next four nights. His unease vanished. There was no recrimination from the hotel owner, though Douglas thought there was a smirk as they crossed in the corridor. The woman's man was nowhere to be seen and the woman did not leave the room except to use the toilet. Once she simply raised her cotton dress and sat on the hand basin and relieved herself.

During siesta time, when the heat made walks impossible, he read to her from the Bible and from *Ivanhoe*, both books his mother's farewell gifts. The girl looked up at him from the floor, without any more understanding than a dog, and sometimes asked for water. *Agua* but she said nothing else.

On the fifth night, without rain, the water rose high, the boat was freed and tied up at the landing. He checked the stitches on her face. Far from a careful job, they looked the work of the butcher on a Sunday roast.

One of the ship's crew told him later that the nurse, or the doctor, were not expected to stitch the woman's face with any delicacy, for she was intended to remain marked for life.

When he boarded the boat she was nowhere to be seen. He felt a sense of relief. The pimp, her man, whom he recognised from the bar on the first evening, came up the gangway after him.

'I have to thank you for the care you gave my woman while she was unwell,' he smiled. 'Here...'

The man stuffed a thin roll of banknotes into Douglas's top pocket. It was not more than two pesos, if that. The money was intended as an insult. This was for the benefit of somebody watching from the shore.

'I know you *ingleses* can't...' he said with a gesture of his right index finger pushed into a ring formed by his left hand index and thumb. 'You can't do it with our women.' He smiled, triumphant, knowing that the Scot's fear and incompetence with the language gave an advantage. Douglas took the full blast of his breath without looking away and slid his hand onto the Smith & Wesson. With the gun still in its holster, he fired the one bullet in the chamber.

He felt a searing heat down his thigh and thought he had shot himself.

The man winced and buckled.

'Now...' Douglas stuttered in English. 'Y-y-you won't walk straight ever again,' not sure if he was speaking of himself, or the other.

Douglas looked down to where he had felt the heat of the bullet on his leg. He had shot a hole through his own trousers, narrowly missing his knee. He broke into a sweat.

But the bullet had also travelled diagonally through the man's leg and ankle, ripping flesh and sinew in its journey. The man limped to the gangway and tumbled down onto the landing, to be raised by two men who came out of the shadows.

The crew cast off and the ship slid into the darkness of the brown river.

# Chapter 3

IF VERACRUZ, MEXICO, was the first European city of America, then the last was Buenos Aires. Never again would men use their economic might to create replicas of European cities with the profits of three generations of adventurers. Never again would so many palaces rise for pleasure and vanity. The Colón opera house, as famous as Milan's La Scala, had opened on its present site in 1908, attracting the best performers from all over the world. The palace of the Papal Nuncio, built in 1909 at the same time as the army club and, the following year, the naval centre, were three images of Argentina's wealth built with near-imperial riches as symbols of achievement in land-ownership. The sumptuous residences punctuated avenues in the city and its suburbs. They were set in French and English gardens, according to the financial and cultural loyalties of the proprietor. The buildings were used no more than for an occasional wedding or family anniversary and remained empty much of the year, as absentee landlords preferred Paris. The British, who had helped to make the fortunes of some mighty families of Argentina, had their palaces too. They were the railway terminals. The Central Argentine Railway's magnificent monument to journey's end had been designed at the close of the nineteenth century by Walter B. Bassett-Smith, a British architect, son of an architect, who had left Argentina to live in Cambridge after bringing English architecture to the Anglican churches and halls, and who had also built a girls' college on the lines of an English public school. And in 1906, in the full season of Argentina's belle époque, Bassett-Smith had built a series of mansions that became stately homes on the remote properties of very rich landowners, beginning with the Martinez de Hoz family's palace in Chapadmalal, on the South Atlantic coast.

The capital's people offered the foreigner their friendship almost aggressively in proof of their existence and capacity to be as good as any place in Europe, for that was the place they most wanted to be. The travel books warned that friendship was just a word, a statement from the lips outwards and not a feeling. In the British, the French and the Germans, but not the Spanish and Italians who were associated with mass immigration and poverty, the Argentines saw their colonial masters and social betters, in spite of Argentina's independence from Spain one century before. Argentines thought of the English as cold and emulated the sense of privacy they attributed to the British. Thus visitors felt welcomed without intimacy. The mixture of cultures exploded into hundreds of expressions which failed to form an identity.

The stories of Argentine fortunes were used as entertainment, to impress the outsider. The Martinez de Hoz family, who had founded the Argentine Club in London, had one son who had kept horses in Paris with which he raced down the Champs Elysee at two a.m. And in 1909 Miguel Alfredo Martinez de Hoz had won the horse and carriage race from Hampton Court to Olympia, in England.

Buenos Aires changed daily. What had been a hovel was razed to make a residence. A mud road became an avenue. A village had become one of the capitals of the world. It was as if Argentina had read, uncomprehending, Filippo Tommaso Emilio Marinetti's futurist manifesto of 1908 ('Only by freeing herself of the stinking gangrene of professors, archaeologists, touring guides and antique dealers,' could Italy be free.). Everything had to be new in Buenos Aires. Nowhere was there any greater evidence of a land where everything was tried and rapidly discarded. The past was not in evidence. Historic houses were demolished to build monuments to the achievements of yesterday. And the historical events of the yesterdays were compressed into unimportant and forgettable statues while the country faced the future. The result was a mixture of styles which made the city a setting for every conceivable taste. Argentina became a country with a European flavour and no *cuisine.*

The combination was a curiosity for Europeans who were delighted by the ostentation of wealth but failed to fathom the way of life with which the richness was associated. In every street there coexisted examples of the eclecticism of the Victorians, the ambitious drive associated with the North Americans and the cultural refinement of the French - all mixed and merged in an unabashed mimicry of the outside. And like all mimics, the Argentines took themselves seriously. People did not see amusement in their own intensity. It was all part of needing to be. And in creating a mixed self in imitation of everybody else, the mystification of outsiders was complete.

South America had always been patronised by Europe like a clever child: original in its way, but not yet mature. Europe had given the region its culture but not intellectual recourse with which to reap the benefits of such a gift. The whole southern hemisphere was left to evolve its own intellect while its soil was plundered by the adventurers of the Old World in the name of cultural advancement. The British saw South America as they did sex, naughty and nice, but bad manners to show too much interest in it. So Argentina tried to be itself, while at the same time being many other selves.

# Chapter 4

THE RIVER BOAT had not completed docking before Douglas leaped onto the cobble stones of Buenos Aires. He took a tram to Retiro and looked for a small hotel, the Central Argentino, across the wide avenue from the station. From there he would explore the city and his situation. His luggage had to be traced.

The hotel manager apologised: all rooms were full. Douglas stood in the tiny hall at the top of the steps up from the street and wondered where to go. He explained that he did not want to impose. Both agreed, nodding without a word. Douglas said he was thinking matters through. After twenty minutes in complete silence, the manager came to him on tiptoe.

'Mister... We have a double room with only one person. But you will have to ask the lady if she does not mind sharing... She usually returns about noon.'

Douglas waited an hour, trying not to look hopeless.

When the woman arrived, he was shocked to find the embodiment of Flora Finching, straight out of *Little Dorrit*. In this case the face was beautiful, whereas Dickens had made Clennam's old flame excessive everywhere.

The beautiful round face smiled with a mischievous chuckle as they were introduced. Mirta, was her name. Mirta, she repeated carefully. She said she thought there could be an arrangement. She led him to a first floor room, chattering all the time, asking about his plans for staying in Argentina. Interspersed with rapid remarks about her timetable and observations about the heat she asked if he was in trouble with the police. He hesitated, said no, and knew that she knew that he was worried. She said that the British had less to worry about than other people. Life was that way.

Mirta nodded towards a screen folded in one corner. They could change behind that, she said, then pointed at the two single beds parted by a large night-table with an enamel chamber pot on the lower shelf. He suggested that she might like the screen placed between the two beds.

'You don't need the screen once you've changed into nightclothes... If you want to sleep in my room you do as I say. Understood?' He accepted. Her tone did not disguise her wish that he could stay to share the price. He was fascinated by her face, which even though fleshy was not fat. She had the attractive joviality of plump people. He looked forward to catching a glimpse of the bulging body below the beautiful face.

Mirta had to go back to work as an office assistant in the Royal Bank of Canada. What did an office assistant do? She helped people. For example, he might like to know that the Royal Canada was the only English bank in Buenos Aires that could exchange any currency he offered and give him a better rate than the Bank of London and South America. All the smugglers used the Canada.

They agreed to meet for supper.

After calling at three banks, he walked to the Royal Canada to see if Mirta's story was true. He found that only the Canada would open an account without references and give him a good rate for his pounds sterling. The thin clerk with a big nose and Brilliantine hair had an unchanging look of polite enquiry. Douglas felt sure his riches would surprise him. The man was trying to overhear one debate about Sunday's match and catch details of another about a rival bank's wages, and watched with the look of a dog at a bone too distant as Douglas unstrapped a money belt and emptied it onto the dark oak counter. Football and pay levels had the edge over the customer's fortune: one hundred pounds in coins and notes. The thin man counted slowly as he listened to his colleagues.

At the *Paraje* (Place) restaurant he ordered steak and potatoes and was embarrassed on three occasions during supper when Mirta caught him staring at her. She chuckled and plunged her spoon into a plate of stew that was spiced with a whole head of garlic. She questioned him through the meal, about his family, about Scotland, about his plans, about how much money he had brought, but she did not mention the police again. His questions were cautious, for fear of encouraging more from her. She answered them all, except when he asked if she had ever had trouble with the police. Her mother still lived at home, in northern Córdoba. But Mirta had fought with her father. During three years she had lived in several houses. The last she had left because the landlord had raped her. She was looking for a place in a good neighbourhood. Douglas thought she might be in her thirties.

'You don't ask a woman her age... Don't worry, you'll be all right with me,' she assured.

They walked back to the hotel after the third cup of coffee and nearly two litres of wine. She stepped out of her summer skirt as soon as he had closed the door and she unclasped the stocking suspenders. He pretended to be looking away and began to move the corner screen towards the beds.

'We don't need that,' she smiled.

He realised that all his fantasies of the day had fallen short of her plans. His heart raced, rose up into his throat and burst in his ears. She stood in her petticoat, the straps marking deep grooves in her shoulders and her arms bursting out of the lace top. She sat on the side of the bed and beckoned him with the warm smile. As he got quite close she announced, 'I am a little overweight for you to come from the front, so I would like you to come in from behind.'

She leaned over the bed and raised her huge backside towards him. He was down to his singlet and cotton shorts in seconds. He had never been offered so much adventure so easily. She handed him a *profiláctico* and he plunged into her with all the innocence and vigour of youthful ignorance.

Youth, wine, strength, innocence, he tried again and went in for more. But she broke wind. It was a long, garlic-smelling fart that floated up to his nostrils and he went limp. Mirta snorted in a manner that Douglas thought was a giggle but it was a whimper. She crawled under the sheets and sobbed. He stumbled back to the other bed, sat there for some few seconds, then put on his clothes and went out to the stairs. He did not notice the condom slide down his trouser leg to the front hall floor. The night porter did not return his greeting but stood staring at the rubber lying on the black and white tiles.

Douglas Noel walked into the quiet city night, tripping softly from his tiredness, the wine and the confusion. He edged through the parked taxis and the landaus for hire and the carts, some with horses snorting, some empty awaiting business in the morning. His feet crunched the gravel in the park in front of Retiro station. The clock atop the tower said two in the morning. Only a few men were about, crossing the square. He trod with care, so that his steps would not make too much noise, which would have been wrong at this time of night.

The dedication on the tower said 'to the Argentine people', a gift from Britain on the centenary, in 1910, of Argentina as an independent state. *Honi soit qui mal y pense*, he read beneath the coat of arms on two sides. England paid tribute to the independence of a nation in which England was everywhere and which English expatriates ran. That amused him and the joke cheered him, for a short time. The ember of his cigarette held his attention, while he wondered what to do. He looked for a time at the lion and then at the unicorn, and then his eyes went back to the lion. The events of the last month were eclipsed by the concrete coat of arms, by the lion and the unicorn. He shivered as he became aware of his own sentiments.

The two beasts became a symbol of home. A choking feeling came up through his body, his stomach went light and empty, his cheeks burned red and his head begun to wave from side to side. While he felt faint he imagined tying a line between the clock tower and home, Heatherlie House, and was distressed to realize that however hard he wished and longed to be there, Edinburgh was not home and that it never would be again, that he had left a place where he had no place and now was without one, without a home or a place. Yet he wanted to tie a line between himself and home, before this chance, here alone with the tower from where the line home could start, vanished.

Douglas sat down on a bench damp with dew. The narrow slats marked his trousers with wet welts. He wondered where he should go, where he should try to find living quarters. First his right eyed clouded, then the left one followed. His head drooped forward into his hands and his whole body shook with sobs.

# Chapter 5

THE BRITISH IN ARGENTINA fled from politics into the observation of wildlife, took part in sports and made their jobs and careers a matter of serious concern. They tried to ignore the fact that new historical cycles were launched every week, perhaps because the country was young. Europe foresaw disaster in the markets and in their politicians' denial that catastrophe was imminent. In Buenos Aires the evening papers threatened unparalleled bleakness. The gloom was blown away by dawn. The approach of real hardship was reflected in the number of clairvoyants who advertised in the newspapers and by the size of public meetings called by the city's quacks, palmists and *santones*.

People of all persuasions generally agreed that crisis could only be overcome by superior events, such as football.

But sometimes, even soccer caused deep difficulties for life and allegiances. Chelsea club had played five matches in Buenos Aires, as part of a South American tour, in May and June 1929. Before, during and after each event, the British community, Anglo-Argentines at large, all suffered the secret split of wanting the visitors to win, because they had come from 'home', not wanting the local team defeated, being able to praise the players of either side only when in company of the committed supporters who were clear about their loyalties. Chelsea won two games, lost two and drew one, which was a diplomatic triumph. At the start of June, Chelsea had been beaten 3-2, in a match interrupted by a Chelsea foul that brought about an invasion of the field. Police charged the crowd to prevent the visitors being beaten. The next day the *Buenos Aires Herald* and the *Standard* football correspondents produced the most convoluted prose to condemn the crowd for running onto the field, without being too harsh, and to scold Chelsea for the foul, yet not reproach the Londoners too harshly.

Buenos Aires then moved to Montevideo for what was to become the first World Cup in July 1930, with thirteen countries participating. The referee blew the whistle five minutes from the end of the final between Uruguay and France, thus ensuring the home team won. Nobody was happy, certainly not England who did not take part. *The Times* of Saturday, 19 July, ignored the final and reported the celebration of the centenary of Uruguay's 1830 constitution, at which occasion HMS *Dragon* was present, as were 1,600 Boy Scouts from Argentina and troops from Brazil. In Buenos Aires, excitement grew around political disenchantment. Argentines, immigrants, expatriates and even English-speaking residents became greatly excited about a series of nationalist lectures auguring a great new age. Patriotic army officers were planning to overthrow the civilian government.

On 6 September 1930, everybody had a share in events. Soldiers went into battle against rebel hold-outs, politicians defended themselves against abuse and public beatings, bank clerks left their jobs to march alongside nationalist demonstrators and the landladies of the old city *pensiones* filled sacks full of pamphlets collected from the pavements for use in the boarding house lavatories. Toilet paper was as scarce as cash, but sold better than bank notes.

On 7 September, the *Buenos Aires Herald* reflected the apparent popular joy in headlines that ran right across the front page. General José Félix Uriburu took over government. He looked a constipated Fascist sympathiser whose claim to reliability was that he went to mass and said six Hail Marys each time he heard an oath. 'End of personalist rule. Army cuts the Gordian knot. Wild enthusiasm greets overthrow of Irigoyen', the *Herald* shouted. 'Argentina now finds herself ruled by a junta whose civilian members are conspicuous for their wealth, aristocratic birth and conservatism,' wrote The Manchester Guardian, as reported in the cables of the day. Under the heading 'South American revolutions', though only the one coup was mentioned, the paper said, 'The root cause of all these revolutions is economic: the low price of the commodities exported by the South American republics, in the case of Argentina meat and corn in particular.' The great powers of Europe preferred the root cause to remain, because industrialization would be deeply undesirable. Pravda, in Moscow, said the coup 'is a big victory for the United States over England and represents a new accentuation of the Anglo-American struggle. One can scarcely doubt that behind the backs of the insurgent generals stands the dollar diplomacy fighting the diplomacy of the pound sterling.'

Why did they waste all that space welcoming Irigoyen just two years before, if they were going to get rid of him with so much glee so soon? The members of the English Club asked with a sense of deep bewilderment. *The Times's* editorial said that, 'There is an ironic pathos in the contrast between the popular hostility that has compelled the reluctant resignation of the old fighter and the remarkable enthusiasm that carried him into power two years ago.' But at the English Club, on 25 de Mayo street, members settled into the native spirit of events, in which were established the arguments that the man really had to go. Every member of the Club knew a general, or at least a colonel, who explained the coup, and things were going to be all right. For those members who read Spanish there remained a little puzzlement as to why one of the country's leading poets, the modernist Leopoldo Lugones (1871-1938), had actively supported the nationalist coup. 'The hour of the sword', the well-know poet had called the change of government.

Argentina's great men now were the generals, because they knew what was right for the country. Not really, really reliable, because the English club members felt that Argentines never were, but the best of a bad bunch, no doubt.

The British boasted about the land as if it were their own, praising its wealth and this new breed of Great Men. People kept telling one another that this was a time of great men and big decisions. The leading civilians in Argentina sat on the boards of British companies, alongside the expatriates who sat with them. The great men among the Anglo-Argentines were the managers of the old companies, such as Agar Cross, suppliers of windmills and farm gates that marked the remotest wilderness and became part of the country's iconography. The centre of Buenos Aires was a place for British business and there the great men congregated, their influence spreading through the provinces as over a spider's web from the city-centre building which housed the Embassy and the Royal Mail Lines.

The Associated Press agency reported that Washington had officially stated that 'Closer cooperation between the United States and Argentina is likely to result from the overthrow of Irigoyen... Despite the occasional exchange of courtesies between President Hoover and the former Argentine president the lack of cordiality on the part of Sr Irigoyen towards the United States had long been manifest...'

To the British in Argentina by far the leading information was high on the front page in those difficult days after the coup: 'The Prince of Wales: Visit welcomed by new government. Foreign capital will be treated with all the consideration it deserves...'

By 8 September, the *Herald* reported, soldiers in the streets had fired at each other, against the ships in the harbour and the crowds. After a wild night of shooting, bloodshed and rioting, nobody was clear what was going on but then the city fell quiet.

In the British community, the sensation was the publication of Cecil Beaton's *The Book of Beauty*. The London photographer's collection included an entry and the picture of an Argentine *belle*, Miss Clarita de Uriburu. 'She is one of our most important Venuses, for she is absolutely new, witty, pretty, and the result is ridiculously attractive.'

In Buenos Aires society personalities were beside themselves with joy: the flesh of the native aristocracy had made it in the metropolis.

Soldiers everywhere made the city less grand. Troops in uniform robbed the streets of their liveliness and gave the great houses they occupied the smell of barracks. The city of which Le Courbusier had said, according to the newspaper *Crítica*, just one year before: 'Buenos Aires is stupendous and could become the most beautiful in the world,' looked more unattractive now. Tanks and troops had that effect on places.

# Chapter 6

**D**OUGLAS TOOK ROOMS in the Calvet building, at the corner of Avenida Leandro Alem and the Avenida Corrientes. His bags had been sent there by the Phoenix Hotel porter – assuming the inevitable destination of single, male expatriates. A message tied to his trunk said that Mac and the Chilean drunk were fine, not dead. The semi-literate hand added the courtesy that the writer hoped Douglas was in good health and that he would always be welcome at the bar. He left his luggage untouched and with the delight of a man who is free once more ran the six blocks to the bar on Avenida Córdoba to thank the owner. After an hour, with celebratory *ginebras* burning his bowels and with babble about the great friendship of Scots and Galizian people turning in his thoughts, Douglas went to pay his bills at the Phoenix.

The news that he was back in Buenos Aires would reach the hotel soon enough and it would not do to evade payment. Gossip would have got around. The Phoenix was a stopping place for the community. For most of the English coming to town from the 'camp' it was the next best thing to their own club, and cheaper. It had been built in 1891, almost as an afterthought added to the Pacific Railway shopping and business arcade. The hotel's grand ballroom was used for English community weddings, anniversaries and special receptions in 'camp week' in mid-winter during the annual cattle show. The balcony over the entrance hall was occupied by an orchestra, sometimes all women, as in Vienna, that played to the arriving guests.

A letter from his mother, forwarded by the shipping agents, brought cuttings from *The Scotsman* and a few items of family news offered as a token of affection. There had been a train crash, one neighbour had died and another had given birth to a daughter. The Anglo-South American Bank announced that Chilean nitrate had almost doubled for the quarter, compared to 1927. In Edinburgh, Chile and Argentina were much the same. The Argentine peso was quoted at a shilling and nine pence. That was about all the *Scotsman* knew of South America, and much more than his mother cared.

The Calvet building, property of a family of vintners and wine merchants, stood on the corner opposite the central post office. From its cellars came the heady whiff of wine shipped to the docks and from the railway nearby, for distribution to all points in Buenos Aires. The upper floors of the six-storey building were private apartments used mostly by English lodgers whose landladies were widows, or the wives of alcoholics and dissolute men, or the permanently infirm who only showed they were still alive at Christmas. The building, known to the English-speaking community as the Old Calvet, was a landmark. Its leaded roof, with Parisian *mansards* and the long balconies, had been visible from afar to incoming ships and approaching drunks. For many it was a symbol of the European look of Buenos Aires. Inside, the damp air from the River Plate made men's ties look like mushroom farms and one long-suffering Dutch tenant's clogs grew fresh sprouts each spring.

At street level, partly inebriated by the aroma emanating from the large goods entrance that led to the cellar, sat the emaciated and ancient warehouse porter, Matías, a station below that of the residential porter. He befriended Douglas in the first five minutes. The newcomer had looked with interest at the cobbles set in semi-circle patterns on Avenida Corrientes.

'Imagine starting on the first row of cobbles and having all that still to do,' Douglas remarked to himself aloud as he looked up the avenue running away from the port.

'You think only one row at a time, just like in prison: one day at a time,' Matías explained slowly, to match the speed of cobble laying. After some evasion the porter said he had spent time in prison for severely maiming his lover's husband. That had been many years ago. He surveyed the cobbles with a sense of property, for he had helped to build this avenue and for that reason had found a job in a place from where he could watch over the road. With him was a dog, so old and thin that fleas only stayed on him out of solidarity, for they could have found more warmth on the dog's skinny master.

The city's air filled with the dampness of the river, with the pong of the sewage and the rotting vegetation that flowed down into the Plata from the upper Paraná. The southerly breeze brought the smell of blood from the new Anglo slaughter house in the South Dock. Contrasting with the odours of progress and pollution, parks in the city, patios in the slums, mixed the scents of jacaranda, eucalyptus, mimosa and wild roses.

The landlady on the fourth floor put Douglas in a room with a Jamaican trader, and over tea and scones he saw his fellow lodgers smile knowingly. The trader, dealing in stinking hides and spirits, snored and farted through the night and each who had suffered him had fled. The landlady rejected complaints because the Jamaican produced a tin of Capstan cigarettes for her every time he came to stay.

At breakfast on the second day, before the household emptied as each man went to his work, all were surprised to see Douglas smiling, well rested. The third day was the same, and on the fourth the trader moved to another boarding house, leaving the newcomer a room of his own.

Much later, when Douglas was admitted as a man among equals, he told his tale. On the first night, the snoring had been unbearable. On the second, after three hours of exhausting wakefulness, Douglas got up, shook his roommate half awake, kissed his unshaven cheek and muttered, 'Sweet dreams, lover man.' After that the trader sat on the edge of his bed for the rest of the night.

Douglas settled in with a group of men of his age, the kind who laughed at other men's affairs and who gave rolling pins as engagement gifts. There was a constant flow of men from up-country railway branches and depots who celebrated a brief escape from the wives they would always remain married to, out of habit and because their jobs depended on cautious comportment and conventional customs. The only affairs they could contemplate were with the wives of their juniors or with local women.

There was too a regular traffic of short-term Irish guests, farmers on business. In spite of the sun and their new life the Irish retained their special whiteness: the only way they could take any colour was by copious drinking. And even then, the bloom that this brought to their cheeks was betrayed by eyes filled with weariness. The cloud of the age of ages in their look would only sometimes be cleared away, and never on Saint Patrick's Day. They had been born tired of time, exhausted by the search for a destiny that would bring them some comfort and justice, after a history of despair. Their clothes were garments out of the nineteenth century, with perhaps a modern cut here or there to make an elegant neckline or higher hem.

Antonio, an Anglo-Irish lodger known as 'Anguish' for short, fell in love with the landlady's daughter. He could never find her alone though he knew that she responded; her warm smiles were full acknowledgement of his blown kisses. She was in his dreams and he even thought of her in his bath, and then in his confessions at the Irish church where the priest advised prudence and said that Anguish would be better cared for by his own kind. The priest often had to convince the Irish lads to mend their ways. Very often too, at the end of the month or in July at the Cattle Show the priest had to sweep through the brothels and recover the boys before they could spend all their savings. They were married off to the wall flowers described as nice Irish girls, rounded up at 'Camp week' dances. The collective wedding parties were such that sometimes they made the crime pages in the evening papers and were recalled for years after. Mrs O'Toole, who cleaned and ironed for the reverend father at the Holy Cross Church, called these occasions the 'spectaculate conception' of each year.

Anguish said that he would have none other than *La Verónica* with whom he was deeply in love. The landlady kept the adolescent in bloom safely from him. Anguish decided that the only way to win and secure her, for he was sure he had already well wooed her with his eyes and blown kisses, was to compromise her before an audience of *ingleses*. This would force the mother to relent for she would never want it to be known that she kept a scandalous house.

On a day like any other, that happened to be Sunday morning after Mass, and in spite of Douglas's warning that he was not very fond of Sundays, Anguish devised direct access to Verónica's bedroom by-passing her mother in dramatic fashion. He asked Douglas and Harry, an English accountant, to winch him down from the roof on the furniture hoist to the level of the fourth floor, from which hanging position he would enter the girl's room.

The landlady was out, but she tended to lock her daughter in when the men were about the house, dismissing the girl's complaints with a mother's argument that such was best for her child whom she did not want to see suffer.

Anguish was mistaken. The landlady was at home, bathing and painting herself for a fantasy encounter with a widower from the Great Southern Railway who had moved, in deep grief, to her lodgings and with whom she was thought to have flirted quite seriously after only three weeks.

As bad luck is an accumulation of misfortunes, Anguish and friends mistook the bedroom window. Anguish was lowered until he was sitting in front of the senior woman's chamber. There she stood, with her ample breasts bared before the mirror in the wardrobe door, her chubby hand holding tweezers with which she plucked at hairs that ringed her saucer-sized nipples.

Anguish was stunned by such sights as he had never seen and forgot to call for a change of plan. She caught sight of him in the mirror and went for him with a broom. He waved to be raised, but the pulley sprocket stuck and high above Avenida Corrientes's cobbles the Irishman swung helplessly, thumped by a broom swung by a woman in too great a fury to cover her bosom.

Matías, the wine-cellar porter, came with an oil can and chain spanner to overcome the jam.

The two lodgers who had operated the furniture winch without success never knew the full story, despite being as close to the events as they had been. But it was later said that Anguish, under siege, threatened the woman that he would report fully on his view of herself. She was then convinced of the wisdom of allowing Anguish to see her daughter, to tell Veronica firmly, for she was young and could be impressed by his deep voice and prospects, that he was the man she would marry because that was written in the air. Anguish promised to love her for ever until they tired... he meant died. The priest at the Holy Cross agreed to marry them after some more severe words about a wedding outside of the community, and Matías left his stool by the street cobbles to be one of the ushers in the church.

# Chapter 7

WHATEVER THE POLITICAL WEATHER, every Anglo-Argentine waking hour was spent watching the progress of the princes, the Prince of Wales and Prince George, down through South America.

There were more important events taking place. But nothing was as noticeable as royalty. For example, there was a Londoner named Cyril Taylor who flew a small single-engined open cockpit Comper-Swift across the Andes, from Santiago de Chile to Mendoza, in Argentina. Cyril was thirty-five and had wanted to fly the Andes since always. Flying had been his greatest ambition, he had told his friends who went fishing on the waterfront on the River Plate. And so, in January 1931, on a weekday when he got time off work, because he could not wait for a weekend, he unfolded the skeleton and fabric and took the noisy moth-like machine swerving along the line of Andean passes, flying very low and without any ground support. When he landed in Mendoza, he was declared a hero on both sides of the Andes. For an Englishman it was a little, and only a little, like flying from home to home. Chile was very pro-English, and Argentina wanted to be so very much. The papers in both countries splashed Cyril's adventures across their front pages. But then the papers and the readers thought no more of air pioneers. The glamour of royalty was enthralling.

The Royal Tour by the princes was a sales drive to prop up British commercial strength throughout the continent, but mostly in Argentina. His Royal Highness, Edward, Prince of Wales, who someday would be king, had been in Buenos Aires in 1925 as a salesman, largely to beat off the growing influence and fortunes of the rich Americans from the very rich Unites States' industries.

By 1927, Argentina had become the largest buyer in the world of US-made cars and tyres. A brand new Chevrolet sold for £375 in Buenos Aires and the order books were full, though there was not so much demand for the Cadillac, which sold for £1,650 in the showrooms of the South American capital. There were 19,300 automobiles in the streets of Buenos Aires, many of them made in USA. The 'bloody Americans', as they were described by the British, were everywhere. The British had a share of the public transport system, apart from the railways. There were 3,500 electric trams operating in the city, but English manufacturers were losing out in consumer sales.

Such a serious situation, as were all matters commercial, could not dampen enthusiasm in anticipation of the Princes' arrival. Preparations included a vast trade fair by British business in Buenos Aires and fantasies of romance by Anglo-Argentine virgins.

The Princes' progress was reported daily as from their landfall in Peru. The South American correspondents of *The Times* kept the news on the Royal advance flowing from Monday, 16 February 1931. They had arrived in Lima on the previous Friday, from Panama. From the Peruvian capital they flew to attend a reception given by the British Community at the Arequipa Club. Then to Cuzco and across Lake Titicaca on 18 February.

As the Princes left Peru, army forces in Callao revolted against Colonel Sánchez Cerro, a jumped-up, aspiring despot who had thought his time had come and had deposed President Eguía. Sánchez Cerro was forced to announce that he would not run in the forthcoming elections, but these would not be held anyway, at least not until an assembly had been elected to reform the Constitution.

Bolivia was, at that moment, an altogether far happier arrangement. 'La Paz, 19 February. The Princes are *muy simpáticos.*' They had received an enthusiastic reception. The newspaper *El Diario* welcomed the 'heir to the throne of the greatest country in the world'. Now, that was what the British wanted to read. *La Razón* published a ten-page section in English. 'Bolivia owes much to British capital and enterprise. Our country has a deep feeling of gratitude.'

The royals flew to Antofagasta, Chile, two days later, just as Communists were reported to have taken the town of Encarnación, in Paraguay. The Princes were far from that, however, when they landed gently on Valparaiso Bay on 24 February in a Sikorsky amphibian plane, escorted by six Falcons. A call at Grange School was a local success when the headmaster was told to give his fifty boys a day's holiday to mark the visit. President Ibañez 'spoke of the gratitude of the Chilean nation for the unswerving friendship of Great Britain. The Prince of Wales replied in Spanish' and then played a game of polo.

But if sport was of interest to royalty, it was sport that was turning nasty at their next destination.

'There is serious tension at the present moment between the Governments and peoples of Argentina and Uruguay. Bad blood was engendered about a year ago over an international football match played in Montevideo in which the Uruguayans defeated the Argentines. Ridiculous as it may sound, this defeat rankled very sorely...' wrote the Buenos Aires correspondent of *The Times*.

Public feeling against Argentina was being whipped up in the streets of Montevideo by refugees from the September (1930) coup and by dozens of central Europeans who had been deported for their Anarchist sympathies. Fully aware of their fate should they ever land in Europe, the alleged Anarchists had jumped ship in Uruguay, 'likewise, many Anarchists from Buenos Aires have gone of their own accord to avoid the attentions of the police...' reported *The Times*. Buenos Aires and Montevideo needed each other as neighbours and rivals, and 'in recent years not only Montevideo but several Uruguayan seaside resorts have been largely patronised by Argentine tourists, attracted by the gambling facilities at the official casinos and also by the excellent motor roads.'

*The Times*' leader on Wednesday, 25 February, said that 'Time was not so very long ago, when Englishmen would justify their feelings of innate superiority by pointing to the failure of foreigners to realize the importance of cricket and football...' But now, 'we have much to learn from South America about the real importance of football matches.' The editorial writer recalled that there had been great enmity shown at the first international tournament in July of the previous year. 'The football match, coming as the final round of a tournament between two neighbours with such long memories of each other, took on a symbolic character. The 90,000 spectators indulged in orgies of partisanship which led to insult and injury...'

The evening papers in Buenos Aires said the First World Football War was imminent. There were, however, not enough serious casualties, so the idea of war was put aside. The tension and the insults were such that Argentina would break relations with Uruguay in 1932.

# Chapter 8

DOUGLAS FOUND A WOMAN who looked clean and appeared to be helpful in one of the better brothels of the *Bajo*, the section of the port-side avenue which ran south from Government House. She had thin blonde hair and a square jaw, her body felt bony, her shoulders jagged. She looked what she was: a lean and hungry central European. He thought that if he had tried harder he might have secured a woman of greater beauty. But he lacked the confidence and decided that he could evolve improvements on the woman in his fantasies. He felt pleased, a little smug even, that he had found the guts to get himself a woman. He became contented in the assurance that she was the best his abilities could conquer.

He would have preferred an English girlfriend, but there were none available on request. There was one, from a family in the southern suburbs, by name of Margaret Kelly, but he did not dare approach her. She, and a cousin named Mary, disowned by families who had made their names unmentionable, gained a comfortable income from 'English' bank clerks and railway supervisors and lonely bachelors who wanted to play 'Mums & Dads' and sometimes 'Babies & Doctors'. Douglas thought that because the Kelly woman and her cousin were from the community they would be without disease, the British Hospital offering prostitutes a free and discreet medical service. But he knew that his belief was prejudiced make-believe. His real fear of them was that they would talk, which they did, and his weaknesses and failures would become known to all Buenos Aires on any night the girls got drunk with their customers. Already Douglas had caught up with some of Mac's history, his first British acquaintance in Buenos Aires, through the women's gossip. Mac took either Kelly or her cousin out on each of his visits to the city to play 'father' to a temporary 'mother' and speak of conception. This exercise, it turned out, was a yearning for a child conceived with a woman and then lost in his vanished youth.

There were no respectable houses on the *Bajo*. Most of the better kind were well away from the port.

No sooner had Douglas finished with the woman at their first assignation than she followed him back to the Calvet. From that day on she spent every possible moment with him, sneaking into the building unseen, then leaving quietly to attend to her other customers. Often she followed him when he went to call at city offices, where he thought he had employment prospects or had been recommended for a job. In the afternoons, sometimes three or four a week, when the house was empty, Eva, for that was her name – all Poles seemed to be called either Eva or María – would sneak into the building alone, so as not to be seen with him. From the toilet she would bring to his room an iron bowl of cold water and wash him and herself with a clean teacloth, which she would rinse later and hang from the window handle. This washing routine would be followed each time he came. Then she would kiss him and perhaps they would start all over again, while she thanked him for the kindness of small presents which he added to her rates. She helped him overcome his premature ejaculation and beat his shyness with the efficiency of the more experienced. They would stop and she would get off the bed and smooth the sheets when the voice of the newsvendor shouting '*la Quinta*', the 'fifth edition' of the afternoon papers, rose to the window from the corner below. There was enough time for her to dress, which she did untidily as she draped her scrawny figure, and leave the building before the first of the lodgers returned from work.

Some months after his arrival in Argentina, Douglas was offered respectable employment with William Cooper & Nephews, importers of veterinary and farm products. One member of the Cooper family was impressed by the certificate in farming proficiency from the Edinburgh and East of Scotland College of Agriculture. The diploma had been awarded at the end of a five-week course for farmers in foods and feeding stuffs, veterinary hygiene and book-keeping. Not many Britons went for jobs with qualifications beyond school matriculation exams. Cooper & Nephews immediately arranged a training course for Douglas to become accustomed to local names and practices at several small farms on the outskirts of Buenos Aires.

He saw less of Eva and she resented his absence. Lightly at first, but later more vehemently, she accused him of straying because he had a proper job and could not be seen with a woman of her position. Her voice rose when she said 'position' and she hit the letters 'p-o' with a blast of her lips. She was right, of course and he knew she was, but he strenuously denied the accusation. Douglas had been warned by his fellow lodgers about the strength and unpredictability of jealousy of women in Argentina, immigrants or not. If they were outsiders the sense of demand and possession was a local aspect quickly acquired.

One Sunday afternoon, when he came home from a tennis match at the YMCA, she gave him what he forever regarded as his first real copulation, a complete climax for both of them. After they had relaxed she said simply: 'There, that is what you will be missing.' He smiled thinking the remark to be jealousy. Later, they went dancing at a night club on Avenida Corrientes, a street of lights and entertainment only a few blocks up the cobbled avenue from the Calvet.

At midnight, intent on overcoming the distance of the separations of the previous few weeks, Douglas asked Eva to marry him.

He was not wholly convinced that he was doing the right thing with the right person, but he felt honourable. It seemed the right thing to offer. She shocked him by saying, in her heavily accented Spanish, that marriage would be like taking her work home. When he said he wanted her to give up the game for him, she shrugged, then let out a full laugh which sounded too loud for her small frame. Eva walked him back to the Calvet in silence, but made no move to slink into the building. She stepped back on the pavement and raised her hand to the height of her flat breast and from there she waved him goodbye.

She did not return the next day. He went in search of her to the brothel where he had found her only a few weeks ago. Douglas was laughed at when he asked for Eva in his own accented Spanish. What man would want something looking like a plucked and starved chicken? The porter said he had much better women if the *caballero*, the gentleman, would like to look.

When Douglas insisted on knowing Eva's whereabouts, he was told to go to the home of Frau María. The porter used the word *casa* – house or home. The doorman, dressed in a shabby vestige of evening dress, said the madams had *casas*. At the elegant apartment overlooking the posh Plaza San Martín, a very good address indeed, Douglas was told that Eva had been sent on a one-way ticket to a Polish Club, in Lima. He thought he heard Frau María say 'sold', but he was not certain. She spoke in a strange sort of English.

'*Zey* will find her a good old man for husband. Young men should not try to make wives out of whores. Such women are better left for old men. *Zey* play well when old men play bad. So old men like it that way.'

Frau María looked at him with great sympathy, whether it was honest or not was irrelevant. 'Poor boy, forget her. Find another. There are so many, much better, eh! Life is full of better partners if you simply *sink* your mind to making them better. Sink of Eva as a picnic, a thing for once, and then to *somesink* else. You cannot have picnics all the time. Men need wives who are women, not picnics.

'She was no use to me and no use to you. Friends, my good friends, complained. She had pear-ship...' Douglas looked puzzled, 'You know, pear-ship...' He struggled with the word until he realized that Frau María meant 'pear-shaped buttocks', a firm form, bottom heavy.

'And she was flat. Her nipples were so small I was so afraid a friend might hit her with a fly-swat and cause an injury. I got her given with a delivery of three good ones. Those Migdal group were terrible. They always were getting rid of women. For them it was the same to send them to Buenos Aires as to kill. But nobody wanted to shoot them.'

Frau María suddenly looked at Douglas with a reserve of fury her voice had kept hidden. 'On Sunday, she said you were so kind she was falling in love.'

'She is a Pole, man, and zey have smaller brains, the Poles. Zat's why zey come to Argentina. In their country their own men, even their fathers and brothers, ze Jews, send them away. Pogrom, *shmogrom*. They use that as an excuse to get rid of women without fortune or future. The Argentines buy them cheap. Virgins have better price. The police put up notices in Poland. Do you know? 'Beware of Argentina men. Danger of abduction.' And still the fools they come.

'Why do you do zis, you stupid men? Why you fall in love? It is bad... for me... and for you Engliss...'

'Scots!!'

'Ah, so, ya. Scotch, big thing. So you too are sensitive. Stop zis. You are stupid. Eva will make a good young wife for a good old Pole. You English never learn, you want to have a girl's body and save your conscience by imposing protection on her inferior mind. Same way you made the Empire.

'I know you British: I have read Shakespeare and that tells all. In *All'swell zat end'swell*, you know, Helena she says: 'Bless our poor virginity from undermines and blowers up!' Is there no military policy, how virgins might blow up men?'

'In a whore the heart remains virgin, always. And if you blow that up you leave her nothing,' Frau María said.

Of all the people to give a moral conclusion, a madam seemed out of place, but Frau María was very much in place.

Douglas went back to the Calvet drained of feeling, but filled with the Madam's ethics.

The encounter with Eva had been brief, spread over a few weeks. The first few days had felt like much longer because of his embarrassment at stepping out with a whore. He felt that he was being unfaithful to his class, to a social group. The same must be the case with married men when they are unfaithful. They feel awkward when walking accompanied by the partner that is not the one known to a peer group. That feeling never goes away, Douglas advised and asked himself. As the sense that she was an unworthy and shameful partner became less of a burden, he had enjoyed her company and then began to feel comfortable with her. Then the passing days seemed shorter.

On his return from meeting Frau María he found a telegram from his mother. Such urgency and expense from Edinburgh was out of order.

'HAVE READ "THE ROAD TO BUENOS AIRES" STOP WHAT A DIS-GUSTING COUNTRY YOU HAVE CHOSEN.'

It was his mother's last direct communication. After that, all her messages were sent to her daughters, to be forwarded to Buenos Aires to her younger son, for his attention.

Stunned by such sudden maternal rejection, Douglas set out to look for a copy of the book that had inspired such wrath. The search took several days. At Mitchell's Bookstore he found that it was sold from a stack under the counter. The book, by a French journalist, Albert Londres, offered 'the astounding revelations of the traffic of women', according to the dust jacket. The *Spectator* said the book gave 'an appalling picture of the world trade in women.' And the *Times Literary Supplement* found it 'vivacious, graphic and witty, and giving an amazing picture of Buenos Ayres.'

*Typically English review*, Douglas thought.

That was when he began to put together the pieces missing in the puzzle that was Buenos Aires. The brothels that he had visited and those he had only heard about up until then had been easily ignored, put aside with a strenuous tennis match on a town court or a morning rowing on the river. The question of how the women were employed had been dismissed. Douglas had heard about the establishments but was unaware of their employment policy, though he had at times wondered why Eva, a Polish woman, was working in Buenos Aires. Frau María took matters as a fact. The prostitutes were referred to as business women, never as fallen women (which the polite English residents called them from time to time). The trade was controlled by several groups. The French syndicate, operating out of Marseilles, had given the city the *Franchuta*, a word that came from conflating *Francesa Puta*, or 'French Whore'. And it was the custom of Argentine women to feign a French origin and accent so as to charge higher rates. There were smaller French groups and a powerful Italian *Maffia*. One of the largest operators was the Jewish Polish syndicate, Zwi Migdal, supplier of women to the brothels of the Americas, from Chicago to Buenos Aires. Operators picked up women in Central Europe among the destitute. They were the females whose fathers could not pay for a wedding, or whose husbands had vanished in one of the frequent evictions of Jews and would never be able to find another spouse in their environment, or single women with few prospects and even less hope and they were promised marriage in South America. It was the promise of food, regular meals and a bed that attracted them most. Virgins were prized. On arrival in Argentina, with very little ceremony and no mention of earlier promises, the women were put in the charge of Frau María or her likes. Others were auctioned like calves at the cattle market. After a bath and a change of clothes they were informed that they were there to please paying men. If they refused they would get a hiding such as they had never had from their fathers or estranged husbands. Some were married to the flotsam and jetsam in the bars of Buenos Aires to secure legal entry but were controlled by pimps. The Frau Marías were known as managers, or *la señora*. And 'nice women' were the society ladies who were sometimes called on to protect the managers of the businesswomen from police harassment, for a share in the profits, which were plentiful enough to ensure reasonable incomes for all.

The society ladies were married to rich men who spent their money in Europe, travelling there on the Hamburg-Sudamerikanische Line, which was preferred because its ships sailed at midnight, with deck lights ablaze and two bands playing *Deutschland Uber Alles*. Royal Mail Lines had unfashionable afternoon sailings. The Germans took good care of the regular passengers, who brought back the women to the likes of Frau María.

Douglas's encounter with 'Eva the Polish pro', told in confidence to one man at the Calvet, was soon turned into one of the great affairs of the boarding house. What his fellow lodgers most wanted to know was how she had entered the building and they asked for descriptions of what had taken place in his rooms. Douglas also reported on his meeting with the fat woman in the hotel in Retiro. The lodgers were shocked, not about the encounter, but about her size. 'You are a fool; and she sounds like a witch...' he was scolded. Douglas heard himself say, 'No, she wasn't that. Witches don't cry. She cried, remember.'

After some time in Buenos Aires, Douglas found that he had only one local friend and not many Britons he could call close.

'Eva the Polak', as she had now become in his memory, had shown him a city that was healthy, raw and inspiring, a world of convivial masculine chaff and of depressingly exploited women who made their wages out of favours that they were unable to enjoy. Eva had led him through the red-curtained doorways of brothels in the Boca and to the brawling sexuality of the bars on Paseo Colón. She had introduced him to public coitus when she pointed to women straddling men who sat at tables drinking their *ginebra*. And she encouraged him to peer through the torn slits in cotton curtains where he saw couples in half-naked commercial intercourse in small nooks at the end of dark corridors, near the kitchens of bars on the *Bajo*, that rightly named low, port area.

Eva had also introduced him to her only Argentine acquaintance, who would become his friend. Carlos Prieto, in his mid-twenties, had been found living without embarrassment at Frau María's home, where Eva had lived briefly before moving to a room in slum lodgings. Prieto, as he was known, with no first name, said he was an artist – of poor quality – with a desire to portray the prostitutes of Buenos Aires in action and at rest. He relied on parental subsidy to pursue a law degree, with which he would seek a few good property transactions that would make him rich and allow him time for his art.

Prieto was determined to find Douglas a job 'more creative than putting strange powders on plants and pushing pills down the throats of cows. It is dangerous: it is abnormal to be so concerned about the welfare of animals. You might fall in love with a cow, or become a vegetarian.'

Against his better judgement, Douglas was convinced: he postponed joining Cooper & Nephews on the grounds that he had to complete an appointment with a furniture supplier with whom he had a contract. Cooper senior, the only surviving nephew, was not well pleased and held forth about moral duties and responsibilities. Finally, Cooper decided to endure the postponement, in exchange for a letter of intent to join, as the company had paid for the new recruit's training.

Douglas trusted that he could remain one step ahead of Cooper if anything better developed, and began to help to make antiques out of new furniture for merchant class sitting rooms. The job, at a Frenchman's carpentry, taught nothing but a firm pulse, required to drive a needle fine drill bit into the legs of chairs to make them look attacked by ancient woodworm. This fault supported the salesroom claim that the items had been rescued from *estancia* houses owned by patrician families. The carpenter bought good, expensive nesting tables, small chests and bedside shelves at Maple, the English store on Esmeralda Street. With generous splashing of dark fruit juices and Atkinson's gentlemen's toilet water, the polish was spoiled but the wood remained with a lasting perfume, which added to the sales price.

The trouble with such employment was that the Frenchman had to keep away from police by regularly moving premises. This made Douglas's workplace something of a mystery tour and produced a renewed sense of being on the run, which soon became exhausting. After three months the Frenchman fled south to a village which put the Calvet building too far. Douglas resigned with regret. The risk had been considerable but the rewards, in daily pay and danger bonuses as well as literary lectures on all of Europe's current authors, had restored some of his reduced savings and filled him with new knowledge.

The French craftsman gave Douglas his first workplace farewell party with homemade paté and a local fizzy wine the quality of which the carpenter admired at every sip. He was thinking of going into adulterating white wine to sell as champagne.

In the evenings, if Douglas was not too tired, Prieto taught him how to tap dance. After three weeks, they put on an act in the basement theatre of Güemes arcade, on Florida Street. Seamen from all over the world came to the theatre bar for the women and to read the shipping schedules which were pasted up by the reporters from *The Standard* and the *Buenos Aires Herald* – in exchange for free drinks and gratis access to the late strip show.

As the tap dance routine improved, it became a popular number between the bawdy acts and grotesque stripping by fat women – who arched back in spider position, to offer the audience full inspection of their genitals – and men with freak-length penises.

After one month of fairly intense tap dance shows, Prieto and Douglas had the courage to join the female strippers and the transvestites who crossed Florida Street to *L'Aiglon* bar, there to embarrass the theatre patrons who had fled without putting anything in the hat passed around just before the final curtain. *L'Aiglon*, in spite of its seedy custom late at night, was a popular and well-regarded café that remained open until dawn. There the two men touted for a better class of engagement. Sometimes they tapped to a jazz beat played by a band at the *Richmond Bar*, across the street from the theatre, on Florida. That proved their undoing. One day an elegant-looking gentleman came up to the stage and threatened Prieto for having dared to address his daughter: Prieto's father was informed about the night-time occupation and the tap-dancing career came to an end.

Douglas was relieved that life on the stage was over. He had been seen at the *Richmond* by one member of the Cooper family, who begun a tirade about dishonesty and disloyalty, when an elegant little tart with dyed blonde hair snuggled up to the man and put her hand in his trouser pocket. The man shivered at the surprise grip on his testicles and winced at being discovered. For Douglas, it was an assurance that he was safe. But he began to wonder how long he could stay on the edge of the shadows.

Prieto took Douglas on a tour of the artists' studios and private galleries, using the expatriate Scot's search for employment as an introduction by which to promote his own work. Thus Douglas was introduced to Benito Quinquela Martín, a young and successful painter with the appearance of a nonagenarian national monument, who announced to his visitors that 'I was born in the Boca and I shall never paint anything else but my neighbourhood.' This was a district of Italian immigration, impoverished families living in corrugated sheet metal houses and fishing boats moored in the Riachuelo, polluted by the blood and effluents of the meat-packing houses. Quinquela Martín's subjects were the men, the carts and the stevedores of the Boca. Local society was beginning to buy his naive lines of men climbing the gangways of foreign steamers, workers bent double under the weight of sacks of grain or beef quarters, which made Argentina's wealth.

From the art world, in which both failed, Prieto led the way to a crime writer on the morning paper *El Mundo*, published by the Anglo-Argentine Haines family, shareholders in the British-owned railways. Prieto's idea was that Douglas should translate the foreign news dispatches from the Havas-Reuter agency.

The crime reporter turned out to be a character even wilder than Prieto in his plans and projects. Roberto Arlt, a man in his thirties, launched forth in great knowledge of chemistry and described his admiration for Dr Crippen as an inventor of the near-perfect English murder. After two hours of close description of a catalogue of inventions to make synthetic fibres and explosives, the writer suggested that they should all go to supper. With only a passing apology for his poor spelling, Arlt left his copy with the editor, Alberto Gerchunoff, formerly of the newspaper *La Nación* and shortly to return there in desperation, who was fending off an irate Jewish immigrant deeply offended by Gerchunoff's stories about Jewish life in Argentina.

The three men went for a meal. Over a thick steak, much of which Arlt sprayed over the table as he spoke, the reporter described with photographic detail some of the goriest murders he had written about, using his knife to make sketch lines on the meat and with interjections in English. Then he took Douglas to task as a spokesman for Scotland, accusing him of responsibility by proxy for the failure to organize the socialist revolution against English imperialism. Arlt spent an hour in praise of Russia as the guiding light of a new age, drawing a picture of the country with travel book precision from Minsk to Vladivostok.

Douglas fled back to the feasible fantasies of the English-speaking environment.

# Chapter 9

THE TRADE FAIR in Buenos Aires in March would 'show that the British empire is still commercially virile,' wrote Sir Eric Drummond, in a study on Latin America and the League of Nations. But Argentina was, Sir Eric thought, passing through a difficult period. Argentina was always passing through some sort of difficulty.

On Tuesday, 3 March 1931, *The Times* reported that the princes had entered Argentina by way of northern Patagonia. And for many a maiden and so many men, in Buenos Aires, that is where the stories begin to be augmented by apocrypha concerning the princely nights of passion. *The Times* did not say that, but it was the rumour among the better classes in Buenos Aires, who expected the visit to be something special. At the Jockey Club and elsewhere, even in suburban gardens, not a few mothers said over cocktails in the late summer evenings that they would not mind at all, in fact they boasted about the very possibility quite openly, if their daughters were left in the family way by either of the princes. They spoke in terms of a 'roll in the hay' and 'buns in the oven' and other clichés to show how open were their minds.

People who said they knew about the princes' activities claimed that the Prince of Wales drank heavily and that at least one young Argentine woman had seduced him. The idea of bearing the future king's bastard, as in other times women had borne the sons of great warriors, was an attractive proposition in elegant society, according to the people who assured that they knew about these things.

The princes stayed at an *estancia*, Picanew, in Rio Negro, the property of the British-owned Argentine Southern Land Company, and crossed by rail to the Ortiz Basualdo family *estancia* at Huemul. The competition to show the greater hospitality led men out of their senses, and out of pocket. One laid a red carpet over several kilometres from gateposts to grand entrance. The princes reached Buenos Aires by air on 5 March and General Uriburu, the president, held a banquet the next day. The Prince of Wales was back in the whirl that had so exhausted him in 1925.

The Buenos Aires British Empire Exhibition opened on 14 March 1931; four days after *The Times* published a special Argentine Exhibition Number, copies of which found their way to Buenos Aires in time. 'The great Republic of Argentina has paid to Britain a practical compliment that is unique. Never before has one country been permitted to hold an exhibition of its own industrial products in the capital of another...' wrote the special report editor, anxious to please advertisers and counter the paper's not infrequent criticism of the River Plate countries.

The combined capital of the Anglo-Argentine railways totalled £300 million and the network spanned 16,300 miles. Britain sold £30 million worth of goods to Argentina each year and bought £80 million in Argentine beef and grain. Sir Malcolm Robertson, ambassador to Argentina and founder in 1928 of the Argentine Association of English Culture, called Argentina 'one of the most friendly markets that is open to us in the whole world', then warned that cultural links were threatened. 'We persist in ignoring the value of cultural propaganda from which the German, French, Italian, and latterly the North Americans, have derived so much advantage...'

## Chapter 10

OLD MAN COOPER invited Douglas into his office. This alarmed the younger man. No ordinary employee was usually called in. Those who had access and reason to consult the chief, the accountant and his secretary, marched in, back straight, chin up and papers held out in front of them. At the end of each year the old bachelor came out of his corner office and addressed everybody, about a dozen in all in the business. Seldom was anybody called in as he believed that each had their work to do and had to know their job.

'I don't know what it is about you that I don't like, laddie, but I don't. And then again I'm fond of your nerve. I really am fond of you,' he said, coming round his desk and putting a hand on Douglas's left shoulder, offering the view for all the staff in what was referred to as the Main Office. Cooper stood still, in silence, looking at Douglas who tried to avert his eyes.

'I wish I could get angry, but I can't.' The grip on the young shoulder tightened. This was more frightening, Douglas wondered, only a few weeks into his new job, where he would find work. 'I don't quite know why, but you're going to leave us for a few days. The British Embassy wants you, and their word is law around here. Like bloody royalty. Them, aye, and the bloody railway chief. I suppose they do think of themselves as Viceroys. The ambassador is a snob and the trains chief is a lout who won't hear a word about the mess in his freight wagons.'

The old man stopped, apologised for the strong language and told Douglas not to say a word to anybody about his remarks. Douglas promised. He was bewildered by the old man's anger and affection, but relieved that he was not being dismissed.

'But they've asked for you, I can't say no. In fact, it might serve me well to ask them to get our cargo orders straightened... You've got to see the wife of the Number Two at the embassy. She wants a boy she can trust for the royal visit preparations. And so we are to lose your services for the duration.'

Mrs Margaret Handy, second wife of the once-widowed Harold Handy and twenty years his junior, explained in a clipped voice that she had met Douglas's elder brother, a naval officer and a gentleman, at a party in Portsmouth and she had been asked to look out for Douglas in Buenos Aires. This she was now doing.

'He's a jolly good looking man, your brother,' she said. She stared at Douglas for a few seconds, almost as if she was not seeing him, then added: 'It is probably in the family. You're rather handsome yourself.' The voice trailed off in a long 'elf'.

'And you are a very attractive woman, Mrs Handy,' he replied, earnestly, though it sounded like duty. Her smile softened and she looked less business like, but she had been trained to consider any compliment from a younger man to be rudeness, so she recovered some severity. She was at least ten years his senior and her tightly tied-back hair in a bun made her put on quite a few more. Douglas wondered if she had any children, then answered his own question with a glance at the many pictures on the walls and in silver frames on the furniture. They showed older off-spring – at least one was with a young child in her arms – from a first marriage. The photographs stated devotedly and firmly than Handy thought he had enough.

Margaret Handy said Douglas was required to keep a look out for late arrangements, invitations that had not been received, prompt delivery of those missing, checking and re-checking guest lists. She had a social secretary at the Embassy with whom all the work had been done and it had taken her hours, without a thank you from H.E. and not even a 'Well done!' from her husband.

'You men think women are just here to take care of the things you can't be bothered with, don't you?'

She gave Douglas a withering look and for an answer he shrugged. If he had had a choice he would have preferred to be back handling animal ointments at Cooper's.

'And the President's office is the worst of the bloody lot,' she swore without inhibition. 'I asked for a messenger boy and they sent three policemen who would not deliver the order for floral arrangements. So you're going.'

In the hours that followed, Margaret Handy kept a round the clock vigil, arranging secondary protocol. As telegrams flowed in reporting the exact whereabouts of the princes and the increasing number of guests they were collecting in their progress, there were flower-girls to coordinate and rehearse, additional transport to be engaged, new invitation cards to issue and, once, a complete change of venue for a tree-planting ceremony. The ground which was to receive the Royal spadeful was still water-logged from recent freak flooding, so a golf club would have to do.

The Handy couple's home was a grand apartment which occupied one entire floor of a building thrown up in great style twenty years earlier, with the fortune available and luxury of one of the big landowners. It was decorated in a collection of European fashions – they had the money to collect everything. The Handy's obviously needed space for entertaining, perhaps because they had to make sure Harold looked like the next in line to the Ambassador. Every room was in disorder. The three maids, who were either completely indifferent or next to tears, tried to remain in the kitchen, but were screamed for at regular intervals in a torrent of English insults that connected their names in a rush of linked syllables: 'BloodyMartaDamnedErnestaBloodyWhatsit' and the volume grew as the three diminutive girls, half literate adolescents from up country, failed to recognize identity or instruction in the abuse. The housekeeper who normally kept them busy had gone into hospital the week before the princes' tour and never had infirmity been so damnably planned, said Margaret Handy.

The maids were banned from the bedroom and from almost everywhere in the house, as the bed's open sheets became covered in papers, pencils, ribbons for flowers and wilted flowers. Several secretaries came from the embassy to help, but none cleared up after. Douglas was kept running for all of them, often in the unbearable heat of midday. Harold Handy stayed away from the house, returning in the evening briefly to urge his wife, very politely, to hurry and dress for the night's function. By then Margaret Handy was in a good mood, charming, at times seductive, assisted in her buoyant optimism through the worst pressure by several gins and tonic. She would cheerfully leave Douglas in the flat with orders to the maids to give him supper on whatever clear space could be found. He could drink the stock of beer and gin, but was forbidden access to wine or whisky. Late at night, or close to dawn, asleep on the deep sofa in the sitting room (which he had been allocated in the emergency), he would hear her tip-toe into the house, laughing and joking with her husband, until she fell exhausted on the large bed among the papers and pencils. Then her husband would leave, the sound of his departure was so hushed that it was covered by the whirling fans that struggled most of the night to calm the summer heatwave.

In the morning, early, without any sign of a hangover or of being tired, she was also cheerful. Her mood deteriorated during the day and then improved again in the evening. She never told Douglas where she had been the night before, but hinted during those days that the government officials had tried to be intimate or had been rude, or the show they had seen had been a bore, or some officer in the princes' advance retinue was 'A scream!'

On the fifth or sixth morning she woke him from his light, nervous sleep on the sofa with a gentle kiss.

In seconds he was standing as if he had sprung from the bed, grappling with the sheet to keep his singlet and shorts from view. She stood smiling at him, a gown in peach silk covered a matching nightdress. He stared at her flat chest and then caught sight of a firm nipple pushing its shape through the fabric. She looked cool in the rising heat of the early morning. Douglas had sweat running down his chest into his cotton vest. In bare feet, she was a little taller than him.

Margaret Handy moved forward and kissed him on the mouth. Her breath was a blast of brandy and heavy smoking to which was added the foulness of overnight. Douglas imagined his mouth tasted the same; it always did before the first cigarette and he tried to hold his breath as she kissed him, but after a moment he snorted through his nostrils and she pulled back. She took his hand and without a word led him down the long dark green corridor, lined with portraits and European landscapes in heavy oils, to her room where she pushed him onto the bed, his feet dangling over the side. He felt paper crumple beneath him and a pencil snapped, causing a painful jab in his shoulder. She stripped him of the clothes he had on and put his penis in her mouth. He was erect beyond surprise in seconds. And he ejaculated in her mouth soon after her wet lips had begun to run up and down. She looked up, mouth half open, with a mixture of saliva and semen running down her chin.

'Do I swallow?' she asked, her voice half choked, awkward, dribbling from both corners of her mouth. He nodded, remembering Eva, but Margaret spat the mouthful into a towel on the carpet. She remained kneeling on the bedside mat, fondling him, until he was erect again. He leaned back on his elbows and watched her.

'I saw that done last night. We went to San Fernando. I wanted to know what it was like.'

She had returned near dawn, as usual, having travelled one hour north of the capital to what was known among the English as 'Sin City'. Huge suburban mansions, built to imitate French town houses, were used by the prostitution trade and by otherwise respectable families for night-long parties that were referred to as orgies by those who thought of themselves as genuinely respectable. It was not known how many houses were devoted to the flesh trade, or were actually disguised expensive brothels, but there were enough to give the suburb an identity all its own. This was where the young men of the middle class and upward, came to 'make their debut' at sixteen, and where couples came to watch how it was done and to partake if they were so inclined.

Many of the women were brought ashore there from ships in the river, illegal immigrants for the prostitution networks. Drugs were available, imported spirits were supplied by smugglers and occasionally a disobedient girl, whimpering with real reason, received a severe public lashing, for the entertainment of the better-paying customers.

'I saw it last night,' she repeated. 'I wanted to know what it felt like,' she said again. 'Do you like it?'

He nodded, unsure about qualifying his pleasure. 'So do I,' she laughed. She put his penis in her mouth again. He lifted her head gently.

'Your husband... Why didn't you try with your husband?'

'Don't be disgusting. I can't do a thing like this with my husband. Whatever would he think of me, besides... He wasn't there, although I know he's been...' She did not finish. Her face went down again. She nibbled and tugged and licked and sucked. He took longer to come on the second time, but not very much longer. When he came she swallowed. She immediately continued and he ejaculated twice more.

'Do it to me now?' she asked, but it was an order.

There was a gentle smell of sweat and urine as his tongue explored between her creases. She squirmed, then groaned, giggled, quivered, then relaxed. As his tongue rubbed more firmly, she began to groan again, her thighs tightened against his ears; groan, giggle, quiver, relax... This happened several times. He raised his head and moved his body between her legs. But as he got close to her, she slapped her two hands over her crotch. '*Interdit*. No Entry!' she shouted. 'Not that. You're not going in there. Only Harold goes in there. And that's when he asks please very nicely.' She swung her leg over his head and stood clear of him. He looked up at her, frankly befuddled. The front of her nightdress was soaked by his sweat and the saliva from her chin.

The front door opened and they heard Harold Handy's voice at the end of the corridor. 'Good God, he's back! Get out! What on earth...?' Her hissed enquiry about her husband's unexpected schedule trailed off. Douglas collected his underwear from the carpet and lunged for a bath towel noticed earlier and which he wrapped around his waist. As he tried to walk his knees buckled. He felt weak, exhausted from her treatment. He ran down the passage to the main reception area, crashing into the furniture as he went.

'God, you drunk already, Douglas? How the hell are you going to get through the day? You don't look so good'

'Taken by surprise...' Douglas panted 'Going for bath... Didn't expect...'

'Oh, go on then. But do not touch the whisky or the wine. You are welcome to anything else. That's my towel you've got there, I think. God, she is an untidy woman.'

From the bathroom Douglas heard the couple in conversation. The voices were subdued, undisturbed, betraying nothing. When he heard Harold leave, Douglas ran the bath. At her end of the house, Margaret showered and dressed. She ordered the sheets changed and the bed was made. Not a word about the morning passed between them.

Two days later, she woke him again. He was shaken vigorously. But he was rapidly ready for her and in her mouth as she knelt by the sofa. He thrust his waist forward and suddenly went too fast and too deep into her throat. She choked, coughed and vomited over him and the carpet.

The stink of bile and brandy was pungent. Douglas looked at his legs, streamed with her vomit. She did not look up. On hands and knees she faced the carpet, repeating, 'You fool, you fool...'

He bathed and dressed.

She stood over one of the maids who was ordered to clean the carpet with wet rags.

He left the flat without a greeting, went down to the street and felt wretched.

On the last night of the trade fair, Douglas met Prieto at the replica of the Tudor village built for the exhibition. A large notice board promised, **'Better Times for Argentina'**. The evening was warm, but no longer hot as summer slipped into autumn. The days, though shorter, did not give the sense of curling up at the corners as evenings did in Scotland when nights grew longer.

'*Ingleses hijos de puta,*' Prieto protested. He was very drunk and in evidence waved a short necked cylinder-like bottle of Dutch gin. 'I piss on your empire,' he shouted. Douglas sprang back to avoid the splash as the man urinated without direction.

'Prieto, Carlos, this EMPIRE will never end. D'you hear me, because nothing else safeguards my socialism as opposition to it. Nothing is so decadent as Empire and just to spite me it will never go away,' Douglas shouted back.

A man came out of the shadows of the Tudor village with a threatening look. 'If you were really English, you would not be making such an ass of yourself,' he said in perfect English.

Douglas was over his shock in seconds. He had met the man but could not pronounce his name. He was aged about 40, educated at public school in Surrey and in Paris, a lawyer who had made his career secondary to his cultural pursuits – which had earned him Prieto's contempt, because any man who gave up making money when he could was a worm – and he was one of the country's leading literary livewires.

Oliverio Girondo had been one of the founders of the Martín Fierro group of artists and writers who had taken the twenties by storm. Now their revolutionary flame was only a flicker.

He was just back from foreign travel, he told Douglas, convinced that the choice of Argentina was the best in the world at present. Europe was going down the drain. But his eyes seemed to water as he thought of the England and of France which he had so recently left. Those were the cultures he wanted to be part of, but here were the comfort and safety he needed. He had enjoyed being an Argentine in the great cities, a rich man among the impoverished. Rebellion and conformity were in conflict within him, as in most of the Argentines who had spent the last few days at the British trade fair. 'And yet Europe in decadence is still original. We can only hope to be clever in our own decadence.'

'It's a good stage imitation,' Douglas replied looking at the Tudor stage props, his thoughts on Margaret Handy and the previous few days.

Douglas said he was not English but a Scot, for which Girondo apologised. 'But I can tell you have other things on your mind when you say that,' the writer remarked. At which point, almost like a cue for one of the maddest characters in his novels, Roberto Arlt, the crime reporter, made his appearance, demanding to know what they were discussing.

'Decadence and nationality,' Douglas said.

'Decadence, we need decadence, to speed up the revolution,' the journalist and novelist Roberto Arlt shouted. Ever-louder repetition was addressed at a policeman, who fixed his gaze on the group.

Then Arlt turned on Douglas whom he said he had come to see. 'If you are a Scot you are no good for translating my novel *Los siete Locos* (The Seven Madmen). Scottish do not speak English.'

What about Stevenson, what about Scott, Douglas shouted back. They were all shouting except Girondo who could not disguise his strong dislike for Arlt and the man's interest in the criminal classes. Douglas warned Arlt that he might not speak English but he had learned to box at the Edinburgh Academy. Arlt said it was child's play compared with his training in the streets. Girondo propped the drunken Prieto against the Tudor doorpost and stuck the bottle in the drunk's belt. Then he raced to part the squabblers who were shadow-boxing at a safe distance.

At two a.m., at the gates of the Argentine Rural Society which had, 'generously offered its splendid showgrounds and its permanent buildings for an exhibition of British goods,' Prieto emptied the contents of his stomach on the pavement. Douglas saw this as further offence to the land of his birth, and leaving Arlt and Girondo, he swung a kick at Prieto. The drunk sprawled.

The lone policeman was joined by a second and they moved in on the group.

It has never been known very widely, but on that night in March 1931, two of Argentina's leading writers, until then not on speaking terms, a young Scot and another man identified only as 'an Argentine citizen' in an advanced state of inebriation, were briefly detained and rapidly freed by police. The older of the four, Girondo, reasoned with the police that it would be a source of national embarrassment to make an arrest at such a place, and in such times.

There was a note from the British Embassy in the post tray by the coat rack in the hall at the Calvet. All those who had so generously helped to make the Royal visit a success were cordially invited at very short notice, and for this the embassy apologised, to a gathering in the ambassador's home. 'Mr & Mrs Handy have expressed their hope that you will join us,' read an unsigned handwritten postscript.

Douglas dropped the letter in the dustbin and took a bus to Saint Andrew's Scots Church hall, on Avenida Belgrano. There was to be a charity evening of 'Books and Madeira', at which community members would discuss fiction recently read, while Port was served.

# Chapter 11

THE SCOTS COMMUNITY was a refuge for expatriates and aimless nationals who needed a port of call when failure and frustration overcame them. The Saint Andrew's Society of the River Plate was approaching its centenary. The committee and members were true to their origins, but like missionaries who adapt their religions to the practices of peoples in remote places, so did the social calendar adjust to the changed seasons. Burns' Night was moved from January to July, for who could face a haggis in thirty-five degrees centigrade dressed in the regulation three-piece suit demanded by Buenos Aires's male fashion?

The membership was far-flung. The Scots were a group obsessed by a need, almost a greed, to own land. Each Scot in Argentina sought compensation for earlier, ancestral, perhaps only alleged, loss. Although the Clearances at 'home' had begun well near a century before, and the end of the golden age of Scotland's scientific and artistic creativity was also one hundred years past, Clearances and golden age were talked of in Buenos Aires as if both tragedy and triumph had taken place in the homeland only last year.

The English ignored the locals and filled their leisure with English sports and English clubs. The English in Buenos Aires did not think of themselves as strangers. They were aware of the conservatism of their ways but all of them, whatever their income, thought of themselves as an imperial agent of a better people. Feelings were never to be shown. Emotions were wrapped in a tightly tied parcel, only to be opened occasionally in brief private moments. Argentines accepted this and avoided embarrassing the English in their encounters.

The Irish removed themselves from the city to breed great families and start villages in the distant interior, where they tried to keep themselves untainted and unmixed with the local population. But the Irish assimilated by default, for they practiced a secretive if generous miscegenation by their contacts with the women of the land.

The Scots lectured all-comers on the benefits of hard labour, but more often led the listener into endless discourse on their readings of Scottish sentiments. This was why the Scots as a community provided comfort for their kind. Their debate never changed. The Industrial Revolution stood out starkly in their conversation, perhaps because Scotland had been the loser. Scottish writings had made it look so. Their talk was tinged with bitterness at the absence of political power in Scotland and to this they ascribed its cultural stagnation. How many Scots had left their land? Fifteen million, maybe? They had spanned the world, each one proud of the Scotland they had left, each sure they only wanted to return there to die, or perhaps for a dram on Burns' Night, but mostly not at all, for there was nothing there for any of them. And each of the fifteen million expatriates had gone through this same conversation, with themselves or with others, each day or each month, they found they were no closer to home, but neither were they any farther, and there was reassurance in that. Fifteen million men and women said each day that Scots abroad had made the world, and that those who had stayed at home had done so only to destroy themselves.

Because of the political quietude of Scotland, each Scot expatriated made every small incident, from a street demonstration to a shipyard strike, the subject of prolonged and deep examination, until debate raised the event remembered into a full revolutionary occasion. After such evenings of argument, the participants went almost as a committee to Mackern's Book Store – founded in 1849 by a man from Limerick – or to the more recently opened Mitchell's, to order volumes of the newest generation of Scottish writers, Neil Gunn, Compton Mackenzie and Hugh MacDiarmid. It was a sudden rich season in MacDiarmid, or Christopher Murray Grieve as was his family name, for he had produced three books in quick succession during 1925 and 1926 – *Sangschaw*, *Penny Wheep* and *A Drunk Man Looks at the Thistle* – and every Scot in Buenos Aires had read them and then posted the copy on loan to friends on farms in the provinces. Scots could be identified by the books they carried, among which was often the buff-coloured cover of *Blackwood's* magazine, adorned by a portrait of George Buchanan, reproduced since the first issue in April 1817 because William Blackwood had the block left over and saw no reason for unnecessary expense on a new cover illustration. In Buenos Aires the men said Scottish writing had what no other literature could claim. The French novel leaned on ideas; the English on people and places. The Scots combined the strength of those two and generated genius beyond the scope of all others. There was something of the Russian novel in the Scots' literature: the dourness, the greyness of the characters nevertheless glowed with an inner ebullience that enriched the narrative. In Buenos Aires, this conclusion made them proud of their distant home. This was the cultural base the expatriates were supported by to build their own material success in the new country.

Sometimes the arguments would continue in such places as the Dorado Club, a refuge for anglers and alcoholics, founded in 1917 with twenty-two members. This number had swollen to nearly two-hundred as word went around the community that it was also a safe haven from wives and family, because the journey up-river into the islands was seldom a woman's idea of entertainment. There was no fortune there other than male friendship. Dorado was the name of a river fish, nothing to do with the legends of El Dorado.

# Chapter 12

THE GREATER CAUSE of combating foot rot in cattle took Douglas to Concordia, at the top of Entre Ríos province, on the River Uruguay. He was sent there as part of Cooper's sales promotion, 'and you better show increased orders when you get back, laddie.' Cooper's solutions for scabies, *Antisárnicos Cooper*, were well-known in the land, but after the April-May 1929 foot-and-mouth disease scare, in which the United States and United Kingdom had accused Argentina of selling contaminated beef, the pressure was on from government and business to sell Cooper's anti-*aftosa* vaccines. Douglas said he enjoyed his work, but he was more inclined to feel that Concordia was a safe exile from Buenos Aires, than the base-camp for a sales campaign. From there he could watch the world through the four pages of a fortnightly started in February 1930, *The Concordia Chronicle*. This, along with old copies of *The Times*, which were to be found in the reading room of The Victoria Park Sports Club, built on railway property as were many such outposts of empire, kept him quietly linked to the troubles of humanity.

Five men in the advertising department of the Entre Ríos and Argentine North East Railway, a small company with 1,557 miles of track, had started the *Chronicle* as a commercial entertainment and solicited information from residents and travelers.

Douglas, searching for tips about new customers, became a regular visitor at the tiny newspaper office in a shed in the railway yard on the river's edge. Within a week, quite unwittingly, he found himself in the post of roving reporter. Everything local mattered. Brigadier General G.H. Harrison CMG, director of the railway as from February, sent a note to the newsroom every time he bought a round of drinks at the Victoria Park bar expecting the occasion to be mentioned; the ladies' meetings; Saturday's tennis tournament; the whist drive at the club, all had to be announced and reported.

Potential buyers of Cooper's products were promised a personal write-up in the paper of the *ingleses*, which would put the customer well in with the members of the local club. Several local farmers doubled their orders and were distressed to find themselves mentioned only as part of the audience at the meetings of the Concordia Debating Society. However, customers breathed not a word about this, as they would not admit publicly that they had paid the reporter substantially, in orders for goods, to get their names in the paper.

The debating society was encouraged to broadcast a meeting live from the Union Club on Concordia Radio, to be heard up and down the littoral provinces for the first time. The broadcast was sponsored by Cooper and when time came to pay for air time, this was done in sacks of Chilean nitrate fertilizer, which could not be sold in Entre Ríos and Corrientes, because the black, damp earth was so rich it needed no additives.

Douglas's order books burgeoned, so much in fact, that old man Cooper became suspicious and sent his accountant on an inspection tour. Douglas took the accountant, on arrival in Concordia, to the 'historic' – in Anglo-Argentine terms – site of Saint Thomas Church and adjoining Morley Hall, condemned to be demolished to make way for a new road. The accountant was posted outside the church for a whole morning with a Cooper's sign saying the building should stay, for which Cooper's and the local sales rep gained enormous goodwill among the local railway community, who opposed the new road. The accountant returned to Buenos Aires in a fury and threatened resignation if the young salesman was not sacked. But in the meantime Douglas, acting on the goodwill generated by the Church demonstration, had negotiated a reduced rate on all of Cooper's shipments by railway. Old man Cooper had to pacify his accountant and wrote a letter of cautious congratulations, meanly expressed, to his successful agent.

Nothing really happened in Concordia except the past. It was embellished and improved for present distraction.

Apprehension for the future weighed in from years gone by, as small signs of change signaled that the great days of the British railways in Argentina might be over. The *Chronicle* announced staff cutbacks on the Entre Ríos and North East line which would close the advertising department. One of the paper's founders returned to England, one joined the Buenos Ayres Great Southern Railway (5,009 miles of track) and one set up his own photography business in Concordia. His sales slogan read, 'We can make you look natural or beautiful, but not both'.

Douglas was dragged in as a proofreader and sports reporter. With a flair for unabashed fabulation, he reported that Concordia was the cradle of Argentine polo, a discovery made thanks to the investigations of the Cooper's sales representative 'who is also a keen historian'. Thus the first match had been played in the summer of 1874, when mounted police had broken up the tenth chukka to prevent players from murdering each other, later to claim a police victory in the match. The Debating Society called for an inquiry and suggested full historical research.

Those few months in Entre Ríos Douglas savoured for many years after, remembering his season as an honorary colonial. He felt free of the complications of Buenos Aires and out of reach of tyrannical employers and rapacious women. He played tennis with the daughters of railway section managers and took his gins with the fathers at the Union Club or at Victoria Park.

There had been friction between Britons and locals, but, visibly, it had been limited to the, 'Concordia shooting outrage. Bullet whizzes through car', in January, when Messrs Etheridge and West, English motorists, had their Chrysler's crystals shattered. The shot had been fired from a window in the local newspaper, the *Amigo del Pueblo*, which was evidence that not everybody loved an Englishman in Argentina.

Far firmer in memory had been two German aviators who had collected subscriptions for what promised to be a series of hair-raising aerobatics over the port on the river Uruguay. This was to conclude with a spectacular 'death leap' into the river. The airmen cashed a cheque from their promoters in advance, climbed into their machine and soared into the blue. 'Up to the present no further traces of them have been seen!' Douglas publicly denounced the trick. But unlike others he had suspected something; not clear what, it just did not sound quite right. He could not say, maybe it was the plane, maybe the two men... When the fundraising took place at the Victoria Park, he had made a flourish with his cheque, but left it unsigned. The bank had returned it and it was never cashed.

The last of the founders of the *Chronicle* announced that he was leaving Concordia. The railway thought that, in spite of the expense, the paper should continue and in view of his successful participation in the community, Douglas was offered the job of editor. He declined, explaining that journalism had been an enjoyable pastime but would never be acceptable employment in his family. The paper closed on 27 May, 1931.

He stayed in Concordia for a few more weeks, but thought that he had 'adequately managed' the sales promotion 'for which I was posted to this town', he wrote Cooper, and wanted a return to head office. The company chief, fearing that he was in trouble, agreed to his return.

## Chapter 13

NOËL COWARD, playwright and socialite, arrived in Buenos Aires in December 1931, on a South American cruise holiday to escape the alarmingly intense hullabaloo and adulation that he had been enjoying in London. Absence for a few months would build up his popularity, friends advised. The British Ambassador hardly hesitated to ask Coward to give some attention to the community, because the princes had not paid the residents quite enough, which had prompted some unhappy remarks. Coward noted later that 'in fairness to the princes I had to admit that I rather saw their point'. But like a good chap he said he would be honoured to open flower shows and make speeches at community functions. His conclusion, at the time of sailing, was that his public appearances had been short and quite painless and at times even enjoyable. In Buenos Aires, Coward stayed at the Plaza Hotel, but before the end of his visit he called on friends, Leonora Hughes and her husband Carlos Basualdo, relatives of the princes' hosts, to enjoy the lavish luxury of their *estancia*. Buenos Aires, Coward concluded, really knew how to enjoy life. The short tour was later said to have inspired some of the lines in *Mad Dogs and Englishmen Go Out in the Midday Sun*: 'Hindus and Argentines sleep firmly from twelve to one/ But Englishmen detest a siesta.' Although there had been small symptoms of decline, for those who wished not to see it, British influence seemed unassailable. Philip Guedalla (1889-1944), barrister and essayist, produced a travel book, *Argentine Tango*, out of a visit to Buenos Aires, in which he described finding comfort as an Englishman among the natives. 'Argentina has a strong prejudice in favour of Englishmen. The consequence is that British visitors to Argentina know themselves to be something more (or less) than mere foreigners...' Unlike others who were awed by the protestations of close acquaintance, Guedalla wondered if the celebrated friendship was only skin deep. 'You will find Englishmen and Argentines in each other's offices. But how often do you find them in each other's homes? ... That is the real test of intimacy; and it is one that Anglo-Argentine relations entirely fail to satisfy.' The friends fell out more noticeably in July-August 1932, in Ottawa. Argentina, whose entire income was derived from farming exports, had to accept the new tariffs and restrictions offered by Britain and had little ability to negotiate. Britain's colonies wanted preferential prices for their meat at Smithfield Market. Led by New Zealand and Australia, they pressed until they got them. Before the signing of the Ottawa Accord, Argentine beef had undercut the others on the English market. There were no currency restrictions, nor import barriers and the meat-packers of Argentina had the stocks and the ability to push their cheaper meat faster and better. Dr Julio Argentino Roca, Argentina's vice-president, went down in history on 10 February 1933, at a banquet at Claridges, arguing that Argentina felt itself to be part of the British Empire, hinting therefore that it should not be shut out of the more favourable deal to be offered the colonies. But it was too late for that and therefore unnecessary. The banquet marked the conclusion of nego-tiations for what became known as the 'Roca-Runciman' Treaty, between the Argentine republic and the president of the British Board of Trade. The next day, the *Manchester Guardian* commented that Roca's visit 'is a turning point in the history of British-Argentine relations. The long-standing link between the two countries, in both politics and commerce, is a commonplace. It follows that a deep-seated change in the commercial policy of Great Britain must provoke changes as profound in Argentine economics.' Writers and commentators were declaring turning points, watersheds and closing stages all the time. But nobody seemed to know why such endings had to be marked, or even when the golden era had begun. Had a special relationship started early in the nineteenth century with independence, or at mid-century with the railways, or just before the 1914 war, a decade now looked upon as Argentina's *belle époque*? Each person in Argentina had their very own and personal end of an era, after a few weeks, or some months, a number of years, or a lifetime. The country was adaptable to every man's fantasy. The meat agreement announced by Walter Runciman in the House of Commons on 27 April 1933 marked the end of an age of fast money, overnight fortunes, and caused heavy losses to landowners and operators who dared to defy the meat-packing company buyers.

# Chapter 14

THE WIFE OF ONE sporadic lodger from the provinces admitted that she had not known of the existence of latrines in men's toilets until once when she had entered the 'Gents' by mistake. Seeing the porcelain fittings on the walls she thought that the native female peed in public, only to notice that she must be in error when she passed a man at the exit. Hazel's anecdote prompted the line 'Hat sat on the lat', which caused great mirth at the Calvet on every occasion she visited.

The crudity of her anecdote and her lack of self-consciousness in the telling attracted Douglas to her as no other male on the premises seemed to be, including her overweight husband.

In his new job as travelling salesman, he made a promise to visit Hazel Norris and her husband, Philip, at their home in Santa Fe. Douglas's solid employment allowed him to tour the whole territory of the republic, and rapidly to become known among small-holders as 'the *inglés* cattle and plants curer who comes on a horse'. It sounded very agreeable in Spanish. Far ahead of him went word of his ways, and gossip saw to it that his reported success greatly exceeded reality.

At twenty-three, he put to work his humour and improved his slyness to win over the poorest farmers as well as the great farms' *mayordomos*, as the English-speaking managers were called. He presented them with his samples in the course of a little speech about successes in other provinces and thus secured his sales. His inebriate lucubrations for transplanting a non-existent Scottish socialism to Argentina, to compete with the anarchism of Poles and Germans, was used as additional entertainment and considered a treat by local audiences. It did, however, cause eczema at the elegant picnics on the English-owned *estancias*, to which he was often invited because he added a sense of novelty to the small isolated groups. He realized, though, that he had failed to win over this public when he was asked to stand on the outer edge of family and friends when group photographs were taken. They were prepared to entertain eccentrics, but were not happy with radical ideas.

The peculiarities of provincial English-speaking gatherings were part of his introduction to this new life. Theirs was a jolly and comfortable existence, without any mention of politics. When politicians were spoken of it would be only with approval for the most conservative elements.

In Santa Fe, Douglas learned most at the home of Hazel Norris, leading light and confirmed *rara* (strange one) in the provincial capital. Hazel was in the habit of entertaining frequently. Though she felt herself to be several points above the rest of the resident Britons, she made as if she wanted to adapt to the land and its laws. She was in her early forties, a factory manager's wife, organizer of social activities and good works, with two children out of the way at boarding schools in England. She was well acquainted with the local wags and with some of the juicier tales from Buenos Aires as well. Her husband, whom she had married as a young officer before the War, was now a tub four times the size of the man in uniform in the silver-framed picture on the piano.

Hazel was thin and plain, and as shapeless as only thin English women can look in their cotton full-length dresses which they insist on wearing so as not to be seen tempting other women's men. She would invite Douglas to drinks in the evenings, when he could get to Santa Fe. The hot summer nights, scented by a thousand trees and with the damp air from the muddy Paraná river beyond, were the best. Douglas used Rosario as his cattle doctor's base. From there he went by train or was driven north to a point where Hazel could meet him and drive him back to her suburban home. They would chat until the light had gone and the sitting room was quite black. Only then would her husband come home from work.

'You see, Dougie,' she said over and over, her gin content almost as high as her husband's by that time of day. 'The reason why the English abroad have small families is that their men work all day and drink all night.'

She had once shocked her guests, including members of the provincial governor's cabinet, by admitting that the unlimited supply of ice for cocktails came from the city court's morgue – which had so much better storage than her own small ice-box. Her summer garden parties were renowned successes, because the good weather never failed her. She told Douglas that the secret of this was simple. As night fell on the evening of a summer barbecue and as storm clouds gathered, she would light candles and place them in bowls all about the garden.

'The sky gets very angry at seeing flames being lit to challenge the sun when the sun has stopped its light in this part of the earth. In anger, the sky opens and drops buckets on the candles. Once they have done that, the sky is exhausted and there will be no more water for the night. So the parties are always quite wonderful.' She explained this in absolute earnestness.

'Men are just the same,' she said. 'They work themselves into a state and generate enormous heat, but then exhaust it all in one great burst. And they remain quite lukewarm and mediocre for the rest of their time.'

Douglas was never sure what she meant by that – which she said often when drinking. He was baffled by her manner, but attracted by her plain looks and straightforward speech.

It was probably inevitable, he told himself later, that they should become lovers. He could not imagine a love affair with a woman named Hazel and twenty years older, or with a woman with her theories and practices. So he would call her by nicknames to make affection feel different. Both enjoyed their conspiracy: the older woman having secured a fling with the younger man.

The first time they made love was in the exhausted but wide awake hours before dawn after a late barbecue. Her husband had taken his huge frame to bed, the maids had finished cleaning the kitchen. The house was quiet. For many minutes, man and woman sat in silence in the cushions on the garden swing, under a star-lit sky. Very quietly, without hurry or hesitation, as if making love had been part of the night's perfect order, they came together. Of that first occasion Douglas would always remember the downy softness of her crotch, which contrasted with the scouring-pad surfaces of the regularly shaven Buenos Aires prostitutes. He discovered that a woman's breasts were her most beautiful asset. Whatever the age, the size did not matter, he told himself, the shape was always perfect. He would never again call a woman plain.

# Chapter 15

'OF ALL CITIES BUENOS AIRES seems to me the most incomprehensible. Arresting in personality, it is also elusive with a strange and baffling quality that is not of South America. Atlantis has built a new capital, reborn, and Mammon has gone to live in it and the colour schesme chosen is grey against a grey skyline... The city is ambitious, it is also very near to success, and in its projected immensity it is overwhelming... Buenos Aires, with a plagiaristic tendency has absorbed the best of nations... A citizen of Buenos Aires, a *Porteño*, would be ashamed to admit ignorance in any detail of Argentine history, yet that does not seem to prevent him tearing down and destroying the old and the historical... This is Progress, formal, commercialised, solemn even in gaiety. Buenos Aires is intense... Out of Argentina's population of eleven millions, more than two and a half millions live in Buenos Aires. A Chinaman, a Lap, born in Buenos Aires becomes automatically an Argentine...

'Basques and Neapolitans and Poles... an inchoate agglomeration, and the newspapers sold in Paseo Colón give a clue to the creation of a people, The *Porteño* world of Buenos Aires (the newsboy has the *Correo de Galicia* and the *Italia del Poppolo*, and the *Austria Presse*, and the *Jugo-Slavija*, and the *Magyarsag*, the *Kurjer Polsky* and the *Slovenski Tednik*, Ukranian papers, Czecho-Slovakian and Serbian papers, Japanese, Jewish, and Arab papers), and the places where the immigrants used to gather and still come, though in smaller numbers now, are those Italian wine shops on Paseo Colón, the arcades of Leandro Alem with garlic smells and festooned sausages and entrails *a la parrilla*, and beer houses where the *Frankfurter* is popular, and obscene cinemas of the gallic persuasion specialising in a rather tame pornography, and doubtful hotels plastered with shipping announcements. Slow-eyed Spaniards in narrow, striped trousers, a cheap edition of trousers worn as best man at a sister's wedding, in black hats and black shirts and black mufflers and shuffling canvas slippers, smile at hatless Slav and Magyar prostitutes.'

Derek Drabble, *Passenger Ticket* (1934)

# PART II
## 1934-1950

# Chapter 16

T HE FAREWELL PARTY for a Greek diplomat and businessman who had made Buenos Aires the launch pad of his success was announced quietly in *La Nación* in that southern spring of 1934. Douglas was taken to the reception by Prieto, whose supply of fresh acquaintances was unlimited. Prieto's claims to friendship were spontaneous and unabashed, a privilege of the native-born contrasting sharply with the community-conscious caution of the immigrant.

Though announced as a small private occasion, the crowd Douglas and Prieto found at the large apartment off Avenida Santa Fe, on the best side of the city, was vast. The smell of money drew people. The host was commercial agent Dr Aristotle Socrates Onassis, Consul General of the Republic of Greece, according to the notice in the Personals, just below the news that Señora Carmen María de los Ángeles Pereyra de Álzaga Unsué was 'resting at home' recovering from her recent ailment. The Greek expressed delight with his place in the social columns just as the paper's night editor received a severe reprimand for putting news of the riff raff along with the notices from the establishment.

The host who was also his own guest of honour moved through the throng with some difficulty, although keeping as dignified an appearance as possible. He at once enjoyed the attention he drew but was discomfited by the need to see so many people at once. Men jabbering in Greek accosted him. Each was addressed a pleasantry with the faintest of smiles. With that done most of the male guests were ignored; the host-guest's attention was then directed at the more attractive women in their thirties. He seemed displeased by the small company of females in the crowd of men, and probably made a mental note to grumble about this to somebody.

Douglas received a sudden blast of preferential welcome. Onassis said it was an honour to see Douglas there for he was his only English –'Yes, I am sorrrrry,

Scots... British!' – guest that evening. He had invited the British Consul but no representative had been sent from the Legation.

They had met before, at the L'Aviron Rowing Club, one of the French community's main venues, which Douglas had joined in preference to the English Tigre Boat Club because there were more boats available. Onassis was a member not for the rowing but for the contacts the club rooms offered – a better class of Argentine who wanted to boast of French connections. Douglas and 'Ari' were the same age and physically similar, short and stocky. The Greek looked older, helped to appear so by the dark glasses which he wore at all times, by his gravelly voice and by a scent of *Cologne* mixed with the smell of Virginia tobacco.

'After the reception we can go to a *boite*; to talk. I must talk to you. But first I must take care of all these friends. You will excuse me.'

Nobody looked less like wanting to look after anybody than Onassis that night of his farewell party. Prieto nudged Douglas, assuring him that he was on to a good thing.

Onassis livened up, as far as he could allow himself to, in the dance-room at the City Hotel, one of the capital's most elegant venues, two hundred metres from Government House. The orchestra, led by pianist Harold Mickey, a former shipboard music director who had also played for the silent movies, kept the hall active without stop. Mickey was one of the prize catches in the hotel business. In May 1933, aged twenty-seven, he had picked up a contract first offered to the musician and singer Rudy Vallee to play at the City Hotel. William Harold Mickey, from North Carolina, was recording with RCA Victor and was all the rage among the fashionable middle class dancers in Buenos Aires.

Onassis' main reason for wanting to talk to Douglas seemed to be to hold a conversation in English, which he spoke well, and he showed too that he was fluent in Italian, by chatting with a waiter. The Greek interrupted their conversation to dance with his companion, a young singer from the Colón Opera House who told Douglas she would soon be travelling to New York to join Ari. Onassis nodded, but never noticeably agreed. He had told Douglas that he was going to London.

Onassis was mildly affectionate. He would squeeze her hand and point to the floor without a word whenever he wished to dance. He ducked questions, although he seemed to give them great thought, thus enhancing an air of mystery. He described himself as the Greek Consul General, Commercial and Confidential Agent, which added to the secrecy about him. When he spoke of international trade between Argentina, which sold wheat, and Greece, which sold tobacco, he sounded authoritative. On his return from New York a year earlier, he had told newspaper reporters about the good prospects for trade between both countries, and had warned that he wanted more favourable attention from the foreign ministry than it had paid him in the past.

Douglas was entertained by the man's evasiveness which tinged his success with suspicion, or perhaps it was the way a Briton felt about a Greek.

As Douglas thought there was something of the scoundrel about the man when he spoke of his many connections, the Greek remarked, without a change in his voice, 'You listen to me but do not believe me. That is what is wrong with this city, nobody trusts anybody because everybody is lying about everything. You will see...'

Douglas was quick with a rejoinder, 'I listen with interest. Can you ask for more? I have no reason to disbelieve you. You have found success in Argentina. I am still looking.'

Onassis was a millionaire at 27. He had arrived in Buenos Aires in September 1923 on the *Tomaso di Savoia*, with a ticket paid with cash pooled by impoverished uncles. His first jobs had been on the waterfront, as a stevedore, a dish-washer and waiter. At first he had shared a room in La Boca with a distant relative and the man's wife. Later he had moved to a room not far from the Calvet. Between night shifts as an electrician and switchboard operator, he learned Spanish and tried to sell Greek tobacco. It took him a year to place his first bulk order. One hundred thousand dollars worth of Greek tobacco marked the start of Onassis' life. His commission was five hundred dollars.

He bought two suits, some silk shirts, Italian shoes and a *Bordolino* hat, played the London stock exchange and made some more money out of linseed and hides. That was when he had joined the l'Aviron club. In 1929 he became an Argentine citizen. His most regular escort then was the singer Claudia Muzio, whom he had met at the Colón Opera House. She smoked his cigarettes, *Osmans*, in public places and made smoking fashionable, and his sales improved.

Muzio and Onassis sometimes stirred up gossip when they crossed to Montevideo on the night boat.

Aboard, the Argentines of class, married couples, courting couples, adulterous couples, potential suicides, unrequited lovers, homosexual lovers, white slavers, cigarette smugglers, fugitive bank clerks and successful coal merchants with dirty fingernails, danced and gambled in the elegant rooms of the Dodero Line ships, until dawn over the River Plate came with the strong aroma of morning coffee, which is sharpest as night turns to day. As the passengers washed away the gummed-up odours of overnight sweat and sex, they planned a day of more gambling, uncensored films and contraband shopping in the Uruguayan capital, the Montecarlo of South America.

Harold Mickey dedicated an arrangement of Rudolf Nelson's *From the Lift to the Bar Stool*, a song about leaving the bar with a woman and going with her to a room upstairs, to 'His Excellency, the Greek Minister'. Onassis quietly listed the properties he had bought in Montevideo and Buenos Aires. He ran out of fingers and acknowledged the orchestra conductor with a nod, and a half hidden smile directed at his singer companion. Then he described how he had bought six ships in Canada, sold four at a profit, and operated two for his own trade.

'I'll give you a little advice. This country is very wonderful, beautiful, even, but it spends too much time looking at itself. Like some beautiful women, and I know about women here. They do not prepare for the time when beauty is gone. People think only for this week. They think they are clever, and for a time they manage to fool everybody with their cleverness, but you will see... always, always, I tell you, always, they will lose in the end and look the worst fools. Find yourself a ship and make it your fortune.'

The orchestra had been a silent stack of shiny metal and wood for an hour by the time they stopped talking. Onassis had made one glass of Scotch last all night, and at five in the morning he still had most of a double measure. He had referred to Prieto as 'Your secretary,' to whom he would give his forwarding address.

Onassis never left an address, for he had none. Hotels and Greek consulates were his homes, he said as they left the table. The singer looked wide awake and quite bright, in a stunned sort of way, and behind Onassis' back reached for the glass of Scotch before Prieto could get it and gulped down the contents. Her eyes watered. Prieto looked frustrated.

On the sidewalk, the Greek embraced Douglas and shook hands with Prieto. They would meet again, he promised, and once more embraced Douglas firmly. With a whisper like a slowly drawn wood saw, he thanked them for a good men's evening.

Prieto said he was going to bed. Douglas went to have breakfast and then to work. That night he decided that he too should leave the city. If he could buy some land in the valley of the River Negro, where the Southern Railway was offering good terms for fruit farmers and long-term contracts for harvest-time freight, a small farm would be the ship he would take to his fortune. There were opportunities elsewhere in the country. He would have to look into them all when he was travelling in the provinces.

# Chapter 17

DAWN IN BUENOS AIRES was populated by elegant couples in evening dress. Nobody ever slept. To the many locals with sleep in their eyes who filled the night were added European visitors of all kinds and accents who tried to flee Europe but took Europe everywhere with them and added it to whatever was newly encountered. The Compagnie de Navigation Sud-Atlantique, Royal Mail Lines, Blue Star Line and the Hamburg-South America Line offered escape in month-long cruises to Río de Janeiro and Buenos Aires for around seventy English guineas. The German shippers advertised, 'An exceptional opportunity for business people to visit South America... A Holiday Tour to South America by the *Cap Arcona* is the coming vogue.' *The Times* offered to airmail the daily paper, for an extra four pence per copy, to any cruise or tour destination, which made an impressive accessory to a visitor's entrance.

Aldous Huxley, who was just about forty and feeling something of a sage after the success of *Brave New World*, made cruises to distant parts very much a most fashionable thing to do when he published *Beyond the Bay of Mexique*.

Buenos Aires was still growing fast with grand buildings, but it was also more apparently rootless, more noticeably without direction. President Justo had won the elections in 1932 and led the country from the military regime he had supported into an anxiety about a national identity and the role of foreign business in Argentina. The railways were quietly British, but the meat industry was a battlefield for the buyers and traders.

The United States packing companies, known as the *Chicago Boys* after the biggest market in the world, ran the Swift, Armour and Wilson plants, controlled much of the Argentine market and were locked in a price war with the British-owned companies. The British meat business was represented by the Smithfield and Argentine Company, which was small, but the Vestey brothers, Lord William and Sir Edmund, who owned the Blue Star Line, had twenty per cent of the market through their killing plant at South Dock, the Frigorífico Anglo, which had opened in 1927. In Uruguay, the brothers owned the Fray Bentos plant, bought in 1924 from the once German-owned Liebig's Extract of Meat Co.

After the Ottawa conference had restricted entry of Argentine beef to the English market, British companies in the River Plate looked to the United States. Vast quantities of cheap meat for the processing plants were required. Buyers for the United States factories pushed prices down in their deals with farmers' agents. Buyers were rewarded handsomely for good prices, so they shared their commissions with the more accommodating suppliers, but also used part of their substantial incomes to employ thugs to work over the more recalcitrant. The heavies who protected the pimps in the prostitution trade doubled as bodyguards in the meat market.

Evening papers carried reports of fights, brawls and stabbings. Their detail, and their frequency, made the best reading of the day. The cause of incidents was usually given as matters 'relating to the meat trade'. The victims were labourers, servants, never anybody important. Beatings and stabbings were intended as a warning to a cattle supplier, or an agent. Police, government, politicians, everybody but those immediately affected, tried to ignore the growing violence in the industry.

In London, the men of business were worried about Argentina. At a meeting of the Anglo Argentine Tramways Co. Ltd. in July 1935, the chairman, His Grace the Duke of Atholl, told shareholders that there 'had been no improvement in 1934; on the contrary, it has become worse... The persistence and development of wasteful competition has meant further encroachment upon our financial vitality, producing a situation which can only be described as disastrous.' The company's trams had carried 347 million passengers, eighteen million less than in 1933. The receipts were nearly 33 million pesos, 21 million pesos below the levels of 1928. With the pound sterling at 11.45 pesos, the loss for 1934 was £53,653.

Buenos Aires, Argentina, South America as a whole in fact, was to the English at once a form of entertainment as much as a business risk. It was not only the English. No European thought very hard of the long term in Latin America; they thought of profits and dividends now, on good showings that would be reflected in a surge on the Stock Exchange in London. But nobody was thinking of what happened after the profit-taking. What came later was irrelevant. The politics of the place, the patrons remarked in the bars used by European businessmen, were a joke.

*The Times*, Buenos Aires, July 25 (1935) – As a result of the high words in the Senate on Tuesday, which caused Señor Duhau, the minister for Agriculture, to intervene forcibly to prevent Senator de la Torre from approaching Dr Pinedo, the minister of Finance, the Senator and Dr Pinedo today fought a duel with pistols. Neither was hit.

As a preliminary to his duel with Senator de la Torre (who fired into the air) Dr Pinedo resigned from the cabinet, and Señor Duhau, who was wounded by an excited spectator who opened fire on those engaged in the fracas in the Senate and mortally wounded Dr Borda Behere, a senator-elect, has also withdrawn from the cabinet – *Reuter.*

The politics of Argentina were confused, as allegiances moved and changed. The widespread feeling was that nobody was in charge. It was not easy to do business in that kind of climate.

# Chapter 18

BUENOS AIRES WAS ELATED by the visit of Cardinal Pacelli in 1934. This really was a blessing from Rome and a finger pointed from heaven. The world cared for Argentina.

From conversations overheard at the ABC Restaurant, a favourite German haunt near the city's first police precinct, and in the many bars used by the British community, Douglas gathered that the Vatican tour was irrelevant to both groups, but important to some personalities of each nationality. Mr. Handy, of the British Embassy, approached Douglas one evening after work quite unexpectedly and informally and steered him firmly into Lloyds' Bar, in the banking district. The surprise was the greater because the approach seemed quite out of character for a minister of the British Crown. He looked severe and very stern.

Handy explained at considerable length that the Cardinal's tour was unimportant, but it would single out the members of government considered reliable by Rome. These, in turn, would be expected to become Argentina's trusted international spokesmen. The Germans were watching these developments to start trade talks with the said officials.

'England wants to keep in Argentine commerce, and we don't want to lose more than we have already lost, especially not to the Krauts. I want you to keep an ear open for talk at the ABC. I know you go there often. And tell me who the men in their community are who seem to discuss government names and business.'

'Sounds like spying to me,' Douglas said, trying to put a cigarette in his mouth and pour another glass of cider from a jug.

'I call it information,' Handy retorted.

'Well, sounds to me like *Riddle of the Sands* and all that. You know, the Erskine Childers book.'

Handy's mouth curled in a fake smile. He did not like to be tested about his reading. He was an educated man.

'I don't like it. What if I say no?' Douglas muttered after a few seconds.

Handy waved away the idea as completely ridiculous. 'This is a request for a small service to your country. We can't lose our position in Argentina. And of all people, we can't lose it to the Germans. Look at what they did in the war. You were too young, of course...'

They sat in silence for a few more seconds. Handy looked into the street and waited for an answer. Douglas blew his cigarette smoke at the floor.

'Still, what if I say no, what if I am not patriotic. I don't like the idea of spying.'

Handy pursed his lips, looked straight at Douglas and spent a few moments in angry thought.

'I will tell your employers that you refused. That, just for a start. And then I will let the woman you are seeing know what you did to my wife. She told me... And I think you are a disgrace, a rotter of the very worst kind.'

Douglas went white. He burned his trousers as the cigarette fell from his open mouth and he was off the bar stool brushing embers and ash from his clothes. He had a drowning man's glimpse of every moment he had spent with Margaret Handy and imagined her telling her husband it had not been her fault at all.

He became a more frequent customer at the *ABC*. Conversation was mostly in German, and when in Spanish was of no interest to anybody outside the community and family issues.

Douglas grew desperate for information he could pass to Handy. The faces of the patrons revealed nothing. If Handy saw a connection between the *ABC*'s customers and the church, he had a very fine eye indeed. There might be a route to some gossip, or at least a rumour in the restaurant, but it was not immediately apparent. Douglas thought that he might have to invent a report to give to the menacing minister. He decided that he would go to the rally for Cardinal Pacelli to see if he could recognise faces.

Douglas struggled to the front of the crowd on Plaza de Mayo to be able to look across the street as the church and government dignitaries entered the Cathedral. If only the Cathedral had been worth looking at, the rally might have been fun. But it was a mish-mash of fashions following partial demolitions and had been collected and joined together in a large building with a small dome and no feeling of history or piety.

A short distance from him, being pushed about by the swaying and praying crowd, was a short man with a bald head and a large moustache. He was a regular at the *ABC*. Whether he was just an onlooker or an intelligence agent was immaterial: Douglas had a person to point out to Handy.

It was enough; he began to move away. Then a man close to Douglas, in an open shirt and with a huge stomach bulging, shouted an anarchist slogan and added, 'Death to the Pope'. Policemen in the line containing the rolling swell of people looked around and Douglas saw out of the corner of his eye that the little German was pointing in his direction. He started to hurry: the small man had probably pointed at the anarchist, but he might have been pointing at Douglas. The police went for the anarchist. But Douglas swung round, thinking they were going for him. As he turned, his elbow hit something that went squidge on connection. In the following fraction of a minute, Douglas felt a shower of hard truncheons on both his shoulders and on his arms. People shouted, his protests of innocence were ignored. He was dragged away from an angry section of pilgrims and thrown semi-conscious into the back of a police van. The anarchist followed him in, thrown like a sack of something hard.

Bruised quite badly, standing with difficulty, feeling as if he was about to vomit, he was informed at the police station next to the *ABC* that it had all been a mistake. They were sorry, but he was under arrest for breaking a policeman's nose. The anarchist was freed without charges. In the middle of the afternoon, Douglas was also released and he went to bed.

In the evening, sore all over and limping, he left the Calvet to buy a paper. His worst fears were confirmed. *Crítica* had a brief item about the incident. His name was badly spelt but the whole of the community read that paper for its columns of gore in all the crime reports.

Over the next three days, the lodgers at the Calvet reported in detail on each person encountered who had asked after Douglas. He cringed at every sentence. The gossip was everywhere that he had got into a brawl. There was sympathy for his stand against Catholicism, but dominant was a sense that he was a dark horse in the community.

Worst still, he thought, was to receive a short letter in elegant woman's handwriting which informed him that she did not want to be invited out by him again.

Inés was English and he had thought in weeks gone by that he stood a good chance with her. She was having an affair with a recently divorced manager at the Ford Motor Company subsidiary, but on being approached she had welcomed his interest and his invitation to have tea after office hours. She was a secretary, employed in a bank and unlike him had a large circle of friends. Inés had many attractions. She had dismissed him once before, accusing him of a weakness for excessive drink, which at one dinner party they attended as a couple led to his spectacular fall from a stool during an exaggerated guffaw at an insipid joke. He had been forgiven a week later and they had gone to a concert together, after tea at Harrods. Now he was definitely discarded, Inés wrote.

Handy was delighted. With little effort of his own, he had the information he wanted or, at least, a man to watch, so his position and his senior's perception of him were safe for a time. His personal sense of shame had been avenged by the police and he had learned through the grapevine that the subject of his anger had been rejected by the woman he had been trying to please.

'That's it. Dismissed,' Handy said, without disguising his pleasure. 'And you can pay the bill,' he fired as he made to leave the bar to which he had summoned his temporary recruit.

Douglas considered his options in silent distress,

'Fine. So I'm a loser all round. Now there's nothing you have on me. I can tell whom I please about your wife's predilections and what she doesn't give you.'

Handy looked down at him. His cheeks reddened, so did his neck.

'You're finished,' he hissed and walked out.

The radio over the bar played a piece of music by Bertold Goldschmidt, a Jew who had become well known in Berlin. A poem that predicted the destruction of humanity by aerial bombing had been set to piano, percussion and choir. It sounded awful, but suited Douglas's mood.

The barman switched to a tango.

During the next four weeks, Douglas noticed that he was being intermittently followed by a man he recognised from Lloyds' Bar. Robert Wills was the large, tough-looking geezer's name. He had boasted of expertise in guns, pistols mostly, and said his services as a bodyguard to personalities and diplomatic personnel, especially Central European businessmen, were in constant demand. Wills had been twice married and said he would do it again because he enjoyed the comforts and security of matrimony, while it lasted. But at present he had a succession of women who looked to be in their early twenties, averaging about half his age.

Being followed was uncomfortable and vexing, more often insulting, though Douglas was a little frightened as well.

When he tried to confront Wills in the street, his pursuer seemed to melt away and could not be found. He was replaced by an unidentified man. Wills stayed away from Lloyds' Bar at lunch and in the early evening, which was when Douglas could go in search of him.

At the end of a month of this disturbing routine, *The Standard* and the *Buenos Aires Herald* reported that Mr Handy would be leaving Argentina before the end of his tour, transferred to an important post in Paris. There followed several paragraphs of grovelling appreciation of his work in Argentina which had reached a peak in the brilliant coordination of the royal visit.

The sporadic tailing came to an end. Wills was suddenly available again at Lloyds' Bar but volunteered no information about the previous month.

# Chapter 19

M R WOODMAN BURBIDGE, later the second baronet, son of Richard Burbidge, first baronet and managing director of Harrods, London, had travelled to Buenos Aires in May 1913 to establish the store's branch in Argentina. He had sailed back to Southampton in August, having ordered the erection of a building on Florida Street. All the bricks, cement, ironwork, woodwork, windows and installations were sent from England to Argentina and some accessories supplied from the United States. 'At present the great magnet which is attracting the world's commercial needle is South America,' and especially Buenos Aires, according to *The Harrodian Gazette*, in 1913. 'The building was erected in record time for Buenos Aires by working staff night and day, and has caused some excitement in the town besides giving the public in the Argentine a very good impression of Harrods' organising powers,' the house magazine reported. On 31 March 1914, Harrods Buenos Aires had opened its ground and first floors to the public. The inauguration 'was a charity bazaar and the society ladies of Buenos Aires gave their services for selling goods.' The second and third floors opened in September 1914. Some years later, the second baron bought the city's other great department store, 'Gath & Chaves', founded in 1883 by Alfred Gath and Lorenzo Chaves.

The Harrods tea rooms were most favoured by ladies. An appointment there, after an afternoon shopping, was the right stop, to see people and be seen. The tea room was geographically divided, without visible boundaries, into four areas. The society ladies of Buenos Aires took the area nearest the door, for they liked to know who came and went. The British community women always wanted tables by the windows. The German ladies liked the end of the tearoom. They said the heavy curtains which acted as partitions made them feel they were in the nooks of the coffee houses of old Berlin. The women without a clear national identity got the middle of the room. A newcomer might be mistakenly placed once, but the head waiter would never commit the same error twice. And no amount of insistence would win a patron a place outside the area decided by the *maitre*.

The English women in the Harrods tea rooms spoke of maids and shopping and said, 'Thank you, how delightful, very well then, that's fine, what is she doing these days? Oh, did she? You can't really mean that! So good of him, you know, such a wonderful time, how remarkable, really, thank you. Have you heard? Oh, gosh! The BBC said so, and have you ever wondered why Mrs Beeton called her Cookery Book Mrs Beeton's instead of Isabella Mary Mayson's, which was her real name?'

And then they went home convinced that Argentina was a fine place in spite of its politics as long as they could continue to have maids, and tea at Harrods.

The Argentine society ladies were more concerned about who people came to tea with, and where they were going when they left. Their maids were a problem too, and their men were a constant worry...

German women fidgeted, looked alarmed. Sometimes they would hum little songs and laugh, and other times they would blow their nose loudly, as if they had been weeping. Then they would discuss the wrangling at the last board meeting of the German hospital, founded in 1867.

The German community had never been as strong as the British. But though rent by rivalries between immigrant groups who had brought their politics from 19th-century Europe, most of its forty thousand members were beginning to organise their sympathy and support for the new Fatherland.

The Germans had boarding schools – the best-known named after the naturalist Hermann Burmeister, who had died in Argentina in 1892 – newspapers, printing plants and publishers, and the level of their intellectual debate, though described as debased by expatriation, was high compared to that in the British community.

Anti-Jewish expressions were unabashed and recurrent. The mathematician Albert Einstein had been snubbed during his visit to Buenos Aires in March 1925. And there had been overt praise, and material support, for the more notorious right wing nationalist organisations started in Germany in the 1920s.

Prominent among the German community's cultural and political figures was the novelist Max René Hesse. After practicing as a doctor at the German Hospital for seventeen years until 1927, he returned to Germany at forty-two and became a writer. His two novels *Morath Struggles Ahead* and *Morath Realizes a Dream*, published in Berlin in 1933, suited the age's New Realism. The story denounced the corruption of Argentina and of the German community through an idealistic central character whose nationalism and homoerotic relationships pitted him against the social breakdown he saw about him. 'In this country one has only two things in mind: to get rich and to draw attention to oneself,' he wrote. The novels ended in sympathy with the military leaders of the 1930 coup in Buenos Aires, Catholic nationalists who promised the rebirth of a moral Argentina. Jakob Morath, Hesse's main character, was a physician, like Hesse, who went in search of self-realisation through political idealism to escape his routine profession and broken marriage.

The German ladies in the tea rooms at Harrods argued quite passionately, for years, about who the characters in the book were taken from in real life. Who were the doctors, who the nurses?

# Chapter 20

H IS HEART HEAVY, Douglas asked Cooper & Nephews to transfer him to the northern provinces from where he could enter Paraguay and witness what seemed to be the last stages of the war with Bolivia. Everybody who was anybody was going there. In May 1935 he read that the English politician, Randolph Churchill, had been posted to Asunción as war correspondent for the London *Daily Mail*, whose proprietor, Viscount Rothermere, had written that the German leader, Hitler, was 'the most prominent figure in the world today... A man so completely possessed by a great purpose has no use for subtleties and shams...' Douglas did not think of himself in the same league as Churchill, but his presence did add attraction to the war. And if Churchill could connect him with cavalry officers who might like to buy powders and pomades for the welfare of their horses, then a visit to Paraguay would prove very useful.

Paraguay was known in Buenos Aires by the situation of British-owned business in the country and not much had happened there in years. A British doctor, named Macdonald, had been murdered in Asunción in December 1929, but the motive was never known and even if it was, his murder had never made the English papers and had been forgotten. In March 1933 the cricketer Roy Sheffield was arrested for two days on charges of spying for Bolivia. The Essex wicketkeeper had been on holiday on a ranch after he had served as umpire in Buenos Aires for the annual North v. South cricket match, held for the 34th year running.

Douglas had travelled often on the route through northern Argentina, by river and land, selling his animal medicines. On the Northeastern Argentine Railway, and on the small *Ferro Carril del Este Argentino*, he had seen passengers entertain themselves watching the natives from the small local tribes tear one another apart in vicious fights to get at the loaves of bread and pieces of meat thrown from the dining car. The stench of suffering came through the train windows; passengers covered their noses with their coat sleeves.

He had also observed them on the ground. The native people huddled in clusters of mud huts that looked like tiny stone-age villages, set on the edge of private farm land to facilitate access to what owners and labourers threw away. Men and women in their settlements, where they had been corralled by army patrols and government employees in dark suits, were sometimes too disgusting to look at, let alone approach. They would scream, shout and fight to the point of causing serious injury, indifferent to their surroundings. The edges of footpaths were marked by faeces dropped where the urge took man or woman. Women let their menstrual blood trickle, or was it internal bleeding from injury and infection? The blood ran down their legs under thin cotton dresses long discarded by previous owners; men urinated outside their huts, leaving small puddles that children stamped in and splashed one another.

The open sores of age, skin ulcers, burst boils that looked as large as carnations, on the legs and backs of old men and semi-naked crones, stared back at the visitor like spare eyes, as blind as those in their heads. On the farms native Indians were treated as slave labour, at best poorly paid, fed from dustbins and given no shelter. Their life-span was short, their ability to work limited by sickness and weakness.

This was northern Argentina, well removed from the colonisation projects, from elegant residences owned by expatriate farmers and local merchants and from the English club tennis court, which Douglas had begun to enjoy. He felt repelled and drawn by the sharp contrasts of the 'New World' and, afterwards, when he had left behind the smells and sights, he remained mystified by them. He thought of life in the hovels and home in the Calvet; the destiny of one, and the luck of the other, but he drew no conclusions, felt nothing. Helping those people was for missionaries and doctors, not for travelling salesmen.

He crossed into Paraguay at Clorinda, over the River Pilcomayo, near to Asunción. Hundreds of soldiers milled about with little to do. The war was coming to an end and, in any case, had never reached this far south. Bolivia had started the Chaco War in June 1932, when its army occupied the border area at Pitiantuta, in pursuit of a river route from oil-rich Villa Montes through Paraguay to the River Plate. North American oil companies and German officers had encouraged the government in La Paz to attack, after years of border skirmishes, in the confidence that Paraguay was still weakened and low in manpower, since the War of the Triple Alliance had killed ninety per cent of the nation's men by the end of battle in 1870.

Paraguay had beaten off the Bolivian attack in the jungle, but its troops had failed to win the war on the high plateau in the northeast, where the Bolivian soldier was better equipped physically and mechanically. Between them, the two countries had lost one hundred thousand men to fighting and disease. At the start of the war Paraguay's population had been 850,000, Bolivia's 3.5 million.

The troops looked dishevelled, some without shoes, or if they were fortunate, or officers, they wore unmatching footwear. They begged for food, or exchanged it for bits of what was left of their uniform, and approached outsiders with requests for help.

Douglas exchanged an old pair of black leather shoes for a horse which came with a bit and one rein and a sackcloth saddle. It was a very thin, small horse, but its footing was sure and its coat shiny, so there was life in it still. The sergeant who had parted with his mount and the young Scot each felt that they had made the best deal in their lives. The exchange was written down and witnessed by an army scribe who wrote on the back of a miltary telegram which said a consignment of army boots was on its way. The scribe's price was two cigarettes.

Civilians set up small, almost insignificant, roadside stalls to sell limes or *chipá* bread. Smugglers held small stocks, so as not to tempt thieves, and sold single or even half cigarettes. At the river's edge a man who caught small catfish with a whip sold strips of the white meat which a woman roasted on an open fire. The smell of the roasting fish was tempting, but the morsels were minute.

Apart from a couple of cobble stone streets, Asunción was a warren of dusty, or muddy, paths.

Douglas went to visit importers and smugglers to offer his list of products which he assured would save crops and animals after the war. Anybody who could grow food then, he said, would become rich in a short time. They liked his talk, but offered no cash, only barter. Guns, field equipment, harnesses, reins and gear for cart horses – stolen from the dead animals left in the battlefield or killed by the jungle. These were the country's currency and most available. While there was no peace and only truce talks the equipment, hoarded in broken-down farm sheds and railway warehouses, was tradeable. There had been over a dozen pacification meetings but no end to the hostilities.

Argentina's staunchly nationalist foreign minister, Carlos Saavedra Lamas, led each drive to bring the warring sides to talks.

Douglas sent a telegram to Buenos Aires for permission to barter veterinary products for military equipment. While he waited for an answer he went to look for the British war correspondents he had been told were in Asuncion. He did not find Randolph Churchill and assumed the man was covering the war from the attempted talks, or even in New York. A man called Thompson, of the London

*Morning Post*, claimed that he was the only correspondent who had covered both sides and had interviewed the presidents of Paraguay and Bolivia. But there was nobody else.

In the outskirts of Asunción the silence of partly abandoned villages screamed at the visitor that the squalor and sickness, not the war, had killed the men and the women had taken shelter in the city. There was a smell of wood smoke and of the staple *chipá* maize or manioc bread in the buildings. Every possession of value had been moved, or looted.

Once, he urged his horse to hurry towards a man driving a cart, relieved to find somebody in a village street. The cart man was passing through, on his way to the capital, to make sure his son was given a funeral befitting an officer of the 40th Battalion of the Chaco army and that he, the father, would be registered for a war pension due the next of kin.

Would the foreigner like to make a gift towards the payment of the coffin and a priest? The son's body was in the cart, wrapped in sacking beneath a cover of wooden slats laid head to toe, tied down with bailing wire. The dried-out bare feet protruded from one end, the boots and socks that once covered them having been placed neatly by the father's side. The swelling, decomposing body oozed through the slats, but the smell was not too severe. The body was drying faster than it decomposed.

There was nobody to buy farm health goods outside the capital either. Douglas went back to the *Gran Hotel*, to await his instructions. The 'gran' in his refuge was a reasonable overstatement, but it was not the more famous Gran Hotel de Paraguay, where those with power and money stayed. His hotel was a ground-floor only house with about six rooms surrounding an enclosed patio, kept by five women of varying ages. A swarm of flies hung in the air outside the kitchen at the back of the house. At times the concentration seemed to cloud over the sun and the buzzing drowned what conversation was attempted. At least four of the women in the house seemed to be devoted to encouraging every spider on the walls in their web-building by singing words of endearment in Guaraní. Every toad that walked up from the river became a prisoner in the patio. The combination of spiders and toads were the only equipment to counter the flies and mosquitoes that made sleep difficult. Douglas realized that he would not be selling any domestic sprays against insects. Traditional methods applied.

He was the only guest: a bad sign. But the two big hotels in the city were filled with army officers and politicians and some traders that he wanted to avoid. They demanded goods on credit and he could not grant that.

On his third evening at the hotel, after he had watered the horse and brushed it down with a damp rag, he sat in a wooden chair in the patio, drinking beer smuggled from Brazil. The oldest of the women in the house brought a small girl and stood her in front of him. He had not seen the girl in the house and she was probably a neighbour. 'For you,' the old woman said pointing a finger at him and speaking in a Spanish with a sing-song inflection from the Guaraní. He played for time by appearing not to understand her. The girl smiled. The old woman knew that he knew. But when he could no longer evade her glance and her offers, he refused. 'Why?' asked the old woman and informed the girl of the refusal. The girl stepped nearer. 'Because I am a man; she is a girl, very young, a child...'

'Fourteen...' the old woman signalled with her fingers. 'Perhaps...about,' she added, glancing at the girl. 'A good age.' She was small for those few years. She had thick long combed hair.

He stuck to his refusal. The old woman placed herself between the girl and Douglas and looked at him with anger in her eyes. But the anger was only a flash; it did not last.

'Why not? She is healthy. She is clean,' the woman lifted the girl's skirts almost to her waist, showing a young naked body below, with no underwear. There was only a small tuft of pubic hair. 'You are healthy, you have good skin, clean... You white, we need ... Our men went to war, dead, infirm and may never be well. You have no woman.' She shouted all this at him, in a rapid, furious voice. When she had finished, she tugged at the girl and walked away.

That night he was told that there was no food for supper because of the shortages. He went out and found a meal of fatty meat and some green vegetables which he could not identify.

He lay awake for what seemed hours with mild indigestion, waving at the whining mosquitoes, hoping for an end to the sub-tropical night.

Some time after midnight he heard the door open but could see nothing in the darkness. A woman, he imagined it was the girl because of her size, slipped into bed beside him and a small hand felt inside his pyjamas. As soon as he had an erection the woman moved to encourage him to get on top of her. When he had finished and went limp, her hand went back into his trousers. She dried him off on his pyjamas and coaxed him to stiffen. The third time she sat on top of him and giggled and wriggled and bounced up and down, tweaked his scrotum and played with his testicles and finally lay beside him for two minutes, apparently relaxing. She cleaned him with a damp rag that she had brought and silently left the room.

He slept well after that, and the mosquitoes were no bother.

In the morning he noticed blood on the sheet and tried to hide his soiled pyjamas under the pillow. In the patio he found a good breakfast of fruit, *chipá* bread and a cup of hot *maté*. There was nobody about and he left the building quickly after breakfast to do his errands in town. He rode to the ramshackle Guaraní Hotel and studied the guests for possible barter, but left without chatting for long to any one man.

In the evening he found an abundant, in war terms, supper awaiting him under a worn but well-washed linen cloth on the table in the patio. Manioc, a sliver of fish, some leaves, a glass of beer, a banquet. The sheets were clean and his pyjamas had been washed.

After midnight another girl came. He knew she was a different one because she was fatter. The action ran along the same pattern of the night before. The difference this time was that he was woken in the grey light of dawn by a third girl who fled from the room when he tried to open the blinds to see her.

It must have been this girl who came to him the next night, and she was succeeded by yet another after a couple of hours while the night was still black.

By the end of the week three girls visited him in the course of the night. On the Saturday morning he felt drained of strength and could not swing up into the saddle very easily. The old woman brought him a stool to help him mount. He was relieved to find a telegram at the post office ordering him back to Buenos Aires. The offered barter could not be accepted.

As he rode out of the patio, the old woman smiled at him. Several women were with her. Whereas they had been invisible previously, now they had gathered to bid him farewell. Solemnly they nodded a greeting. One of them gave the old woman several bank notes. Another woman ran forward and stopped the horse and shook his hand. Yet another came to him and patted his thigh in appreciation and muttered, 'Good, Good,' in Guaraní. The old woman made a sign with her head that he should leave quickly.

The Argentine health authorities would not let Douglas cross his horse at Clorinda, so he rode it up the banks of the Pilcomayo for two kilometres and paid a smuggler a few coins to cross him with horse. He left the animal with an English acquaintance in Formosa and took the river boat to Buenos Aires.

On 12 June 1935, at the eighteenth attempt, the armistice was signed and the Chaco War was brought to an end. The truce came into effect two days later.

After a stop at Paraná to see customers, he reached the Calvet building on 24 June, as the radio broke the news that the tango singer and film actor Carlos Gardel had been killed in a plane crash in Colombia.

Argentina was in mourning. Douglas shared the grief. Gardel was a star, but he had also enjoyed horseplay and a bit of wrestling with the lads in the YMCA changing room. He had often sung for the members, after a session in the shower. Douglas was among the privileged few who could say they had seen one of the great stars of South America sing a tango in the raw, soaping his crotch and combing his hair as he hit the lowest notes of one of his favourite songs.

Nobody wanted to hear Douglas tell the strange story of his nights in Asunción. One of the lodgers at the Calvet asked if he was sure, very sure, that he had not dreamed it all? 'Wars have strange effects on the mind,' he was told. It was well known that the heat and the awful food could do terrible things to a man.

# Chapter 21

THE *BUENOS AIRES HERALD* ran the news as its third lead on the front page on 25 June. The United Press agency reported the mid-air collision between a plane of the Saco Company, which carried Carlos Gardel, his librettist Alfredo Le Pera and friends, and a tri-engined machine of the Scadta Company. 'The corpse of the idol of the women of Latin America presented a terrible aspect, having been reduced to a carbonised mass with the face contracted with fright and pain. It was identified by the dentures and a ring on the left hand.'

In Buenos Aires, 'a minute's silence, during which the audiences stood, was observed last night at all local theatres as a homage to Carlos Gardel. It was decided that no tangos should be sung to-day at any of the performances.'

The feeling of abandon ran deep in Argentina. Europeans found it difficult to understand such a sense of loss. Philip de Souza's *Tango* had been all the rage in Paris in 1912, but it was over. In the River Plate, the music's fascination lay in its synthesis of Buenos Aires. The origins of the tango may have been in Africa, Castille, the Caribbean, Cuba and Vienna, but its melancholy lyrics about failing love and misfortune belonged to a city of immigrants who had mislaid their past, then constantly tried to recreate it to make bygones somehow more attractive. The opening music of the tango, *Y todo a media luz* (And all in Half Light), sounded as if taken from Dvorjak's Piano Quintet. But the words were melodramatic, noisy lamentations filled with complaint. *Yira, yira* (about a whore at the end of her career), by Enrique Santos Discépolo (1901-1951), pointed to the shortcomings of fickle humans:

> ... when all the doors of the houses
> Where you once went are closed,
> Shut tight against your knocking:
> As you search for a shoulder to lean on,

Seeking to die embracing some friend.
When you left me on the road,
I went from girl to girl
And they all used me.
You will have to witness
Them trying on the clothes
You will leave when you go.
Then you'll remember this sucker,
Who once, even when very tired,
Howled for you like a dog...
Geehra, Geehra...

Buenos Aires tango was pure poetry. It bared the soul. Now its foremost exponent was a mangled mess of charred flesh and bones. 'Others swooped on the riches he had to leave behind,' the tango said. Gardel's life was a tango. His songs and his music had closely described the manic-depressive *Porteño* male and what he thought of his life and of women. It was an embarrassing portrait of wretchedness and misogyny which the north European Protestant could not understand or preferred not to, and thus disguised his own miserable condition. In the tango dance the partners did things standing up which most ordinary people would have liked to do lying down. Embarrassing too was the connoisseur's insistence that tango was serious music, to be explored intimately. Intimacy, for the north European, was not something to sing about loudly.

Gardel had been born Charles Romuald Gardes, in December 1890, at Toulouse, the son of Berthe and an unknown father. In Uruguay, tango buffs said he had been born there, in Tacuarembó. But it was accepted that he had lived in Buenos Aires since 1893. According to the local story, Berthe had departed from France with her child and with the shame of small town scandal, to Buenos Aires, where she took in washing for a living. Her son led an urchin's life in the docks and fled his mother's reprimands to Montevideo at the age of twelve. The picture of her hand-wringing loneliness and the sad lot of the abandoned woman helped eventually to put his Oedipus complex to song and thus capture the sense of urban tragedy that would make him the most popular man in Latin America.

What the European could not stomach was his hair lacquered solid and the dandy's air about him which made his sexuality suspect. He was also a millionaire, which irked the middle classes who believed that singing was not work. He stayed at the Waldorf Astoria in New York, where he had a Plymouth car waiting at the door. An Hispano-Suiza was at his disposal in Paris. His Catalan admirers had given him a Graham Paige car. He owned a film production company, Exito's Spanish Pictures, in which Western Electric had shares, and his films had world distribution by Paramount, where he had a contract that made him one of the best-paid performers in the world.

After death in a mid-air collision the man became a legend.

# Chapter 22

PRIETO HAD THE ABILITY to surmount any circumstance. One moment he expressed an unmatchable hatred for the world, self pity for his own impossibly complicated problems and fell into a deep depression that reflected a sense of inferiority and incompetence. Five minutes later he could be happily embarked on a venture that would surely, he said, bring him success in business and politics. Now he was employed in the law office of an uncle – his father would not have him in his own practice, but had arranged for his son's employment within the family. His aspirations for success in public life were increasingly outrageous and Douglas thought that Prieto's off-the-cuff jokes about the madness of his acquaintances, such as the writer Roberto Arlt, were perhaps a cover for his own increasingly strange behaviour. It became obvious to Douglas by then that the family thought Prieto was, maybe, 'a little peculiar'. Douglas had begun to avoid his old friend, but was compelled to rejoin him on appeal by Prieto or, more disturbingly, by the uncle who employed him. Douglas had been called more than once at the Calvet, summoned by smart white business cards in small envelopes and asked not to abandon Prieto, on the grounds that, 'You, *inglés*, are a good influence. We need your help. If there is anything you want, you must ask us. We are grateful.'

He became uncomfortable, even alarmed. The family meant money, of course. He could not help being attracted to Prieto and his projects. The man's charm and his conviction about whatever he took on invariably drew Douglas into ventures he knew he should avoid. Prieto one day announced that he had been involved in 'incidents related to the meat industry'. He raised and half closed his hand as if holding a gun and his index finger squeezed a non-existent trigger. At first, Douglas did not believe him. The man's politics were too cockeyed to be serious. Prieto's ideological understanding of the world established that it was valid to oppose British meat companies even if that meant appearing to support those from the United States. In Prieto's words, the late president Yrigoyen had been brought down in 1930 because of his support for the old British colonial order. Argentina's future lay with the United States, which was also a young nation and could be beaten at its own game by Argentina, which was also white and European.

They met weekly at Fanny's Bar, on one of the narrower and greyer streets of the city centre, where men alone could pour out their hearts to the prostitutes who used the joint to arrange assignations, or to Fanny, behind the bar, who was mother hen, banker, alibi generator and informer to all her male and female patrons. And she doubled the bills when she knew she had a man or a woman in her grip. Prieto hated her, but relied on Fanny to handle all messages from or for his political cronies. Douglas refused all her services, but admired her and could not keep his eyes off the robust, huge-breasted, middle-aged woman in the mousy hair as she dished out advice or admonition, overcharged customers and short-changed strangers.

Normally, Prieto and Douglas sat at the long wooden bar. The rest of the place was in gloom. The walls appeared to be dark wood panelling, to match the bar. In fact the old wall paper had been covered with a dirty varnish, over which lines had been drawn to appear as wooden planks.

At Fanny's, Prieto, watching the women, became passionate in his attack on white slave traders. Ever since the days of 'Eva the Polak' ('Where is she now? I wonder,' Douglas interrupted, without expecting a reply), Prieto said the pimps' conspiracy aimed to undermine Argentine society and make the country a French colony. It was simple. The French envied the British and the North American influence in Argentina. So they used the Marseilles syndicate and the 'Franchutas' to spread disease and weaken Argentine males. The conspiracy was in the interests of the big corporations. Most immigration was of single males. The Roman Catholic Church advocated the promotion of immigration of married couples, who would be easier to integrate, but it was still mostly the single men who came to Argentina. This was because the Jewish Zwi Migdal group supported the Marseilles Syndicate, because the Jews wanted to destroy the Catholic Church, etc. Hence, Prieto said, prostitution was a useful service to the single male, which big business wanted to control. The immigrants preferred European women to what they called the 'savages' from Brazil.

Angrily, Prieto would shout his disapproval of this anti-Christ trick by foreigners. His fist thumped the counter top. And as his voice grew louder, Fanny would come from behind the till and whack him with a fly swatter. This silenced him, but anger poured fiercely from his eyes.

Prieto had been mentioned in the evening papers on several occasions as he denounced the trade in women, in the name of the Church and the moral fatherland. The response had been a series of anonymous letters left with Fanny which threatened Prieto. Far from cowering and encouraged by what he saw as the 'chance to unmask the enemy', Prieto prepared a small moral crusade with three cronies whom he summoned to a meeting at Fanny's. He would, he said, institute punishment, because the police were too corrupt to defend the nation's welfare and moral health.

With his 'three musketeers', Prieto went to the islands in front of San Fernando, the 'Sin City' north of Buenos Aires, to hunt down 'white slavers'.

In fact, the Rosario-based *Maffia* which had been the principal importer of women for the trade in Buenos Aires was in retreat, under pressure from a lone prosecutor who used Albert Londres' *The Road to Buenos Ayres* as documentary evidence.

The four crusaders never found their target. But they did run into smugglers. A brief gunbattle followed. Against far more experienced gunmen, Prieto's group had no chance. One of his partners was killed. Prieto and the other two escaped alive only because the smugglers stopped firing and withdrew when they realized the enemy was insignificant.

Douglas lived to regret his next meeting with Prieto at Fanny's. It was just after the funeral of the 'musketeer', which had drawn the attention of the newspapers. Prieto was being hounded by enquiries. Fanny warded them off. There was not a spot on his conscience over the death of his companion, but he was angry and looking for revenge.

'There is a woman who runs a racket with children in a house on the corner of Libertad and Avenida Corrientes,' Douglas told Prieto. The information was given to get it off his chest more than to spark action, as the discovery had shocked him. Prieto would understand a story like that, more than Fanny.

'How do you know?' Prieto asked, with an undisguised trace of suspicion that his friend was involved in something murky.

'Because I was visiting some Germans who live next door. I saw the children. They look horribly pale. There are about three of them. They never leave the building. They look about eleven or twelve, but they might be older.'

Prieto's two surviving mates arrived at Fanny's and were informed about the child prostitutes. They blamed Germans, and reduced this to foreigners when Douglas explained that such a view was mistaken. Douglas became nervous. He should not have reported his accidental findings. The men railed not against the evil of the activity, but about the danger to the nation's moral fibre.

After half an hour of discussion, they convinced each other that punishment had to be meted out. Douglas must take them to the house.

He refused. He was shouted at and pushed by one of the men. Without a thought Douglas raised his fist and smacked it into the man's mouth. The man retreated then lunged forward, only to be caught by Prieto. Fanny rammed a broom handle between Douglas and the others. Prieto called calm. He assured his mate that Douglas was a friend. 'So, what am I?' the man demanded and pushed forward again. His mouth was bleeding. Prieto caught him; Fanny shouted that they would all be banned from her place for ever.

That seemed to calm Prieto. He promised Douglas that the only violence would be to smash the property. Douglas allowed himself to be convinced. Such a trade had to be stopped. He made them promise: No Guns. Prieto agreed. Douglas knew all three were armed. He led them to the house.

A small round woman with a greasy apron answered the door and fell back as it was kicked open by Prieto. Douglas waited in the darkened hallway. The three men raced through the house tearing curtains, over-turning furniture, crashing ornaments. There were many shouts and the woman screamed. No children were found. In the shouting one man's voice rose above the rest. It was Prieto's. Then a shot rang out.

They ran down stairs and into the street. In the foyer of a nearby cinema, Prieto told Douglas: 'No children there. But it was the right house. You could tell by the rooms... thick curtains, dark red, velvet wall paper. People don't live in houses like that.' He shook, but it was not fear. An excited fury caused him to tremble.

'The shot...?' Douglas asked.

'What shot?' Prieto played for time.

'Come on, you shit, you promised...no guns.'

'It was a politician. I know him. A friend of my father's. He recognised me... I don't think I killed him. I should have.'

Douglas was very frightened. He walked the few blocks to Fanny's to let her know what had happened.

'You're a childish idiot,' she scolded. 'Fancy telling a madman a thing like that.'

'He's not mad,' Douglas defended.

'You're a bigger fool than I thought,' she replied, and simply ignored him after that.

Douglas went back to the Calvet.

There was nothing in the papers the next day, or the next. The attack had been hushed up.

Prieto stayed away from Fanny's and there was no call to the Calvet from him or any of his family until two weeks later. The uncle sent an office boy to Fanny's with a note and a copy to the Calvet. Prieto was in hospital, in a private room at the Little Company of Mary.

Douglas took him a bunch of flowers, which he carried hanging outside of the tram window so that he would not be seen with them and thought unmanly. Only women carried flowers in public.

Prieto looked terrible. His face was blue, one eye was black and what could be seen of the other was rimmed in blood. His head had been partly shaved and there were iodine tincture marks on the scalp. One hand lay on the bed cover, bandaged.

'They're bastards, Douglas. They were out to get me. You can't expose politicians who bugger little children and get away with it. They sent four men to beat me up... And they shot off two of my fingers.' He began to cry. He looked away and shook with the sobs.

It was something of a shock to see her arrive in the office on Monday morning at the beginning of the month and be shown to a desk which she took as her own. There was no hesitation in her behaviour, apart from a newcomer's doubts about the geography and the location of the material necessary for her work. She was, after all, a competent and experience administration secretary.

He walked across the office, aware that old man Cooper was staring out at him, and offered her his hand in greeting.

'Nobody told me you were coming,' he said.

'Perhaps there is no need to inform you of such matters,' she said curtly.

He shrank. Inés was not putting behind her the incident at the dinner party, or the brawl in Plaza de Mayo.

'I'm sorry. I didn't mean to be rude. I was coming to welcome you. They usually post the names of new appointments on the noticeboard in the hall, but I did not see your name.'

She smiled briefly and glanced at the floor, a shadow of embarrassment in the gesture. Second round to him, he thought. Then she regained her composure and took control:

'Let's begin again,' she held out her hand. He shook it. 'Good morning. I knew you worked here, but I was only informed last week that the job was mine.

I have been off work. I have been ill.' Again there was a shadow of embarrassment.

Douglas noticed that old man Cooper was standing in his office, scowling, so he mumbled an 'Hasta luego,' raised his eyebrows and started to move away.

'Are you still seeing...?' he shot over his shoulder.

'No,' she snapped.

Good, he smiled to himself, and put a little skip into his walk back to his desk. He would play his cards right this time.

He sat staring at her as she went about her business. He liked her, she was accessible.

At four o'clock in the afternoon, he managed to settle down to several order forms on his desk. He felt as if he had been awake all night and sleep had only come with the sounds of dawn. Silly comparison, really, but he had spent much of the day staring at her. Then, as he regained his concentration, there was a long shadow across his desk. It was old man Cooper.

'Listen, laddie,' the chief said shaping the words carefully in a manner that clearly betrayed controlled anger. 'I've watched you gawp all day and do nowt work. No, I don't mind you gawping and I don't mind you staring at the new secretary all day. But I do mind you doing it in my time, and on her first day of work. So, laddie, would you like to explain yourself.'

'She makes a better picture than...' and it was obvious he meant Cooper.

No sooner had he said that than he was eager to apologize. This was no way to play his cards right. He was in a mess again.

'Sorry,' Douglas said. 'That was unnecessary. I do apologize. And, yes I met her some time ago. And I shouldn't have been staring.'

His apology was blurted and completed rapidly, to deflect Cooper's huge fist, tightly clenched, which had risen level with his chest and then, without opening, was lowered slowly.

'If I could just stop thinking for a few moments that you are a good salesman. Then I would punch your face in and bash that lip of yours... You deserve it...'

'Yes, sir, no, sir. I am sorry...'

'But I think of your damned order books and I hold back.' Cooper forced a smile. He swung round and walked away.

'Sorry, sir,' Douglas called after him.

In spite of his impulses he waited three weeks. The waiting was helped by a week's tour to La Pampa, but even in absence, it was difficult. He sneaked a peep at her passport as it lay on her desk one day, and saw that she had arrived in the country in 1926. She had never left: there were no consular notes anywhere. She was a year older than he was. Her occupation was entered as 'governess'. He decided that must be a mistake for private secretary to a cinema actress.

He did not mention hangovers during the week. He tried to get to bed early so as to look wide awake in the morning. He arrived punctually to work at 8.30 and made the first round of teas and coffees for the dozen or so people in the main office.

Then he invited her to tea at Harrods when they left the office at six o'clock.

He sat staring at her. She had dark eyes and her hair was also quite dark, slightly curled. She had been born near Liverpool, but her mother was Argentine-born, married to an English seaman, who had died when she was a little girl. Her grandmother was Peruvian, but she had never met her. She lived with her mother. Her name was Inés Louise, after her mother.

'What a pretty name,' he mumbled. She smiled at him, amused by his effort.

'No, I mean it. I like your name. In fact, you know this, I like you. That's why we're here. I think.'

She smiled some more and he felt very wobbly and light in the stomach.

They agreed to meet again, to go to a concert at the Colón Opera House. It was her choice. His heart sank and he tried to delay setting a date. He preferred tea at Harrods, so that he could look at her. She said she would feel safer if their meetings were arranged outside of the office and not discussed in work hours, except in an emergency.

'How does Cooper feel about his staff going out together?' she asked.

With the certainty of absolutely genuine information about which he knew nothing, Douglas said, 'He doesn't give a damn. Pardon the language.'

'I don't believe you.'

He walked her back most of the way to her home on Peru Street. She asked him to stop twice, to catch her breath. She said she was a keen tennis player, but she had not been well.

'When you are well, we must play tennis,' he said. To hell with concerts, he thought.

He ran most of the five blocks back to Plaza de Mayo and then, almost automatically, stopped outside Fanny's. At the door he prevented himself from going in, waved at Fanny who probably puzzled over his long absence. He ran on to the Calvet.

# Chapter 23

THE ADVANCE of modern technology had Buenos Aires enthralled. The local English-speaking community were very proud of one Mr Charles Abbott, on the staff of the Shell petroleum company, who had flown a Fox Moth across the Andes. It had taken him just over two hours each way between Mendoza and Santiago, as part of an experiment towards opening a new air route.

For North American residents a new age was to be born with the imminent arrival of the Douglas Aircraft company's new twin-engined DC-3. The 21-seat passenger plane build for American Airlines, to beat the 14-seat DC-2 built for Trans World Airlines, flew its maiden flight over Santa Monica, California, on 17 December 1935. The new thrill in modern aviation was due in Buenos Aires soon.

The French community was quietly proud of the popularity in the city's bookshops of the French edition, and of the translations into English and Spanish, of the two books by Antoine de Saint-Exupéry, *Southern Mail* (1929) and *Night Flight* (1931), in part based on his experience as a pilot in Argentina's air mail service, the Aéropostale, operated by the French. Of all the pioneering airmen, the French in Buenos Aires held him highest.

Saint-Exupéry was in his late twenties when, in October 1929, he had arrived in Buenos Aires to work as a pilot. At the time, the US company, Panagra, with tri-engine Fords, had started the Miami to Buenos Aires airmail service, which took nine days. The French had been competing hard to keep and expand their share of the developing world postal network.

His duties had been to extend the service south through Patagonia to the Straits of Magellan. The first plane he used was a Laté-26, with whose 450 horse-power engine the pilot hugged the ground and braved the Patagonian winds. The service operated L-25s and the larger Laté-28, as well as the Breguet 14 and Curtiss

Lark. In these machines the French-run Argentine post spread to Asunción, then to Rio de Janeiro, which was a major stop on the South Atlantic mail routes.

The Frenchman was a social butterfly, active participant in 'orgies' and bouts of drinking, at the end of which he had to drag house guests out of the bath to be able to wash before going on duty. Worst of all, he wrote only occasionally to his mother in France and was not too punctual in his remittances to her. That's what people said about him. Whatever the truth may have been, his advantages, a substantial wage and the ability to travel up and down the country quickly to attend parties, assignations and poker games, were all part of a privileged life.

His book *Southern Mail* was set in southern Europe and North Africa. *Night Flight* takes place in great part over Patagonia, but extends to other provinces of Argentina. The sense of the solitary struggle of the postal service pilots, alone in their tiny cockpits, bumping through banks of cloud high above a vast and hostile plain, captivated Buenos Aires. The romance of air travel was discussed at every social gathering.

The sudden death of Robert Bontine Cunninghame Graham in Buenos Aires shocked his many admirers. The *Buenos Aires Herald* reported on 21 March 1936 that the 'great stylist' was dead. 'Don Roberto' was a popular figure in the city and his demise while on a visit seemed unfair. The British community felt it much more than Rudyard Kipling's death in January.

Those who had seen him at close quarters or who had known him were far fewer than was apparent from the conversations in many cafés that morning. Everybody had a tale about Don Roberto. His appearance, that of a twentieth-century, cleaned-up Don Quixote, with body so thin he had to walk sideways against a strong wind to avoid being blown away, inspired more apocryphal stories than the dozens of real anecdotes generated by his full and adventurous life. Writer, traveller, Socialist, founding activist of the Scottish nationalists – Hugh MacDiarmid had complained that he was 'one of those damned aristos' who got involved in the politics of the people – and Liberal MP. Cunninghame Graham was also an enthusiast of everything South American.

At the age of 84, and after a long absence, he had returned to Buenos Aires. During a visit to the museum in Luján, rich in the gaucho and nineteenth-century memorabilia about which the old man had built his fantasies, he had caught a cold as the late summer cooled suddenly. The cold had become pneumonia.

Cunninghame Graham had been visiting Buenos Aires and other parts of the country and continent since his adolescence. His affection for gaucho life, and for the gaucho's attachment to his horse as instrument and friend, had developed in the writer a bond with the land which went beyond mere romance. His love for South America had been described as a dream which reality could not keep up with. *The Review of the River Plate*, in December 1899, had remarked that, 'It is a good many years since Mr Cunninghame Graham was in this country and he was a very young man at the time. This accounts for the curious half-reminiscent, half-dream-like tone of his Argentine tales. The life of which he wrote has almost passed away.'

Graham's admiration for Swiss-born traveller and, briefly, teacher in Buenos Aires, Aimé Felix Tschiffely, who had taken two horses, *Mancha* and *Gato*, from the southern Andes through the length of the Americas, was as much based on the friendship of man and horses as on the journey, which Graham saw as the epitome of adventure involving two inseparable animals, man and mount. Tschiffely had once asked Graham what he would like to be if he could return in another life. The Scottish writer said he would like to be a *gaucho*, as he had been briefly in the 1870s. The *gaucho*, in Cunninghame Graham's writing, was represented somewhere near to William Wordsworth's depiction of the yeoman farmer, rebelling against the corrupting elements of industrial and capitalist progress. Perhaps Graham even saw a parallel in the crofters who had been oppressed by new landowners unsympathetic to the smallholders and highland farmers.

'He would have been conspicuous in any age, but was most conspicuous in one to which he did not seem to belong,' said the obituary in the *Manchester Guardian*, reproduced by the *Herald*. 'He would have done very well as a Highland chieftain, leading his devoted clan to battle (himself in faultless tartan) while he sang a Jacobite war song which he had composed and set to music... His appearance was just a little elegant. Singularly handsome, keeping his slim and active figure, his thin and adventurous face, his mass of grey hair and long pointed beard, like a Spanish knight's, he was always most scrupulously dressed in the accepted fashion. 'He is, I regret to add,' wrote George Bernard Shaw, 'an impenitent and unashamed dandy'.'

Buenos Aires had welcomed him on his arrival in February in the manner reserved for very special guests. A crowd had assembled in the port to meet his ship. A crowd had also hung about the Plaza Hotel waiting to see him during the few days that he was able to step out into the city's sweltering heat, before he had fallen ill and died on the last day of summer.

## Chapter 24

'WHATEVER HIS POLITICS, he is with God now,' a priest remarked to Douglas as they waited in the crowd outside the hotel. 'You're the man who got into trouble when the Cardinal was visiting, aren't you?'

The priest introduced himself. Father William Furlong, Irish with a strong Argentine accent in his English, Jesuit priest, born at Fisherton, in Rosario. He said that Cunninghame Graham should be buried in Argentina, for this was his real home. Douglas was indignant.

'He's a Scot, for Christ' sake, he belongs there. And he is bloody well going back.' In fact, the newspapers had already announced that Don Roberto had expressed to his companion of 26 years, Mrs Toppie Dummett, that he wanted to be buried in Scotland.

The crowd grew noisier as the coffin was brought down from the fifth floor of the hotel and put on a horse-drawn carriage, behind which walked Tschiffely's horses, *Mancha* and *Gato*, brought to the hotel through the good offices of a local worthy, writer and friend of the dead Scot, but too late for Don Roberto to 'meet' them. This had been one of the expressed intentions of his return journey. He had even brought a small bag of oats from their former owner, which he had intended to feed them in a symbolic mission of friendship.

Douglas and Father Furlong walked behind the now famous little *criollo* horses, fighting for a place among the pushy, affectionate throng that was anxious to be part of something important, up Avenida Santa Fe to the *Casa del Teatro*. There the coffin was put on public view and there the floral tributes were delivered by the dozen.

Douglas first tried to punch his way through the crush, but his new-found companion said it would be undignified for a man of the church to start waving his fists to gain entry, however Irish.

They withdrew to a bar nearby to watch the arrival of the city's notables who came to pay their respects all through the muggy evening of the first day of autumn. Even President Justo visited. The floral wreaths were so numerous they were stacked on the pavement of Avenida Santa Fe until they could be found a place inside.

Cunninghame Graham 'put us on the map', Furlong told Douglas. 'He was the most publicised, and most representative, author in the present day of what I call *Southamericana* – it is that genre of travel writing that runs through the nineteenth century, which gave Argentina a great part of its early literature, its iconography and a sense of romance about itself. The present *Southamericana* is not the same, it is not so pioneering as it was a century ago. But even now it still captures an atmosphere of the country we would like to have, because we think foreigners want us to be as they see us in their writing.'

William Furlong S.J. was a historian, whose special study was, among other things, early British settlers and merchants in Buenos Aires. His conversation became a lecture.

'The trouble with Don Roberto is that he was at once lovable and wonderful to read, yet he was a romantic and never became a great writer. We like him because he came from Scotland and made us feel important. That means we have little self-respect. We enjoy the eccentricities of a European because it makes us feel good. And because Graham was only a visitor, his strange romance with Argentina is easily accepted. Now take W. H. Hudson, he was a good man, you know. But he never came back. And people who did not read could not know him. Hudson really penetrated this country when he wrote down his life.

'When Rabindranath Tagore came to visit Victoria Ocampo, in 1924, he went around asking people if they knew anything about some wonderful books by a man called Hudson. Nobody had heard of him. Ford Maddox Ford, Galsworthy, Conrad, all said Hudson was one of the great writers in English, but by then he was not ours. And he should be ours, even if he did write in English and left Argentina because he could not make his life here. He hated the immigrant Italians here, you know, because he said they shot little birds.

'People are now saying wonderful things about Cunninghame Graham's writing about Argentina, because he has just died. But Hudson was the better writer, he was a stylist. Graham was a *raconteur*.'

Douglas had come upon Hudson at twenty-one when Hudson had been dead six years. It seemed strange to find a writer in English proclaimed by the priest as a classic of *Southamericana*.

The British community was largely unaware of its cultural surroundings, unless these had a strong link with commerce. The favoured reading was John Buchan's *The Thirty-Nine Steps*, which showed great understanding of Scots, and his *Prester John*, which had little compassion for Africans. The western novels of Zane Grey, melodramatic cowboy stories which the author produced by the dozen, had a wide readership in Buenos Aires.

Douglas and Furlong argued at length on that day of mourning about the names they could include in their listing. Douglas suggested that John Masefiled could, at a pinch, be included in *Southamericana*, but they moved on without agreement. Masefield had never been to Argentina, though he had spent several weeks in Chile in 1894, at the British Hospital in Valparaiso, recovering from illness. In 1913 he had written the poem, 'Rosas', set in Argentina and based on the mid-century dictator who had ruled the River Plate with an iron fist.

At the end of the century, William Bulfin (1862-1910), had achieved some popularity in Buenos Aires and Dublin with his stories of life in Argentina in *The Southern Cross*, the Irish community's weekly. His collected stories, *Tales of the Pampas*, had circulated among the Irish community in a print-run of five hundred copies, but now he was almost forgotten.

Furlong was final. 'Bulfin can stay, but Masefield is not in my classification. He was never here; he wrote a poem based on newspaper reports. Otherwise I'll also have to claim Eugene O'Neill. He lived in Buenos Aires you know, before the war, in 1910, but he was a drunk and a drifter. He worked for a few weeks in the Swift packing house, and some people say he took a character from there for *The Iceman Cometh*, but I don't think I want him for my list. Though God pardon me for being so unkind. I speak of putting people in a literary geography.'

There was Walter Owen, born in Glasgow in 1884, at the peak of his popularity, not for his poems, which he published under a pen-name in *The Standard* – it would not have been right for a Scot in the import and export business to be seen to be writing poetry – but as the translator of José Hernandez's gaucho epic, *Martín Fierro*. The translation of the sixty-year-old book had rolled off the presses of Basil Blackwell in 1935. For his efforts Owen was the toast of the English-speaking community, the guest of honour and principal speaker at countless receptions and club gatherings. He had to autograph menus and napkins at lunch and was celebrated by Argentines as the man who had made Argentina's classic known to the whole world... well, to that part that could read English.

Douglas remarked that there were no women among the authors. Furlong retorted:

'This is a young country, a man's place. When societies are more advanced there is room for men and women to work on equal levels, as in Germany, I think. But not here, not yet.'

They grudgingly included Lady Florence Dixie's *Across Patagonia*, published in 1880.

Argentina as a place of romance was under a cloud. Strong nationalist expressions began to tarnish Douglas's enjoyment of the country. A journalist in his late thirties, Raúl Scalabrini Ortiz, was mobilizing public opinion, through publications and lectures, to call for the nationalization of the British railways. The British countered with anonymous pamphlets, which described and celebrated their contributions to Argentina's development.

From the Casa del Teatro, Cunninghame Graham's body was put aboard the Blue Star Line's ten-year-old *Almeda Star* for the journey home.

## Chapter 25

DOUGLAS AND INÉS decided they would get married in November 1936. It was not the extended courtship that Buenos Aires standards expected, but they had known each other long enough to decide.

In the months before the wedding they lunched and dined together almost daily, when Douglas was not travelling out of town or visiting fruit plantations in northern Patagonia. In the midday break, he helped her search for furniture for their home on the fourth floor of a new building on Avenida Córdoba.

Often, he spoke of the land he would like to buy to become a farmer. She said she could not face living far from the city. Evenings were spent at concerts at the Colón, at the cinema, or listening to the author Victoria Ocampo lecture on English writers. She was especially entertaining in the post-script to her talks when she would discuss world personalities encountered in Europe or who had been her guests at Villa Ocampo, her palatial family home north of Buenos Aires. She knew everybody, it seemed, and rumour had it that to escape a loveless marriage, she had been the lover of not a few. Victoria's lectures made Douglas and Inés feel that the Britain they had left a decade before was not so far away. They needed that reassurance.

The Spanish Civil War came closer as Argentina opened its doors to refugees. One hundred thousand men, women and children fled to Buenos Aires, making the war something in which Argentina was involved. Real tragedy added to disaster at the start of spring, when news of the murder of the poet Federico García Lorca reached the River Plate. García Lorca and the Chilean poet Pablo Neruda had been in Buenos Aires together for the great meeting of international writers organized by the PEN Club in 1933. García Lorca had become a star encountered daily in Buenos Aires. He had stayed at a hotel on Avenida de Mayo during that hot month of October when writers from all over the world were visiting the city.

A man whom Argentines felt had been in part their own was snatched from them.

'You start to get acquainted with these people, and almost immediately somebody says they are dead. They seem to be saying that about everybody nowadays,' Douglas remarked.

Inés understood the grief of Victoria Ocampo at the homage to García Lorca, and listened to the recollections of every word that the Spanish poet had uttered during the PEN congress. But Inés was a woman preparing to be wed. She had other priorities.

Douglas and Inés worked on a wedding list at *Wright's Bazaar Inglés*, a store started in 1879 as Simons and Wright. The shop had been on Avenida de Mayo since 1922 and Charles Wright had bought out his partner in 1931. English plate and crystal made it the British community's favourite expensive gifts store, handy for wedding lists.

She ordered her dress from Harrods, not white, but a very elegant outfit that could be used for special occasions afterwards. 'Besides, we've been around a bit and it seems quite hypocritical to wear white,' she told Douglas.

Douglas ordered a suit from James Smart's, a long established English store started in 1888 by two of the sons of the original Smart, of Edinburgh. Wright's and Smart's were considered the best. And Harrods too, of course.

They booked the fourth of November at St John's Cathedral, a mid-spring wedding.

'You know, marriage is not such a bad thing,' Father Furlong told Douglas with a chuckle. They had got accustomed to meeting for coffee or tea in a bar on Callao Avenue, near the Jesuit college of El Salvador.

'How would you know?'

'I've seen so many. They look like fun... The pleasures that the spirit can't offer, at first anyway, the body certainly provides.'

'Funny, you seem very much a man of the flesh, Guillermo,' Douglas said. 'How come...? Well, you know.'

'I'll make a shocking confession, among friends. God already knows, and tolerates this. The flesh needs dedication, enjoyment, devotion, attention,' his voice was deep, rich, lustful. 'You have to celebrate love... I mean good fornication... like a Christmas mass, and then have time for vespers for prayers of thanks. That is if you really enjoy it. I decided when I was quite young that I had no time for that kind of love. I thought that I was better employed in the celebration of knowledge. I needed to devote time to learning about the past of this strange country of mine. I have become a man of history. In a country that can't be bothered with history and is not old enough to repeat its mistakes, I want to keep the records that will caution my students against future errors.'

'Keeper of records, keeper of history, in a place that tells itself it has no history or spends too much time trying to correct history to contemporary will. What a responsibility,' Douglas cut in. 'And how idealistic, or is it arrogant, to think you can caution people against repeating their mistakes. I prefer a good woman...' he paused. 'Sorry, that was crude.'

'And I'll be even more crude. I became a Jesuit to escape your good women. I find them repugnant, in body and function. History is a better lover; she, have you noticed that history is a woman in Spanish, is prepared to give all of herself, and the greatest satisfaction, in exchange for just a little flattering curiosity. It is a far more generous affair...

'You would really enjoy the glory and mystery of the Catholic ceremony,' Furlong said, abruptly changing the line of conversation.

'Anglicans are Anglo-Catholics and high enough for me.'

'Yes, make the best of it, if that is what you want,' Furlong said.

'I was once in love with a Franchuta...'

'A real one?'

'No, she was Polish...'

'I meant a real prostitute. That is very romantic.'

'She was a real one, in a way, but not really. She still bothers my memory and I feel bad about it.'

'Is this a confession? I could take confession in the chapel.'

'No, it is a conversation, which confession is not.'

Father Furlong was taken aback a little. 'You mean you think you are still in love with the woman. That spoils a good chat, which is why I would have preferred it as confession. You know something: I am bored with men who are about to be married, or who are already married, who decide to tell me that they feel bad about old flings. I have never had a fling, I don't want one and I don't see why men should come to me with their boring old beddings just because I'm a priest. Grow up.

'You're not in love with that woman, nor do you feel guilty in your thoughts now that you are going to be married.

'You are fantasising. Something which remained unfinished and which was made impossible by events that I ignore might have become a solid relationship, complete with adventure, informality and inconformity. All of that is a thrill you would not be able to handle. It did not develop, and it did not because it was not meant to. That is destiny. The guilt you think you feel is only part of the excitement of the fantasy.' Furlong fell silent.

He looked straight into Douglas's eyes. They held one another's gaze for some time.

'Phew...' Douglas sighed, pulling out of the connection. 'Was that anger, preaching, or a lesson from history?'

'All of that.'

They laughed.

Furlong sighed. 'I wanted to meet you from the day I read in the papers about your punch up in Plaza de Mayo. Our chats are better than anything I've had before we met. I knew it would be a good association when we spent all those hours talking about Cunninghame Graham.

'I wish you all the happiness with Inés, because you care for her. You love her, you have said so many times and I believe you. Make the best of life. I'll be at St John's, but I won't stay for the party. I don't like parties where you don't know most of the people and you have to make small talk with all of them. Conversation is impossible. You understand that. You and I like conversation.'

From the ceremony on 25 de Mayo at St John's Pro-Cathedral – which was just inside the centre of the city's commercial and banking district, but uncomfortably near the whorehouses and red light bars of the Bajo – the bride and groom and their guests walked along to *calle Peru*. One of Inés's friends, a woman named Chubby Bailey, who was not chubby, had organized a small wedding party. Chubby was very thin. She was also wealthy, as she had sold all her late father's railway shares on the London Stock Exchange.

The hostess exuded the confidence of new found riches as she fussed over the small group of guests. Inés's mother, Panchita, sat in a corner and reminisced about the seamen she had met in her time, before and after being married to a master mariner, but she showed little maternal pride. She said that marriage was something people got into because it was expected of them, but there were more important things in life. She did not explain what they were. Several of Inés's friends were there; so was old man Cooper, regretting that Inés had decided to resign and look for work elsewhere. Two of the lodgers from the Calvet were also invited. Prieto came with a silver cruet and shook everybody's hand with his left, keeping his right, minus two fingers, hidden in his coat pocket. He quickly withdrew, smiling uncomfortably and half bowing to each person who threw a polite greeting his way.

Douglas helped stack the plates in the kitchen, in spite of the two maids engaged for the evening by Chubby. He was on his best behaviour. These were the people who had seen him fall off stools, drunk, and he was anxious to wipe out that memory.

Chubby Bailey sent the maids out of the kitchen and then put her arm around Douglas's neck. Her face went close to his.

'Look after her, Dougie. Look after her and love her...'

There was an urgency in her voice.

'Why?' he asked foolishly.

'You haven't talked much, have you? Well, she is a great woman and she'll be a great mate.' The pressing note in her voice was gone and she was now only making the trite remark of a slightly tipsy wedding guest determined to sound deeply loyal and concerned.

The conversation, after the professional photographer had left, was mostly gossip. Douglas found, to his discomfort, that he had little to contribute because he had usually chosen different company. He told everybody about the flow of lodgers at the Calvet. But he insisted to one and all that what he most wanted was to buy land to farm on, which was what he had come to Argentina to do.

At midnight, he told Inés, 'Well, Mrs... Time to walk back.'

'Walk, you can't walk,' screamed Chubby. 'I've got a car to take you. Besides it's miles. I have to look after you, Inés. I want to be godmother to the first one, remember.' The women giggled and there were ho ho ho laughs from the men as they went down to the street for the send off. Chubby produced a bag of rice and the couple were showered with it. One grain lodged uncomfortably in Douglas's ear and he wriggled his little finger in his ear until the rice was dislodged. He felt embarrassed, but the guests on the pavement screamed with laughter.

They were to spend the night at the Alvear Palace Hotel, the most elegant in the city, return to the flat in the morning and take the evening boat to Montevideo for their honeymoon.

The honeymoon suite at the Alvear Palace had been decorated with flowers sent by Chubby. Inés had trouble getting out of her dress and fell on the bed in her petticoat. She laughed loudly but she was exhausted.

Douglas was a little apprehensive about what should happen next. Apart from what was revealed by swimming costumes, they had not seen much of each other's bodies previously. While he was thinking this and taking the cuff links out of his shirt, he heard her sigh. She was asleep. 'Some wedding night,' he said to himself.

The night was warm and the curves of her body showed through the sheet. They woke at dawn, brushed their teeth and made love. It was easy, it was quiet, it was gentle fun. Douglas felt deeply in love. He would always love her. He liked it this way and she enjoyed it too. They made love three times. Later they lay quite close together and smoked from a packet of Players that had been one of Chubby's wedding presents.

'I'm going to like this,' he said, with a peck on her cheek. She smiled. They got ready for breakfast.

# Chapter 26

MILDRED BAILEY SANG 'Thanks for the Memory' in 1938; it was a popular hit all over the world. Count Ciano, Benito Mussolini's son-in-law, said of the pilot dropping incendiary bombs in Abyssinia that the aesthetic elegance of seeing an Ethiopian going up in flames was pure art, the ultimate the surrealists could aspire to.

In February 1938, Argentina got a new president, Roberto Ortiz. Although he had come to power in the atmosphere of fraud that had dominated the decade, he was seen as a decent man. But he was ill and unable to cope with the looming crisis. The poet Leopoldo Lugones, the greatest of the modernists the country had produced, drank a dose of poison one cold grey day in a small hotel on an island in Tigre, north of Buenos Aires. He was 67 and he had taken his life when seized by bitterness at the nation he saw all around him. His early socialism, his liberalism, eventually his nationalism and his unofficial role as ideologue of the 1930 coup had all failed in a society ruled by corruption and greed. His death was followed by that of the poet Alfonsina Storni who walked into the sea south of Buenos Aires to escape her cancer.

Britain's stake in Argentina was sixty-seven per cent of all foreign investment. The United States had twenty-one per cent.

In January 1939, Lisandro de la Torre, former senator and defeated fighter against corruption, also committed suicide. He had even lost his own land in Córdoba province through fraud.

Disaster was the backdrop to Josephine Baker's tour of Buenos Aires at that time, to entertain the people who had read all about her singing and stripping in Paris.

On 21 August 1939, the Polish liner *Chorbry* docked at Buenos Aires on its maiden voyage. Among the many rich and elegant aboard was the Polish writer Witold Gombrowicz, then aged thirty-five, travelling to write about the voyage.

He had had one successful novel, *Ferdydurke*, published the previous year. He did not like Buenos Aires. It was too far from Europe, he was not known at all here and it would take years before he could expect his writing to be introduced to a Spanish audience.

But it was in Buenos Aires that he stayed when, the following month, Germany invaded Poland, Britain declared war on Germany and Gombrowicz had no home to return to. As from September 1939 the Tortoni Café, on Avenida de Mayo, became his residence. He disliked the lacrimose Argentines who recited sentimental poetry and sang noisy tangos, but he filled his diary with stories about them and he could play chess for hours on the stone-top tables with only the purchase of one cup of coffee. He was never short of somebody to play against and in spite of the patrons, the Tortoni, inaugurated in 1858 on a street that would become a Spanish style avenue in 1888, had transplanted and adapted something of an old world air that Gombrowicz missed when away from Paris.

The British community was alive with good causes to help the war effort. *The Standard* and *Buenos Aires Herald* carried daily and extensive reports of events on all fronts and items of patriotic support from the empire and the dominions. For all Argentina's neutrality, private pro-British action was intense and enthusiastic.

As the first year of the war came to an end the community in Montevideo and Buenos Aires marked the anniversary of the scuttling of the *Admiral Graf Spee* after the Battle of the River Plate, in December 1939.

Britain launched high profile action to secure trade with its old customers. Sir Granville Gibson and the Marquis of Willingdon announced to members of the British Chamber of Commerce, during lunch at the Plaza Hotel in December 1940, that Argentine importers would be offered new facilities and encouragement by Britain, which 'will always be Argentina's oldest and most trusty friend in the old world.' The speeches filled three pages of each of the English-language papers.

Lord and Lady Willingdon attended St John's Sunday service, which as usual was broadcast direct by *Radio Mitre*. Prayers were for Argentina's neutrality and British victory. The Toc H League of Women Helpers made appeals for dolls and toys of every kind for poor British children; Dr Smith's Memorial Patriotic Guild held fund-raising fêtes; newspaper readers were urged to *Be Businesslike, buy British* in full-page advertisements; the British Society's Patriotic Fund announced a Melting Pot Sale; and the ladies knitted socks and the men sold raffle tickets, forever. The Fellowship of the Bellows collected cash to build Spitfires for the Royal Air Force.

President Ortiz was pro-British and ill, his vice-president, Ramón Castillo, was pro-Nazi and conspiring to seize government.

Nearly two thousand three hundred men and women from Argentina volunteered for war service. The many funds recorded the donations from eight thousand individuals, in addition to institutional and corporate gifts.

Peru and Ecuador went to war, Reuters reported on Monday, 7 April 1941, but nobody noticed. In August a ceasefire was agreed in Rio de Janeiro.

The writer Stefan Zweig and his wife committed suicide at Petropolis on 3 February 1942. They had recently moved to Brazil from Britain. 'He was an exile in time from the nineteenth century, and his death may perhaps be attributed to his weariness of wandering,' said a short obituary in *The Times*.

Then, on 22 August 1942, Brazil entered the war against Germany. German submarines had sunk Brazilian ships and made inaction impossible. The *Manchester Guardian* said that 'President Getulio Vargas has shown that even a dictatorship with totalitarian leanings can be American first and can prefer to stand with the democracies.' Uruguay's declaration of war followed shortly, after a German U-boat torpedoed the ship *Maldonado*. Uruguay had already suffered the humiliation of a Nazi plot to turn the country into a farming colony to supply food to the Third Reich. For the British in Argentina the declarations were at once good yet disheartening. Only Chile and Argentina continued to have diplomatic relations with Germany. The writer Victoria Ocampo devoted a special issue of her magazine *Sur*, started ten years earlier, to a 'Homage to Brazil'. The edition, launched with ceremonies and speeches, irked the government in Buenos Aires which was trying to maintain neutrality – on the grounds that Argentina had nothing to gain from entering the war.

# Chapter 27

DOUGLAS VOLUNTEERED for war service but was told at the British Embassy that as Inés was with child there would be time after the birth.

She miscarried.

He stayed to comfort her and to try again.

The war was long and far away and could wait for him.

He met Witold Gombrowicz at the Tortoni one afternoon and together they went on several visits to the provinces. The Pole, complaining about Argentina almost without stop and often getting seriously drunk, said he wanted to develop a business project. He had discovered that motorcar tyres were selling for enormous profits. He planned to smuggle tyres in from Brazil and flood the Buenos Aires market, thus being able to generously subsidize Polish writing in exile.

Douglas gave it some thought but after one exploratory trip up the River Uruguay, to check the strength of border positions, he decided that he would not help Gombrowicz. He said it was not a venture for a family man.

'You don't have a family,' the Pole remarked brutally.

'I'm trying to have one,' Douglas replied.

He knew that a few years earlier, if the idea had been put by Prieto, he would have fallen for it and tyre smuggling would have become their activity. But he was not prepared to leave Inés for any longer than necessary.

He noticed that sometimes, when she said she was not feeling well, her breath smelled foul. It was not when she had a menstruation and there were no outward signs of ill-health. But the sign that she was not well inside was the awful bad breath. When he asked once she dismissed the question by saying he was rude and inconsiderate. He thought she might be consulting a doctor, but he was not sure. If she was unwell, she was not telling him.

Douglas became resentful at her secrecy, but did not mention her possible ill-health again to avoid hurting her. When she was well, they had fun. They would spend weekends playing tennis, or he would hire a boat and row her out to the islands. She enjoyed that and they both revelled the secrecy of landing on one of the many uninhabited islands on a Saturday afternoon and making love quietly on the damp soft soil. Before sunset he would row back to Tigre, usually with Inés fast asleep in the stern seat.

They bought a plot of land in a southern suburb, Ranelagh, because the traffic manager at Plaza Constitución, the Victorian-style terminal of the British-built and owned Great Southern Railway, lived in Ranelagh. The manager said that he thought that he would be in charge of timetables for the rest of his career, and when he stepped down he would have a word with his successor to make sure the trains stopped at Ranelagh at the right time. The small station eighteen miles from Buenos Aires, watering stop for steam engines, thus had an excellent service, one commuter train arriving there each evening 'just on gin-tonic time'.

Inés and Douglas built their own house in Ranelagh and called it *Shangri-la*, the idyllic place in James Hilton's novel *Lost Horizon*.

Ranelagh might have been named after Ranelagh House and gardens, an eighteenth-century pleasure gardens next to Chelsea Hospital in London. It might have come from another Ranelagh, in London's East End, or it could have been named after Ranelagh in Dublin. Nobody knew. The British-owned Southern Land Company had started Ranelagh with ten English-style detached houses in 1913. The village got its first taxi in 1930, driven by one Harold Welbourn, known to some as 'Well Worn', a man who had been born feeling tired.

The tragedy of war in the world all around them was broken down into many smaller individual tragedies. Inés became pregnant, but miscarried again. She had been expecting twins.

With Inés in deep distress about her inability to bring a child into the world, but determined to keep 'a stiff upper lip' the moment she left the British Hospital, Douglas went to find the doctor who had looked after her for some years. But if he knew of anything wrong, the medic was not saying. Douglas met a wall of denial. He felt guilty about going behind his wife's back, simply because he had achieved nothing.

# Chapter 28

A NEW SET OF DICTATORS made their appearance during the afternoon of 4 June 1943. The army removed President Castillo, who had forced the resignation of the dying President Ortiz in 1942. A junta took power. Suddenly, in a matter of hours, every government office was run by small men with low foreheads and partings in their hair that looked as if made with an axe.

The take-over proclamation was standard military copyright repeated in all the coups and attempted rebellions of the last twenty years: 'To the citizens of the Republic: the armed forces of the republic, loyal and zealous guardians of the honour and the traditions of the country, as also of its welfare...' and so on.

The toll of two short gunbattles between rival army factions was thirty-two dead and seventy-five wounded, many of them civilians trapped in two buses that were fired on.

Argentina remained pro-German and the United States and British spokesmen were concerned that they could not change the course of the country's foreign policy.

Among the military was a popular colonel, secretary for labour, Juan Domingo Perón. Public attention and admiration concentrated on him at all official functions. He and his fellow-officers were described as pro-German; they were wined and dined at the German Embassy, people said, but he kept smiling and said nothing. Perón had been in Italy and Germany before the war, but now he was not saying what side he was on.

The trade unions became his most ardent supporters as Perón used his labour office to give them power, funds and the promise of more. Previously there had been powerful men and women who wanted to keep workers poor. But the people in the unions would win through, he said, because this was their country and they should have access to all that was in it. In exchange, all he wanted was a little backing from them, so as to help him get what he wanted for them. An aura of intrigue surrounded his every move and appearance.

It was in January 1944 that he met his new girlfriend. She was introduced to him at a charity for the people of San Juan, left homeless by an earthquake that damaged seventy per cent of the provincial capital. Perón, a widower, was from then on seen in her company. A radio drama actress and B-film player, she looked radiant. She delightfully offset the serious demeanour of the middle-aged colonel. Evita Duarte was in her early twenties.

# Chapter 29

FOR INÉS THE SPEED of events was important, but irrelevant. In that same January when the earth under San Juan shook, her first son was born alive at the British Hospital. At last she was a mother.

There could be no greater joy in her life.

She was in her mid-thirties and she had feared that a family would never be for her. She had become desperate and now that was over. She was frail and the child was not a bundle of health, but for Inés and Douglas this was an amazing turn in their luck. The maid from up-country was soon joined by a nurse, to help Inés with the sickly child, but the home of the newborn was a happy place that summer.

There was strong reason for good cheer everywhere. For some time, the British community in Argentina and their friends knew that the tide had turned in Europe. A man at the *Buenos Aires Herald* said that it had become obvious that the allies were winning. At the start of the war the Germans in Buenos Aires sat in the front on the trams and local Britons had taken seats at the rear. In 1944, British residents moved to the front seats. Germans sat at the back, near the door so as to be able to get off faster.

Argentina remained an exciting place. Everybody was saying that they would make a new start when the war was over. Everything would be fine. Douglas set his heart on buying a piece of land for a small fruit farm, probably in the south.

And then, finally, on 27 March 1945, as Britain prepared the funeral of Lloyd-George and General Eisenhower announced that the main German defence line had been broken, but only then, Argentina declared war on the Axis: 'for the purpose of identifying the policy of the nation with that common to the rest of the American republics,' General Farrell's presidential announcement said.

The atmosphere of domestic ferment was overwhelming. Rightwing nationalism was born between repudiation of the declaration of war and seeing in the military government the channel for all their dreams against the Europeanised liberal elite – whose most visible spokesmen were the writers Victoria Ocampo and her magazine *Sur*, and the writer Jorge Luis Borges.

Perón was at the centre of a political storm of his own making. He had given many people a glimpse of something better and even if they did not know very clearly what it was they had a feeling that nobody, and certainly not Perón, could stop them searching further for days of greater comfort. Perón seemed, at once, delighted and terrified by his own machinery.

North American businessmen arrived in great numbers. And they were liked. They were easier to speak to than the serious and superior Europeans. The chummy superficiality of visitors from the Unites States won friends. The men's brush-short hair in 'crew-cut' style and their colourful clothes singled them out. Perón, ambivalent as ever, took a dislike to the Americans. He preferred the company of Europeans, the enemy he knew. Their formality suited his officer-class mentality.

The difference with the old days, long-time residents said, was that it was not easy to know who could be trusted any more. People were informing on their bosses at work, maids were reporting the mistress of the house, and friends were falling out over political matters. The British community had never seen that happen before.

Colonel Perón, minister for war and de facto vice-president, was the loser in a power struggle and was put under arrest. Eva Duarte launched a campaign for his release with the benefit of all her acting career and good contacts in the radio stations.

Inés was pregnant again.

'It's hard to think how you got pregnant again, with all that is happening around us,' Douglas remarked.

'Easily, my dear, I'm delighted to say.'

They were happy. He knew that they were very much in love. The boy was recovering from a terrible first year of ill health and Inés was expecting a second child. It was a comfortable pregnancy, but she was exhausted. She spent most of the time in the sofa or on the bed, or in the garden if it was warm enough, with her feet up.

'We might think of going home, one day,' Douglas said. 'To visit. Fares are cheaper and it would be time to go back and see the family.'

'That will put paid to your dreams of a farm,' Inés said. 'It'll be one or the other, but not both. The hospital bills have been too big. I'm sorry we've cost you so much in doctors.' She laughed, but they seldom spoke of that side of things. Her health had cost them most of their savings after paying for the house. But times ahead looked good.

Inés began to bleed at the weekend.

Douglas made her as comfortable as possible in the front porch, where it was sheltered and warm. He took her cups of tea and got the maid to make a large fruit salad. When he spied on Inés he saw she was crying. But she hastily dried her tears whenever she heard Douglas or the maid approaching.

He telephoned the British Hospital and was advised to wait. A general strike had been called in protest against Perón's arrest and the hospital warden could not say what staff they would have available. It was better to sit tight at home.

On Tuesday, Douglas decided to get Inés into town, to be closer to the hospital. The bleeding had not stopped. He telephoned Chubby Bailey who said she would prepare a room.

Douglas carried Inés to Ranelagh's railway station. She complained in embarrassment, but did not fight him. The maid came behind them carrying their overnight bags. The nurse and the maid would stay in Ranelagh with the boy.

He was surprised how light Inés was and said she should put on some weight to help the future child.

'I'm not light,' she laughed. 'You don't realize how strong you are.'

He did know he was strong, his body was thick-set, overweight, in fact, but his arms were like steel, tested often on the farms he visited, when he had to hold down a sick or a panic stricken horse, or feed medicine to a cow. That was the life he enjoyed, not desk-bound work at Cooper's. But Inés was too light for a pregnant woman.

It was evening on the 15th when they reached Chubby Bailey's flat on *calle* Peru. The taxi driver said he was not working the next day, as 'things in town' were getting so uncertain. The hospital said that if Inés was in town and comfortable she was better there than at the hospital. It was not clear how 'things in town' were going to develop over the next few days.

On the night of 16 October the General Confederation of Labour called on workers to demonstrate for their hero's liberation. Individual unions advised their members to march on Government House to force Peron's freedom. Their call was taken up by Perón's girlfriend Evita, who had by now clearly exchanged her film and radio career for political aspirations as Perón's mate, and used her radio contacts to call for a mass turnout. However, Evita stayed with relatives, out of the city, in the farming town of Junín.

Early on the seventeenth, with Inés safe in Chubby's home, Douglas decided to make the short dash to Cooper's office to look at recent correspondence and put his in-tray in order.

The streets had been alive with people all night. Cars sped round corners, sounding their horns regardless of the hour. Angry exchanges had been heard often. Calls of 'Viva Perón!' were frequent, almost as if they were a password.

At mid-morning columns of men and women thronged the streets. Some of the groups seemed to be walking somewhere. Others milled about trying to decide whether to merge with a passing column. Men ran up to small clusters of people and shouted instructions. Here and there Argentine flags were carried, but mostly it was a crowd without flags, without organisation. They were Perón's *descamisados*, his shirt-less ones, so named by the colonel because they were most often seen in their singlets or undershirts – shirts were kept for Sunday best, jackets, if they owned such garments, were for weddings and funerals.

On the way to Cooper's Douglas changed plans. He had never seen so many people in all the streets. And they were a peaceful crowd. This was something new. Loud hailers called on union members to strike, peacefully. Most union leaders were trying to regain the leadership that they feared lost if Perón went down for good.

He hopped on a tram, one of the few about, crammed with passengers. He rode with it for only a few meters before the crowd became too thick for the tram to move. These were the people of the country that he had lived in for nearly two decades and whom he had never before seen.

More were arriving every minute. Meat workers from Avellaneda came in their thousands from the south side. The meat packing plant workers, the most militant in the labour force for over a century, had long become Perón's principal source of support. They were not alone. Railwaymen were out on strike. Men and women employed in the small industries run by British, French and Italian families, and which dominated the working class suburbs south of the city, risked instant dismissal by joining the march for Perón. It did not matter. They had taken action independently of their bosses and the voices on loud hailers were congratulating them, egging them on. Messages from Evita came across the Plaza, strong, loud, read over a hailer on the top of a car surrounded by the crowd. The colonel's lady was their rising star and her name and her words were loudly cheered.

People sat on the stone edges of the fountains in the square in front of Government House, removed their shoes and socks and stuck their sore feet in the water. They had never walked so far in their lives and they had started very early.

Douglas moved among them under the warm spring sunshine. People were excited, but mostly curious. Some of them, even in middle age, had never seen Government House. Though they lived only a few miles south of the city, there had never been time enough off work, or the curiosity, to come and see the pink palace from which the country was ruled. It was not their business to see such things. Government had never been anything to do with them. Until now.

The smells of working men filled Douglas's nostrils. It was a mix of wine and sweat; of men who had worked in all weather ten or twelve hours a day. They had the pungent odour of factories, dust and perspiration, dried and then exuded several times in the day. Douglas had smelled this on the farms visited, but never in the city. It was a rich human stench and it was not offensive.

By five o'clock in the afternoon radio stations were announcing that Perón was back in Buenos Aires, at the military hospital. Crowds gathered there and shouted their support for the police. '*Viva la policía!*' was not a chant often heard, but the force had clearly shown allegiance to the Peronist movement. During the day, police road blocks had been abandoned by personnel so as not to clash with marchers. There were reports of shooting incidents between rival factions. Several unions advised caution and opposed a general strike call by the trades union headquarters. Printers, builders, the Democratic Shop Assistants' Committee and others called for calm. They were ignored; every street in the city seemed overcome with the excitement.

Some shops opened to sell food and drinks to the crowd, but as streets remained full of people owners closed their stores. The crowd concentrated outside Government House and called for Perón to come out onto the balcony. President Farrell assured people that their hero was free but they demanded to see him. Sometime before midnight Perón, looking unsettled and pale, made his way to the balcony facing the Plaza. His speech was drowned by the crowd's greeting.

The radio said he had resigned from the army, sacrificing a general's palms to become 'the people's colonel'. There was a roar of pleasure from the crowd. When their hero went inside again, slowly, very slowly, the crowd began to thin out. It was very late.

Lloyd's bar stayed open. The proprietor thought it his duty to provide a meeting point for his long-time European patrons. It was also his way of overhearing their crisis conversations.

Robert Wills, a regular, was the centre of attention. He claimed to have been Perón's bodyguard through the months of campaigning in the factories and meat packing plants. The Englishmen drinking with him were undecided whether to trust him or cold-shoulder him. Douglas had not seen him for some time. Their eyes met and Wills walked over to him.

'Hullo, Dougie,' Wills was jovial, confident.

He carried a closed shoulder holster and a gun in his belt, and for the benefit of the custom at Lloyd's bar he was not hiding either. 'Sorry about that thing, lad. Had to do it...'

'Had to do what?' Douglas asked.

'Follow you around. Sorry, bit of British Embassy business. Forgotten what it was now. Remember?'

'No,' Douglas lied, but ten years and more had passed. It was strange that Wills should be speaking to him now. Unless he wanted those who knew the past to keep quiet about it, and the reminder was intended to do that.

'Good times ahead, Dougie... Let me know if you need anything. I think I'm on to a good one,' Wills insisted.

The cleaning woman held court.

Elsie 'Sniff', whose surname had been mangled somewhere between London's East End and chronic hay fever in Buenos Aires, said she knew the colonel.

'And what a gentleman he is, I'm telling you. I know him. I've done for him and a proper gentleman he is.'

Wills approached her, soured at losing his own status as the main source of interest.

'He's had a crack at you yet, Elsie, has he?'

She never stopped cleaning the counter top, or so it seemed, but the wet rag in her left hand was next seen draped over the patron's face. There were several nervous laughs.

'You just watch it. And mark my words. If the colonel puts his plan for government into practice, you're all going to jump. Because I've heard him talking mornings when I've been cleaning 'is 'ome. And he's going to put this place right, I'm telling you. And you know I don't speak for nothing. All your lot are going to watch your Harrods tea go cold. And then you'll come and ask me. We've got a great man coming there and this country needs him.'

Wills decided it was not a night to be on the wrong side of Elsie and he walked out silently.

Elsie said she knew nothing about Evita.

'Why can't a widowed gentleman have a bit on the side, I ask you.' She roared a rasping smoker's laugh that sounded like the slow striking of a hundred matches. She described Perón's small flat in detail. Douglas was given a full description of the colonel's crockery, furnishings and how many uniforms he had in the house. Elsie said she used to tell the colonel about the English people she met at Lloyds. As if by a flick of a wand, her audience vanished.

Douglas walked back to Chubby's with all the day's gossip. Inés was asleep, but he sat up until dawn discussing the events and his own prospects.

The next day's papers reported every detail of the demonstrations. It was only now that Douglas had any idea what Perón had said from the balcony. 'Workers... Nearly two years ago... I declared that I had received three great honours in my life, namely those of being a soldier, having been called a patriot, and of being named Argentina's first worker.' What complete lack of modesty led a man to declare himself the champion of the people? The military had never worked for a living. They only dressed to collect their wages.

'You won't be able to speak like that outside these four walls,' Chubby warned him. 'And even inside, you'll only upset Inesita.'

There was no way of moving out. The city and transport were getting back into order very slowly. The railway bridges had been raised to stop people travelling into town, but people had crossed the Riachuelo boundary by small boats all day. Those who had been afraid of the idea of floating on water in a wobbly rowing boat, which they had never been on in their lives, walked the long way round to reach road bridges and had reached the Plaza de Mayo anyway. The British ambassador, Sir David Kelly, had visited the navy minister to ask that everything possible be done to protect British-owned railway property from damage. But it was the wrong door to knock on. The minister for the navy had been responsible for Perón's arrest.

Douglas left Inés at the British Hospital and for the next ten weeks, nearly up to Christmas, visited her every day after leaving the office. On weekends he went in from Ranelagh, with the boy.

In May 1946, Inés gave birth to a daughter.

'Now we can be a real family,' she laughed. She was still very thin.

In June, on the third anniversary of the 1943 coup, Perón took office in the full dress uniform of a brigadier general. His rank, which he had cast off on 17

October, had been restored and he had been promoted. Perón was back in his beloved army uniform and he had an adoring crowd cheering him.

Bob Hope, the stand-up comedian, and his wife Dolores, came to the Buenos Aires American Club for the fourth of July. Harold Mickey was host band leader. It was a show of strength and good spirit by the community.

# Chapter 30

THE NEWS, WHEN IT CAME, was a terrible blow. Nearly a century of British management of the Argentine railways was about to end. Perón had announced that he would nationalise all foreign-owned public services. It was part of his election campaign.

But when the news was published, it was a shock.

Men whose fathers, sometimes their grandfathers, often their whole families, had been employed on the British railways since 1863 now were faced with new masters.

For many the change meant adjusting from expatriation to exile, or to assimilation; it was not clear which was worse. How could they begin to absorb the idea of uprooting themselves from a home that was theirs as comfortable outsiders? They would be forced to become natives where they lived and felt deeply at home, where they were acknowledged residents and British always. Britons had come to know the country, the land, better than a majority of the native born. They had business and clubs everywhere. The sons of Italians and Spaniards did not move from their front door, but the British had travelled the map. Yet while they had been intimate with the soil, they had been alien to the people.

That had been their triumph and their failure. The British community, like all expatriate groups, was without intellectual orientation. The major signs of the British Empire were its clubs and its churches – often its cemeteries also told part of the story of imperial progress. The sporting and social centres that Victorian England had encouraged in its colonies had become homes away from home to an international class with no great cultural enterprise outside of the pursuit of commerce. So when a nationalist general with some reading and a gift for words had come along, the semi-colonial structure had fallen apart. In fact, intellect was the most feared subversive element in the expatriate communities.

When the announcement of outright purchase was made, after more than four months of arduous negotiations which on several occasions had threatened to break down and during which every Briton in Argentina had hoped they would fail, it came as a death sentence. The *Standard* and the *Herald* filled their front, back and several inside pages with details of the transfer, the contract and reaction in London. The settlement covered eleven railway companies, five forwarding agencies and transport firms and two omnibus companies. The price agreed was £150 million sterling (2,482.5 million pesos), of which £126 million was in blocked Argentine sterling balances in London.

'The final sum agreed represents a compromise between the original Argentine offer and the British demand... The outright sale is generally considered more satisfactory to Britain than the mixed company originally proposed...' *The Times*, in London, commented on the morning of Thursday, 13 February 1947: 'The passing of the railways into Argentine hands will certainly please the Argentine people in general, who have never had much love for foreign-owned public utility companies, and who regard the possession of their own railway system as a matter of pride and prestige.'

Winston Churchill accused the British Labour Party of short-sighted policy, throwing away the chance of a mixed company that would secure Britain's continued influence in Argentina. Labour had, he said, sold the railways to pay for Britain's false teeth, mindful of the forthcoming national health service.

But Britain needed Argentina's blocked sterling to pay its 1945 debt to the United States and was well rid of the railways, which were in dire need of maintenance. The railways would have reverted to Argentina automatically in the mid-1960s, but nobody could wait that long. Sir Montague Eddy, who had signed the sale agreement, described it as, 'A reasonable compromise – and reasonably satisfactory to both sides.' Because he was hoarse, his assistant spoke after the signing ceremony, which 'brings to a close a connection of 90 years... We have never failed for one single moment in carrying out our obligations to the country...'

On the older railways in and around Buenos Aires, elegant, grand ladies, widows mostly, sat quietly in a first class carriage, their parasols folded and held tightly against their knees. They would ride for one, maybe two stations, not to go anywhere, but to refresh the memory of a ride on a British-owned railway, and in grateful recollection of their late husbands, engineers or managers on the line. Then they were driven home by chauffeurs, taxis, or friends.

Every station was festooned with flags and coats of arms. 'Ours', proclaimed the slogans on the steam engines, 'thanks to Perón.'

Perón's next plan was speedy industrial progress. The mailsacks full of hard currency and the stacks of gold bars piled high in the Central Bank shrank as purchases of capital goods and products were bought for cash. This was the new Argentina.

The language of government became more demagogic and intemperate. Evita, now Mrs Perón, created a Foundation which carried her own name and which distributed clothes to the aged, bicycles to children, medical facilities for the poor, and the crudest of political epithets to her critics who were all branded members of the oligarchy or their sepoys. From the rich she demanded donations for her Foundation.

Most political issues were outwardly settled by forced half holidays during which factories were emptied and workers bussed to Plaza de Mayo to hear the wisdom of Perón.

His luck held. Even on rally days that seemed doomed to be rained out, the clouds opened and the sun shone down on the gathering. Those occasions of suddenly improved weather became known as 'Peronist days'. Perón's enemies were reminded of the 1930s, when Nazi party meetings were equally climactically favoured. This had been known as 'Hitler weather'.

# Chapter 31

THE TELEPHONE CALL from Government House came the day that old man Cooper announced that he was retiring. He said he was tired of this country and of trying to run a decent business. Import duties were rising, orders had to be handled through a central institute whose every employee wanted a kick-back, every Peronist functionary claimed to be entitled to a 'commission', and remittances for orders abroad were blocked. In the two years since Perón came in, Argentina's economy had encountered severe difficulties. When all the world was making money out of the end of war, Argentina was losing it. Cooper said he did not understand the country any more. He said that several times. It was time that younger men took over.

Then the telephone rang.

The male voice was abrupt and when Cooper remonstrated about impatience, he was rudely scolded for speaking Spanish with an English accent. The message was clear, though. Douglas was required to be at Government House at 7 a.m. the next morning. Might the man say what for? No, that was not his job. The *Señora* wanted to see him.

Cooper was beside himself. He wanted to leave the country that afternoon, bound for anywhere. He thought of contacts in the police force to secure immediate issue of a 'good conduct certificate', without which a foreign born national could not leave. And he would not be allowed to travel to Montevideo because Perón had made it almost impossible, as reprisal against Uruguay for harbouring his critics.

'I don't know what you've done, laddie. But I can only say I'm sorry for you.'

He still called Douglas 'laddie' and still, after all these years, he was ignorant of the country he had spent his life in.

'I hope my business is not ruined because of you. What is going to happen? You don't know what these people can do to us.' He muttered on, shouting at times, grumbling. He sat at his desk and held his head in his hands and was not reassured by the staff who tried to comfort him. All he had ever wanted in the last twenty years was a quiet retirement, and now this had happened.

Douglas reminded Cooper that they did not know the reason for the call. The staff seemed satisfied with that and Douglas felt in control. He was not sure that he felt comfortable though. As Cooper was in a panic from the time the telephone had rung, he had not identified the caller and had no reference at Government House. It took Douglas most of the afternoon to trace an employee who confirmed the seven o'clock appointment at the *secretaría privada*.

What terrified Douglas was having to call Ranelagh to tell Inés of the summons.

There was a long pause on the line when he told her, and finally she just said, 'Look after yourself.' He knew she was hating every minute of his absence. Inés was afraid, but not saying so. She would never admit to anybody that she was nervous. She put the phone to the boy's ear and Douglas was delighted to have his first telephone conversation with his four-year-old son. He had not thought of doing that before. The brief exchange filled him with pride. He was the father of that little voice at the other end.

He decided to spend the night at the Phoenix Hotel, so as to make it to Government House on time. The appointment sounded reasonable, as Perón got into the office very early. The general had joked about his early starts: the army had trained him that way. 'Start early, bugger knows why, but early,' Perón cracked.

In spite of Cooper's warnings and fears, Douglas slept soundly. The night porter woke him at six with a cup of coffee and asked after Inés and the children. There was a genuine interest in the enquiry. Douglas and Inés had used the hotel often over the years. In the early days the porter had always winked at him as they left. Douglas was sure the porter thought both the children had been conceived at the Phoenix.

The respect and deference with which Douglas was met at the security desk in Government House filled him with a warm glow of importance. He was taken to the Señora's chief secretary's office and given coffee and *croissants*. Over the next three hours he was regularly offered coffee and more rolls, and American cigarettes, and every now and then an inner office assistant came out to say the Señora was not on her way yet, but would soon be, there had been a special audience at the residence, then finally she had started out, but had stopped on the way to receive the greetings of a group of party workers.

He read the morning papers, all of them, then studied much Peronist party literature, was informed of the history of the woman's branch of the party as told through the speeches of Evita and settled down to read the massive volume that was Argentina's Five Year Plan. A secretary who seemed to smile at him with excessive warmth, as nurses sometimes do before serious surgery, offered to telephone Inés and to tell her that nothing much had happened.

At ten o'clock it was obvious that the Señora had arrived somewhere in the building. People stood at their desks, coffee cups were hidden and men and women picked up stacks of papers. Half an hour later a young army officer came out to say that the Señora had to unveil a new bust of her husband at a factory in La Plata and she would be grateful if Douglas would travel in the car with her, so that the conversation could take place in comfort. The young officer smiled all the time and sounded very respectful to both his boss and Douglas. He apologized for the bother and said that Douglas could return immediately to Buenos Aires by train, if he wished, or stay for the unveiling ceremony and return with the retinue later. Douglas knew that he was not being offered a choice.

The process by which he was frog-marched to the waiting car, ordered to stand aside to wait for Evita to take her seat and then be invited to sit next to her, was a disconcerting military operation. The ceremony in La Plata was due to start at 12 noon, according to the officer. They started on the fifty-two kilometre drive along Route One with twenty minutes to go. The outriders signalled the start, tyres screeched and they were off. Douglas was ignored for the first ten minutes, as Evita went through some papers with the *aide-de-camp* in the front seat. All the time that she spoke to her aide her right hand was in the air, waving at well-wishers who shouted support and signalled their affection. She never looked out. She had her blonde hair tied in a bun and wore a business-like brown suit, with a carnation in the button hole.

After ten minutes, with her free left hand she shoved the papers at the aide and with a smile said, 'I hate this stuff, you go through it.' '*Si, señora.*'

She offered a half apology for the previous ten minutes delay, but not for the earlier four hours. She put her left hand on his right and said, 'How do you do?' in English, but immediately went into Spanish. She had been told many things about Douglas. He wondered if she had the right person and what was to come next. She praised him for his Spanish, which she said had no trace of an English accent. He said he had once had a girlfriend called Eva, regretted the blunder, and was guilt-ridden that he had brought the past back to his lips. She perceived his discomfort and ignored his remark.

Waving all the time, and looking straight ahead, she gave him an efficiently abridged version of the Peronist campaign programme, listed the wonders planned for the new Argentina by the general, and described the remarkable character of *el lider*. The monologue finally led into the creation of the Eva Perón Foundation, her own base on which to build better conditions for her beloved people.

She kept her left hand on his. It was not a sign of trust or endearment, merely of control. Their hands lay there, one over the other, on the leather upholstery of the Chevrolet adapted for official functions. She looked attractive, but gaunt. He remembered a photograph of her which he particularly liked, taken before they reached power. She had shoulder length hair, the top button of her blouse was open and she was wearing baggy slacks. She looked extremely sensual. Reproduction of that photograph had stopped since she entered office in 1946.

'I was an actress,' she informed him unnecessarily. 'So I have known what it is like to see the whole film being made in colour, because they can do that in the laboratory. But the film comes out in black and white. So, because of my position, I see things in colour. But I know that the rest of the people can only see things in black and white.

'My work, Mr...' she struggled with the pronounciation, then said *Dugla* 'is to bring about the day when everybody, all the people of Argentina, all the *descamisados*, not just the rich people, can see life in colour... I want the day to come soon when even my people's dreams will be in colour.'

She turned to him, she seemed quietly pleased with the formulation of her political aspiration. She sighed. Her breath was foul. He was reminded of Inés on the days when he knew she was not well but would not admit it.

'Have you been unwell?' he asked with urgency, beyond the breach of protocol, to discover what might be wrong with his wife. Eva Perón turned her face away and looked ahead, without a word. She took a deep breath.

'And this is where you can help me,' she announced.

The clock on the dashboard said half-past twelve. They were leaving the southern industrial belt, where they had to slow down the most for well-wishers, and now the large black Chevrolet began to gather speed on the open cobble road.

'The foundation needs money to carry on its work.'

Jeeeesus Christ, Douglas thought. Now what?

'But Cooper's is a small firm...'

'*Dugla, Dugla...* we know that. Small companies must give as well. They must give their share, they have made money here all these years and given nothing to the people...

'But, I am thinking much bigger. Not Cooper, your friend...'

Douglas was puzzled.

'Eh?' He wanted a cigarette, but she did not smoke and he dared not produce his packet.

'You know... Your friend. We have been told about him and how you met... Onassis...'

He felt his skin tingle and he was numb. She was smiling at him, a cold smile, but a smile no less.

'That was ten years ago, at least,' Douglas said quietly, delighted to find his voice.

She was very serious.

'We know...,' she smiled knowingly. 'We know your work in a British company. We know you live well. We were told about your friend, Onassis. We are going to invite him to Argentina, for the Mar del Plata film festival.'

'That was ten years ago, *señora*, really. I have never seen the man since his farewell party and some drinks. That is the truth.'

She was certainly not smiling now. And she was taking a deep breath again to let him have a piece of her mind. Douglas had heard about her temper. She was not taking this from anybody.

'Did Robert Wills tell you I knew Onassis?' Douglas blurted, and watched her let out all the air she had prepared for the blast. Her hand came off his.

Recently, over a drink at Lloyd's bar, Douglas had told Robert Wills about his one meeting with Onassis. It was an injudicious and boastful tale to tell, but had been delivered to counter Will's stories about being Perón's bodyguard. For the sake of a little more influence, Wills had passed on the tale.

Their conference was over. She thanked him for his time and tapped the aide on the shoulder. 'Stop!' she ordered. '*Si, señora.*' The driver started and immediately switched off a siren. The outriders were crowded around the car in seconds.

'Out!' she told Douglas.

He stood on the side of the empty road to La Plata. A man and a boy selling fruit by the roadside looked at him without a word. It was about five kilometres back to Ranelagh. Douglas started to walk.

# Chapter 32

LAWRENCE GEORGE DURRELL hated the Argentina of that time. And from the day of his arrival, aged thirty five and with his wife Eve at his side, he could not see his way to getting out fast enough. 'Larry' Durrell had been posted by the British Council, which he hoped would earn him the foreign service points that should take him to a more likeable destination. His writing career was at the delicate stage between obsession and renown. Argentina, far from the world's publishing centres and Durrell's beloved Mediterranean, was not the best place in which to pursue literary success.

In November 1947 he wrote from Buenos Aires to Henry Miller, with whom he had begun a correspondence in 1935,

> This is a perfectly fantastic country: but then so is the whole continent. The interesting thing is the queer lightness of the spiritual atmosphere: one feels buoyant, irresponsible, like a hydrogen balloon. One realises too that the personal sort of European man is out of place here: one cannot suffer angst here only cafard. So much is explained here about the American struggle, the struggle to get de-personalised. Because this is a communal continent; the individual soul has no dimensions. In architecture, in art, religion, it is all community – skyscrapers, jitterbugging, hyperboles – it is all of a piece. [1]

In March 1948, he expanded on this slightly to tell the author of the *Tropics* that 'Argentina is exactly like the USA in 1890 – full of tough go-getting tycoons fighting over the undeveloped riches. The weak are driven to the wall... Everyone with any sensibility is trying to get out of this place, including me.' [2]

1 The Durrell-Miller Letters, 1935-1980. Edited by Ian S. MacNiven. Faber/Michael Haag
   1989. Page 218
2 Page 223.

More informative, but equally bitter, were Durrell's letters to his friend, Mary Hadkinson, in Paris. On 7 February 1948 he wrote to her from Buenos Aires.

You envy us? Argentina is a large flat melancholy and rather superb-looking country full of stale air, blue featureless sierras, and businessmen drinking *Coca-Cola*. One eats endless beef and is so bored one could scream. It is the most lazy-making climate I have struck: not as bad as Egypt, of course: but I'd give a lifetime of Argentina for three weeks of Greece, fascist or no fascist. Here one is submerged in dull *laisser faire* and furious boredom. People quite nice in a very superficial and childish way. I think the States would be better. However I'm contracted for a year so I can't think of escape until next March. The only fun is horseback riding, we do plenty of – across the blue sierras, *á lá* Zane Grey. But it's all very dreary really. As for the meat it's rapidly driving me vegetarian – next week I move into Córdoba, my new post, and take over amid polite bowings...'[3]

In March 1948, Durrell wrote to another friend:

Finally I have to rest in Córdoba, 'the Oxford of Argentina' as they call it, rather misguidedly I think. It's a variation on a small Henry Miller town in the dust belt. The people are charming but zombies...

On the whole I dislike Argentina heartily. It is empty, noisy, progressive, money-ridden – all the sins including those by Coca Cola Inc. and Buick. But I could stand all of that if only the climate were not like a piece of wet meat laid across the nervous system. Life goes on in a muted sort of way – as when you press your hand on the piano strings and play. No concentration, no power of holding on to things: and yet they eat meat here as the staple instead of bread... The irony of lecturing about Shakespeare in this ambience is something perhaps only Shakespeare would enjoy. I don't. [4]

Two more letters to Mary Hadkinson later in 1948 testify that acquaintance with Argentina slowly bred interest and tolerance.

3 Lawrence Durrell. Spirit of Place. Faber 1969. Page 94
4 Page 96

Meanwhile – the Argentine – O dear, this boring tedious town. Food very good. Easy life, but the climate is desperately exacerbating – electrical storms four times a week – temperatures going up and down – One new delicacy as fine as anything the Chinese thought of – called Palmita. It's the white heart of a small Brazilian palm tree, tastes like a mixture of oyster and asparagus – a lovely taste – yes, horses and cows, there is nothing else – We ride one and eat the other interminably...[5]

Durrell's complaining was as much about the British Council, then a Foreign Office branch into which were sent those who were awaiting better postings, as about Argentina.

Since I am not a bugger, a Catholic or an Earl all the royal roads to advancement are blocked. Meanwhile the Council are cleverly making use of my literary reputation and paying me the salary of a junior lecturer.

This place is crawling with Jesuits like black beetles. One can't mention Freud without everyone having an orgasm and telephoning for the police. But the climate... beyond words. Never have I brooded so long, so consistently, and with such fixity of purpose, about suicide. [6]

His last letter to Mary Hadkinson from Argentina reflected his anger at the environment. His ill-humour was so marked it was almost that of a film character, so crabby it seemed to be designed to entertain. Nothing suited him.

We have just travelled 300 miles thru a wall of yellow dust to TUCUMAN to lecture, past a dead salt lake which is worse than Sodom and Gomorrah to look at, thru a landscape so flat and barren that it was really a nightmare. Tomorrow I FLY TO Mendoza – at the foot of the fucking Andes to perform the same office – gabble, gabble, gabble. Next to Rosario – in the heart of dust-bowl ugh! [7]

5 Page 97
6 This letter is undated, headed only 'Argentina', and was written to Mary Hadkinson in 1948. It was not published in either of the two collections of correspondence. Durrell's year in Argentina did produce a collection of his lectures, A Key to Modern British Poetry (University of Oklahoma Press, 1952). At the end of his Preface, he wrote: 'In conclusion, I am bound to thank the British Council for permission to reprint these lectures, the composition of which helped me to pass away a year in an uncongenial climate to our mutual profit.'
7 Lawrence Durrell. Spirit of Place. Faber 1969. Page 97

Perhaps the English, the Scots, all the British, had never really understood the country they claimed to be fascinated with. Each visitor sought an England, or a Greece, or a Germany, on the River Plate. What they found was a combination of Europe and America of their own making. Each then picked out the worst and best for recollection. The worst justified departure; the best, nurtured by fantasy, would encourage men to extend their search beyond their mixed feelings. It had always been thus. In 1826, Sir Francis Bond Head, an engineer living in Edinburgh, was contracted to travel to the River Plate Provinces' to inspect the British mining interests there. But his enthusiasm and romance were tempered by reality. Bond Head's conclusions revealed that the means for easy survival led to greed and rapid corruption. [8]

In February 1948 the novelist Christopher Isherwood visited Buenos Aires. He was on a holiday between books, travelling from New York to the River Plate. His quiet surprise as he progressed through Central and South America was recorded later in a book, *The Condor and the Cows*. [9] Buenos Aires banks 'have a definitely British atmosphere; they recall the solid solvent grandeur of Victorian London.' The people's 'faces – regardless of the racial origin – have a placid, somewhat bovine expression. This is hardly surprising, considering the amount of meat they eat... Every self-respecting boy must have a past, to take with him to the altar. And after the wedding, of course, the real fun begins – because, then, you are in a position to "betray" and be "betrayed"... These people are still living inside an old French novel.'

Isherwood enjoyed reunions in Buenos Aires with friends from his Berlin days. He was pleased with gatherings with the writers María Rosa Oliver, staunchly left wing and yet very much part of the old landed upper class, and Victoria Ocampo, increasingly anti-Peronist. Of his friends, perhaps the most notable was Rodolfo Katz, 'one of the very few people I have ever met who has really read, studied and digested Marx,' who may have been used in part for the Communist character in *Mr Norris Changes Trains*. Katz had come to terms with capitalism and in Buenos Aires had founded a weekly newsletter, *Economic Survey*, which was considered the most authoritative source of economic analysis and forecasts in Argentina. [10]

8 Sir Francis Bond Head. Rough Notes Taken During Some Rapid Journeys Across the
    Pampas and Among the Andes (1826). John Murray, London 1861.
9 Christopher Isherwood. The Condor and the Cows. Methuen. London 1949
10 Rodolfo (Rolf) Katz died in Bariloche, Argentina, aged 75, on 11 February 1975

Victoria Ocampo and María Rosa Oliver, wheelchair-bound but surprisingly energetic, introduced Isherwood to a world that was vanishing. Through the two women he peeped in on scenes from a novel set in Central Europe in the early twentieth century. People had failed to preserve their fantasies in the old countries, so they had transported them, complete with all accessories, to the new land. Titled women in vast palatial properties, with English grooms for their beautiful horses, entertained the visiting author. This tough old aristocracy was under threat from Perón's government and from the new millionaires he was encouraging. The old Europeans claimed an unequivocal right to being the sole authors of Argentina's history and, through influence, real and imagined, had resisted industrialization and modernization. The old class had grown up on the land and the farming wealth had made Argentina one of the rich nations of the world. They could not admit that time was passing, that Argentina had to change, and that Peronism was collecting praise for introducing progress. Ironically, the vernacular aristocracy were admired by nationalists who followed Perón, yet were also proud of the presence of old world decadence. There was no special reason for such pride, but the old oligarchy that had taken refuge in Argentina did give the country a touch of class.

Isherwood left Buenos Aires after three weeks, still in a state of bewilderment about the Argentines' concern with honour and virility. He admired potency, which in a way seemed to fit in comfortably with his homosexuality, but too much 'macho-ness', as he found in Buenos Aires, made him recoil.

The parting shot, in *The Condor and the Cows*, is for Eva Perón.

(It is not) the obscure little actress who is the sinister figure; it is the beautifully poised, graciously smiling First Lady of Argentina, President Perón's legal and all-too-influential adviser. She may have been a bad actress once, but today she is a highly efficient demagogue. She may have been vulgar and noisy and temperamental; now she is coldly vindictive, ruthless and ambitious. It is even believed that she may wish to become President, after Perón's term expires. Under the present Constitution, Perón can't succeed himself – though, of course, he wouldn't have much difficulty in getting this rule amended, if he chose to do so...

Perón's chief propaganda-drive is directed against Great Britain, not the USA. It centres on the Antarctic – or, at any rate, that segment of it which is directly south of Cape Horn – and also includes the Falklands and their dependent islands... I don't think the British are much alarmed by all this.

Perón's education ministry had ordered every school in the land to teach children that the Malvinas were an integral part of Argentina's territory, inherited from Spain and usurped by Britain. *Las Malvinas son Argentinas* was a sentence that every human being repeated from his or her first day at school.

John Dos Passos, the North American novelist, also visited Buenos Aires in 1948. He wanted to investigate Peronism, but found that United States citizens were not welcome. *Time* magazine had reproduced a silly remark about the national hero, General José de San Martín, picked up during the repatriation of some patriotic family remains. The magazine had said that San Martín's parents' bones had returned that year, and his horse's bones would be sent for in the next. At every customs post in Argentina, officers searched luggage for copies of *Time* magazine. Smugglers of anything else had a field day.

In 1949, Perón ordered his party in congress to vote for constitutional reform which would permit his reelection.

# Chapter 33

INÉS BECAME ILL in that year of constitutional reform, although she had been in poor health for some time. Doctors found her illness disturbing but would not tell her their diagnosis. She knew, though. Of course she knew, as the probing of her chest became more difficult, operations more painful and her confinements at the British Hospital longer.

When she was allowed to go home, all her energy went into putting the house in Ranelagh in order. Her small children spent every possible minute at her side. Her son remained sickly and weak with asthma, but her daughter was all that she had wished for, healthy, robust, joyful. The girl was the child that Inés had ached for during the years of miscarrying.

And now, after all this time of hoping and more hope, she was being taken from them.

At first, the parting seemed prolonged, the distance between them growing very slowly, and no permanent farewell might ever have to be said. But then the distance grew more quickly. Inés felt she was being tugged away from her babies as she stretched out to try to catch their hands. There came a time when she could hardly hold them on her lap. Then she could only just sit them beside her in bed. She tried to stroke their heads, run her fingers through their hair; they faded as she looked at them, she blinked and refocused, but her sight became dull with weakness. She tried to smile at them. Tried to wave, she could hardly make out their faces. And then they were going, slipping away, out of reach of her extended arm.

Inés died in February 1950, *Year of the Liberator General José de San Martín*, the centenary of his death. In Europe he was remembered by an equestrian statue on the sea-front at Boulogne-sur-Mer – where he had died in aged retirement.

His bronze horse had been shot through by rounds of aircraft ammunition fired during the Battle of Boulogne in May 1940. Now he had a whole year dedicated to his memory.

Funny how the mind wandered when the arrangements were being made. 'Funeral today, Tuesday 21st, at 11 o'clock at the Quilmes Protestant Cemetery. No flowers by request.'

Life without Inés was the end of... End of what? Douglas wondered. It was not the end of life, except hers, which had ended. But it was the end of happiness, of comfort, the end of expectations, hopes, plans, love, care, meals at the right time. And yes, he admitted, the end of much happiness... Of course, he would try to find that with his two children.

'It is the end of my *Southamericana*,' he said aloud. It was the end of an experiment in contentment, of discovery and pleasant adventure, without too much achievement or the need for much effort.

'The Great Anglo-Argentine Novel in which we have both enjoyed being characters has come to a close,' he said, again aloud, to his son, who lay across his mother's empty bed.

The maid, Fortunata, looked puzzled. 'Are you all right, señor,' she asked. She had been crying. An adolescent, devoted to her mistress, she was as distressed by the loss as by the uncertainty that she faced. Two dogs, a Scottish terrier and a Dachshund, lay very quiet on the cold kitchen floor.

For Douglas, added to the deep grey grief which is the sum of all failures for which there is no word, was the government's increasing animosity towards British presence. Britons were accused of conspiring against the Peronist regime.

As Inés had lain dying, Douglas had joined the Socialist party and had been caught daubing walls with slogans that put in doubt the morals of Evita's mother. In fact, he was right, the bitch was a bastard, but that was not a reasonable argument, the arresting police sergeant said. Because Inés had been ill Douglas was freed immediately.

Perhaps it was time to leave Buenos Aires.

He should have left earlier, with Inés. Born near Liverpool of Argentine-born mother and Peruvian grandmother, Inés had hated the country's politics and Argentina. She had wanted children and lost two, and when two had been born they had been robbed of her by cancer as big as a horror story.

Had she lived she could have looked back on a life which had aspired to suburban comfort but had been steeped in toil, first as a governess, then as a secretary in the opaque austerity of English companies trading in Argentina, in pursuit of the material security of the middle class.

And there had been the sandwiches. She had cut the finest white bread sandwiches for christenings at the Anglican Church in Quilmes, for the flower show at the Ranelagh Golf Club, for sports days at the Quilmes High School for Girls, at the Saint Alban's College for Boys and at the Ranelagh Community School – which her younger brother, a large man called Tiny who had tipped a baggage scales at one hundred and fifty kilos, had helped to build. Anglo-Argentines in their hundreds south of the Riachuelo city boundary had nibbled Inés's sandwiches.

She had wanted her children to be English, if not by birth, then by forced environment. She had sent the boy to an English nursery and to English Sunday school – where it had taken them months to find out that 'lettuce spray' was not an invocation of divine care for the kitchen garden, but a misunderstanding of 'Let us pray'. Her friends had been English-speaking and the village became known as the most English of Anglo-enclaves – barring the Hurlingham Club, west of Buenos Aires and founded in 1888, which had a stronger claim to that classification. Her only native acquaintances had been the shopkeepers. Inés had felt far more British than her Scottish husband, who loved the memory of his native land, but was attached to the contrasting landscape of flat, open Argentina.

Her grandfather had arrived in about 1863 to help lay the first tracks of the Great Southern Railway, from Buenos Aires to Chascomús to Dolores, which British engineers and British contractors had completed in December 1865. The grandfather had gone from clerk to draughtsman to contractor – on the Entre Ríos and Central Argentine railways – and to a comfortable two thousand pounds a year as Resident Engineer on the Pacific Railway in 1903.

She was part of the country, but had never belonged.

The house in Ranelagh became a meeting place for anti-Peronists of varying intensity, critics, enemies and plain undesirables.

Douglas's new housekeeper, a small Greek woman with a young son in tow as a souvenir from residence in wartime Germany, shouted warnings that they would all be caught and imprisoned, that the dictator was a good man, that he had brought order to the country and it was a duty to support him.

Her shouts drove them into the garden, but her fears were greatest then because the loud discussions were noticed by the neighbours. So they all went back into the house and the housekeeper made soup.

The ironing woman's husband was arrested for opposing his union's orders, but he never said why. It was about something to do with asking for better wages when their first daughter was born. Douglas went to the police station to try to get him released, but instead got drunk with the duty sergeant, who asked for a bottle of *ginebra* to declare an amnesty.

The sergeant was never seen in Ranelagh again and the ironing woman's husband was re-arrested and tortured. The night after the 'amnesty', Douglas's two dogs were poisoned, as a warning. Douglas retaliated by going to the railway station and painting in thick creosote the word 'Ranelagh' over the name Carlos Spegazzini, a botanist of Italian origin whom Peronism had honoured by renaming the *ingleses'* suburban station.

'They' came back and stoned all the metal shutters in the house for half an hour, which had the maid, Fortunata, and the children hysterical with fright.

Fortunata's boyfriend, a wiry fair-haired young man, known as *Aguilucho*, went after the unidentified stone throwers and stabbed two. He was not known for his political loyalties, but certainly for spur-of-the-moment urges. That night he had felt like stabbing some people and stabbed two. Aguilucho washed the knife and his hands in the kitchen sink and then vanished to escape police searches.

Douglas was privately grateful for his spontaneous defence, but glad he had gone. Aguilucho would sit at the political gatherings in the kitchen and roll his eyes until only the whites stared out. Sometimes he seemed to get stuck like that. When that happened the discussion would be interrupted as he vigorously banged on his temples with the heels of his hands to straighten out his eyes. Once, Aguilucho – which meant 'small eagle' in reference to the man's long curving nose – had opened his trousers to show the others what a man he was. He showed Douglas and company a very long penis. Then he put it away with an air of defiance and continued to listen to the political discussion.

Aguilucho returned to the house in Ranelagh some weeks later. He accused Douglas of having intimate relations in the privacy of a bedroom with Fortunata. The evidence Aguilucho said, was that she had been washing too many sheets. Her name did not bring her luck. He stabbed her six times and fled again. Douglas took her to the village emergency surgery in a garden barrow. The nurse took most of the night to sew her up.

# PART III
1950-1963

# Chapter 34

NATIONALIZATION MADE the British community feel left out. United States residents thought that the strength of their old rivals was at an end and set up their businesses to take part in Argentina's age of import substitution. North Americans were supplying materials for Perón's accelerated industrialization.

Financed by the income from exports during the war, new Peronist factories produced the Puma motorcycle, then followed with an Argentine version of the Italian Lambretta scooter. Then came a family car with a two-stroke engine, named after the Peronist party, Justicialista. Every Argentine family would have one, the official literature promised. Next came local assembly of the Italian Gilera motorcycle and a small native diesel engine pick-up truck, partly inspired by the German Mercedes Benz diesel, the Rastrojero – the first models were run with tractor engines. It was the best of the Peronist homemade transports.

Every provincial town filled with the rattle of two-stroke engines and with the impatient clackety-clack of the incessant diesels. As in other parts of the world, the sound of the working man's motorcycle came before the first bird calls of the morning.

For the defence of the Fatherland, the new aircraft factory in Córdoba developed a small prototype reconnaissance jet plane, the Pulqui, which made a couple of short test flights. However, Argentine pilots preferred the Gloster Meteor fighter jets bought in the USA. Perón's aim was to create an industrial power in Latin America, but he had spent his reserves too quickly for the drive to last.

Anglo-Argentines grumbled about the shortages of toilet paper and the dark grey white bread, often made from the mill sweepings of wheat and flour as all high grade farming produce was exported to meet the ever-growing imports bill.

People complained, in whispers. University teachers who had critical views had been purged from the time Perón entered office in 1946, when the press had been controlled. The first target, in 1947, had been the British-owned Haines family publishing house, printers of the newspaper *El Mundo* and the popular magazine *El Hogar,* which published stories by Jorge Luis Borges.

The British community felt that not only was its power being whittled away, but it was also losing its symbols of the age of influence. This was particularly the case in January 1949, when Esteban Lucas Bridges died in Buenos Aires, aged 75. His book, *Uttermost Part of the Earth,* a history of the settlements of Tierra de Fuego published in London in 1948, arrived too late in his life to give him the rewards of his long experience and research, and had not been in time either to assist the prestige of the community. The Bridges family's exploits in the south, from the beginnings of the *estancia* Harberton in 1887, were a clear indication of the pioneering spirit and educational devotion of the English-speaking families in Argentina.

The thoughts of expatriates were of days gone by. In the 1950s it began to feel as if those times had never existed. In some Buenos Aires houses, one clock was set at Greenwich Mean Time to remind the dwellers that 'home' still existed. Picture calendars from Harrods – ordered from London, if the price at Mackern's bookstore could be afforded – helped to fix in memory the colours of English woodlands and countryside contours from a sitting-room wall. Britons longed for a return to their 'home'. The England they thought of existed no more and the Argentina they remembered was also vanishing. Before nationalization there had been the security that some would return to die in England, or Scotland, or Wales. Others would die in Argentina and would be buried safely, cosily, at the British cemetery, which had taken community corpses since 1833. Since 1947, return had become difficult, if not impossible, and now there was uncertainty about ending life in Argentina.

Community picnics remained regular features, the social gatherings at *asados* – where language-switching underlined two separate cultures rather than a merged one – were weekend routines. Bridge evenings were always organized, and travel about the country continued to be as free as ever. But Anglo-Argentines felt alien, stared at because of their language, in their own land.

The trains no longer ran on time. In the days before 1948 it had been common knowledge that if a train appeared to be a few minutes late the clock needed adjusting. Now a train could be delayed because the Peronist engine driver called a public meeting to honour the name of Perón in gratitude for nationalization. Nobody could stop the engine driver, who could stop the train.

Things, it seemed, had worked better before 1948.

# Chapter 35

DOUGLAS DID NOT NOTICE the woman who took the stool next to him at the bar of the London Grill. The first sign he picked up was her strong, expensive perfume. French, he thought, without really knowing. He squinted and saw her, slightly over-dressed for late Spring, in a black outfit, elegant. A waiter tried to convince her that the bar was not for ladies. She ignored him.

After about five minutes of trying to ignore her stare Douglas heard himself being addressed in good English with a heavy European accent.

'Are you going to sit here and drink yourself stupid?'

He looked at her without recognition. After a time, the picture of the lean square jaw came back to him. Her face was fuller, not quite fat. It was Eva the Polak.

He smiled, slightly embarrassed at such an unexpected reunion with the past.

Without a word he nodded to the waiter and led her to a table in a concealed corner. Yes, she had put on weight, but it was not fat. In fact, she was quite attractive.

'Aren't you going to say something?' she asked.

'When did you learn English?' he replied.

This time she did not answer, but smiled a little crookedly at him. Her eyes searched his face, inspected his hands and his clothes. If she reached any conclusion her eyes were not telling.

'I've missed you so much all these years,' she said in her funny accent. 'Twenty...' she added.

Douglas went bright red and looked around the restaurant. Most of the tables were empty. There were a few after-office drinkers, some voices in English, but not many. He wondered about the source of her apparent wealth, and smirked at the thought that she might have her own brothel now.

She noticed the start of a smile and returned it.

'Are you embarrassed to see me?' she asked.

'A little,' he admitted.

They ordered drinks, but remained silent. They had still not spoken when the waiter returned, with a gin and tonic for her, *ginebra* and water for him.

She started, then stopped, then announced, 'I thought we could go out to supper. I was going to visit all the English bars in town to see if I could find you. But you were in the first one I went to.'

'I might have left Buenos Aires.'

'You're in the telephone book.'

'True, I hadn't thought of that. Sometimes I've looked for my name in the phone book as a reassurance that I am here, that I belong here. A phone book entry, or your name above a shop entrance are the only ways to reassure yourself that you are part of a city.'

He looked for things to say to avoid asking obvious questions.

'That's interesting. It's years since I've given any thought to where I belong,' she said.

'Well, that's just a little game of mine.'

'I thought we could go out to supper,' she repeated.

'You said that...'

'Yes, but you did not answer. Let's go to another bar. Let's try the Tortoni first. What about supper?'

He hedged, he had two children at home.

'Phone the maid, or your housekeeper, whatever she is.'

He hesitated, but she led him to the bar, asked the operator for the number, and when the telephone rang in Ranelagh she handed him the earpiece. Douglas advised that he would not be back that night. He said he would be staying with friends. Then he spoke gently to the children.

'She'll give me hell,' he remarked.

'She's the housekeeper for Jesus' sake, not your wife. Or is there anything else?'

He only replied that the children missed their mother.

They finished their drinks and took a taxi to the Café Tortoni. She had chosen it for its old Buenos Aires atmosphere, but when Douglas told her about the novelist Witold Gombrowicz, who still used the Tortoni as his social centre and occasional work place, she became quite excited. She had read all his books, in Polish.

The head waiter said the writer had gone to visit friends out of town and would not be back for a week. She implored the waiter to tell her a stream of anecdotes about Gombrowicz. Her laughter was loud and full at his description of the fashionable clothes on the women who came with him to the Tortoni, and the way some of his male guests discussed items in their newspapers, and how Gombrowicz mimicked members of the government.

Tears rolled down her face, flooding ruts in her make-up. When she rushed away to the Ladies' to powder her face, the waiter said to Douglas, 'I shouldn't be speaking like this, you can't tell who is listening nowadays and will report me. It is not safe to make political jokes. But your wife seems to enjoy my stories so much... You are English, no? But the *señora* is not, no?

'Of course, Gombrowicz did not do all those things about the government, only some. But I like to have a laugh at the government sometimes. He is a great man, you know, a really great general. We are lucky to have such a president. Oh, yes... He came here, once, to listen to a poetry recital. But to laugh helps to relieve the tension.'

When she returned to the table Douglas kept to himself that the stories about the novelist were fabrications for her entertainment, but he told her provocatively, 'You've just been called my wife.'

She smiled, 'I might have been, eh?'

He did not encourage her. Apart from that, he was beginning to enjoy himself.

Outside, on the pavement of Avenida de Mayo they debated where to go for supper. He wanted to take her to the Plaza Hotel, make it a real treat. Eva preferred the Alexandra restaurant, named after the English queen and still patronised by the community's better paid businessmen.

'It's early,' she said. 'Let's have one more drink before supper. Take me to the *ABC*.'

Douglas froze. A tiny alarm rang somewhere warning him that this whole evening might be a set up. Then he wiped away the thought and felt uncomfortable at suspecting her of a conspiracy. But she had not yet told him what she was doing in Buenos Aires, whether she still lived in Lima, which was where Frau María had said she had gone, nor explained anything about the source of her well-financed appearance.

In recent times the thirty-year-old ABC had become the watering place of fugitive Nazis, at least that was the suspicion among the English-speaking community. At lunchtime the restaurant filled with office workers from the neighbourhood. In the evenings the bilingual menu came out, in German and Spanish. Douglas still used the restaurant because they turned out a good Wiener schnitzel und rosti and he could ignore the Germans.

There had been numerous stories that Nazi treasure had been brought to Argentina in exchange for an unknown number of blank passports issued through the Vatican to facilitate the escape from Europe of some of the more unsavoury characters in Hitler's government. The reports had not been substantiated, but who needed evidence when there were good, and strong, rumours?

The topic of gold for safe passage was made great use of by anti-Peronists. According to their gossip, former Nazi technicians and engineers were at work on secret weapons projects in Patagonia, perhaps even a rocket programme, and at the aircraft factory in Córdoba. There had been an influx of Germans after the war, but they had been a large community before and Argentina was a land of immigration. The country was a natural haven for Europeans.

'I have come all this way to see you, and the *ABC*,' Eva said as they sat in a taxi again for the short ride to the restaurant. 'I'm sorry, Douglas. I have told you very little about myself. But I thought you had to talk first. You haven't. So much sadness in you. I thought that if you told me about your life it would make things better, like in the old d...' She cut herself short.

'I think we should spend the night together. And talk as good friends, after a delicious supper. After all, you said you were not going home tonight.'

His heart accelerated out of control, but this took the conversation away from the *ABC*.

'That was because I usually stay at the Phoenix when I know it will get late. And you had already suggested supper,' Douglas said, on the defensive.

She started talking almost as the car pulled up on Lavalle Street, outside the restaurant.

'I went on a long cruise, through Panama, to Miami. From there I took a plane, Panair. It is a beautiful flight. Panair... You leave on Monday and arrive on Thursday, and the plane stops in Trinidad, Fortaleza and Rio de Janeiro... But it is so frightening to fly, Douglas I must tell you...'

He held the door open and with his hand in the small of her back gently propelled her forward. There appeared to be a little resistance in her step and he pressed more firmly. They sat down away from the bar and ordered beer.

'Yes, I came to find you. And some other things...' she chuckled a throaty short laugh, looked up at him and then lowered her eyes in sham modesty.

'I've been here a week and I know quite a lot about you. I called at your office. Your life has not moved on much. I came to settle a few old scores. I went to Frau María yesterday. She is very old and frail, and I thought I'd scare the hell out of her. Kill her with a heart attack or something. But she was so polite, said she was not sure if she remembered me, because she'd "taken care", that's what she said, taken care of so many girls who wanted to live in Argentina. She gave me coffee in the same silver-plated coffee cups she always used. It was as if nothing had changed. But she said, "Hasn't the world changed?" I left her without knowing why I had gone to see her. I was looking for some sort of revenge, or at least to say, look you owned me but I've done OK. But there was none of that. She saved my life. A German woman saved me, a Polish Jew... But I couldn't thank her when I'd really wanted revenge.'

'There's a German like that here...' Douglas pointed to a large man, balding, half slumped over the table in a corner near the bar. 'Schindler, Oskar Schindler... He's broke, talks to himself. Apparently he helped Jews in Germany, and now the Germans hate his guts. He tried to breed nutria on land in San Vicente, but it hasn't gone right... He drinks too much... A problem I understand,' Douglas said, raising his beer.

'How do you know that?'

'About drinking?'

'No, damn you, about Schindler...'

'We drink, we talk together... He's in a bad way tonight. His wife comes in to fetch him sometimes and drags him home. It's a long ride out. He wanted to write for the *Argentinisches Tageblatt*. They like him there, because the paper has always been anti-Nazi. But he drinks too much... and often does not finish whatever he's writing.'

'How d'you know that?' she asked again.

'Look, you asked that just now. What is this? You wanted to come here, I am just giving you a few stories about the place... I know because I know. One of the owners of the *Tageblatt*, one of the Alemann family, comes in for a drink, with Schindler. They have a few drinks, talk in German, and tell me in Spanish what they're talking about in *Kraut*. So what's the problem?' He shrugged his shoulders as he imitated what was supposed to be a Jewish English accent.

'My whole family was wiped out in Poland. The relatives in Warsaw and the others in the country, there is not one of them left. They had been lost to me for years, but they were family and there was no need to wish them dead. They could still be family even if I did not know anything about them. Now, there is no family. I have nothing to mourn, not a bone, not a stone, not a name. My husband was also a Polish Jew. Much older than I am. A good man, a very dear man. Years ago, when he wanted a young Polish Jew for a wife he took me because I came with no family strings. He clothed me, taught me, said he did not want to commit the sin of bringing children into this world, and only really wanted to be taken care of by a young woman. He went to Warsaw in '46 to see if he could find any family traces. I had begged him to. And now I also have a telegram saying he died, and the guilt of having asked him to go to Warsaw. I am sure he did not want to die there. Lima would have been better. Lima would have been good enough.

'He had a heart attack and died there, in Warsaw. He left me nine jewellery stores in Lima, and his nice brown hat which I always liked to wear. He never wanted to keep many clothes because he hated the idea of other people stepping into his trousers after he was dead.'

Douglas tried to make some comforting noises. She stopped him.

'Don't... You have your tragedies. And I've got mine. That was why I enjoyed myself so much hearing about Gombrowicz. He's an unpleasant bastard in his books. But I wanted to laugh and I did.'

She changed subject. 'In Lima there is much talk about how the Nazis have come here for shelter. Is that true? I have never seen many Germans, not Nazi Germans.'

Douglas shrugged.

'Let's have another beer and then go for supper,' she suggested. 'They have not done anything to me, the Nazis. But I would like to have a picture of the kind of people who killed all my family, and so many other families.'

He had to admit that he had read about the horror, but it was all a long way from Argentina.

'It was a long way from Lima, too. And my family wasn't that close either. But it was a Jewish family, my Jewish family. And I want to see the likes of people who killed Jews because they were different.'

Four men came in to the *ABC* and immediately got into loud conversation. They greeted the man called Schindler, but he gave them a grunt. His head nodded occasionally and immediately jerked back as he resisted the sleep induced by alcohol and solitude.

Douglas gave a short chuckle. 'There's one of the kind you want,' he said. 'People in here say that's Adolf Eichmann, though I don't know if it's true. It's supposed to be a secret, but people tell you these things here quite casually, and they say it is a secret. He answers to an Argentine-German name, something like Richard Klements, but who knows.'

Eva trembled. She steadied by grabbing Douglas's hand.

After a time she began to laugh. It was a giggle at first, but then became laughter, from the throat, loud, quite hysterical and unstoppable.

Douglas patted her hand, stroked her cheek and pleaded with her to stop, but knew she would not. He had a strong suspicion again that this scene had been rehearsed in some form in her mind many times. And then the moment he had been dreading arrived, as ferociously as she could make it.

She sucked in a deep breath and shouted in English.

'Naat-zee-s! All Naat-zee-s!'

Eva sounded drunk, but Douglas knew her to be sober.

The lone drunk named Schindler was jolted into full consciousness. The four men at the table seemed to be blown apart, as if a rock was thrown in their midst and had smashed the bottles in front of them. When they realised what had happened, one man dashed out into the street, into the evening. The three remaining shouted an oath at Eva in a mixture of German and guttural Spanish. The three looked towards the couple's table. Douglas stood up. He made the first move.

His fist went into the first face. Eva pushed her glass into another face. The third man planted one hand in Douglas's chest with the force of a brick and with the back of the other hand followed the falling figure with a crack across his cheekbone. Douglas felt the hard thud of bone on bone.

Half winded, he bounced up with the glee of a fighter.

Now he was really enjoying himself more than ever in years. He hit the nearest face several short punches, felt a small beer bottle smash on his head, shook himself, shot a jab at a nose that went squish as it met his fingers. He felt his neck gripped from behind and he drove his left index finger into the gripper's eye. Eva's voice chanted on 'Nat-zee-s! Nat-zee-s!' Stupid woman, Douglas thought, behaving like a bar whore. She's going to get herself killed. He felt a kick in the back which narrowly missed his right kidney but caused a stabbing pain in his ribs. He swung round and his elbow connected with an eye whose owner dropped like a sack.

The lone drunk shouted 'Basta! Basta!' over and over again and with the help of the barman he began to part the men and keep them separate. Two men ran Eva and Douglas out onto the pavement and held the door shut from the outside. Eva addressed her chant at the large man. He shouted back in Spanish, 'No Nazi! No Nazi! Understand, please. Oskar Schindler, please!'

On his last entreaty and repetition of his name Douglas clapped a hand over Eva's mouth and dragged her away. There was a deep plea in the man's voice. He was almost in tears. Drunk's tears, Douglas thought.

Once round the corner they smoothed their clothes and he straightened his tie. She gave him a comb with a silver grip and he cleared the glass splinters out of his hair.

Draped on her shoulder they walked into the Phoenix. The night porter looked at Douglas and winked, but demanded to see their identity cards. He suspected that they were not married. 'Señor, please. For you, this once. But the new laws will give us problems. You are a customer, so you must be careful and not cause us these difficulties.'

Douglas was laughing through his pain. He felt his eye puffy, and he had an ache in his side.

In the room they pulled at each other's clothes, removing them roughly and urgently pulled back the bedclothes. Her suspenders snapped loose but she left her stockings on. They fell on the bed and he went into her with all the energy he had shown in the fight. They clawed and squeezed, bit and kissed one another extracting twenty years' worth of absence from every second.

Panting and groaning from his wounds he lay half on the bed and half off it. She laughed loudly and deeply, and catching her breath started licking his bruised eye. She looked at the bed. There were bloodstains on the pillow and sheet as the wound on his eyebrow continued to bleed.

'What a battlefield,' she said looking around at the sheet.

'It'll be sore tomorrow,' he replied, thinking she spoke of his wound.

In the full bath later they nursed each other's welts and bites. She put lavender water on the bruise on his cheek and he howled from the sting. They studied each other's bodies. Both had taken on a few kilos. He tweaked the spare flesh on her waist, she poked at his paunch. He lay back in the warm water and she manoeuvred herself on top of him. She helped him harden and then slipped him into her. It was cramped, but more relaxed than on the bed. After quite a long time, and when the water felt almost cold, they watched the semen floating on the surface of the water and splashed it back and forth at each other.

The night porter provided bandages to cover his eye so that they could go out again.

Supper at the Plaza Hotel was memorable for the cold food. They hardly touched the elegant menu as each put two decades into chronological anecdote. Their conversation was filled with endearments, longings, fresh proposals to carry on with life together and multiple expressions of joy at the possibility of such a reunion. In minute detail they went through the fight and described in boasting terms every move made and every punch received or landed.

Some time after midnight they returned to the Phoenix and went for each other again with volumes of pent up feeling that neither knew they still had in store.

In the morning, in a room where the smell of copulation seemed to float in the air, they again came together. They dozed off, facing each other, in the hot bath.

Over a slow breakfast at a bar on Florida they said goodbye, gently, without hurry. She had a Panagra flight to Lima. They would write to each other and see how they could make things take shape over the next few months.

On their second cup of coffee he became quite nervous and she asked what was the matter. 'The children,' he said. 'I must telephone to see how they are.' He looked around for a 'phone, but there was none in that bar. Next, he told her he might take the day off work and go to Ranelagh: he wanted to see his children.

'Would you like me to come with you?' she asked, and paused, knowing it was the testing point she had been looking for. 'I could take another plane. Anything to postpone a flight. I hate flying,' she was quite off-hand in her remark, as if the delay was not important.

He looked straight into her eyes for some time, then quietly but firmly said, 'No,' and lowered his eyes.

'I understand...' she said, patting his hand.

'No. You don't. I'm not sure that I do,' he replied, pulling away from her.

'I think I do,' she insisted.

On the pavement outside the café they shook hands and walked away from each other.

# Chapter 36

IN SEPTEMBER 1951 Argentina was told that Evita Perón was ill. First she was in hospital for a routine check-up, then she stayed in. The illness was uterine cancer, suspected since some time earlier. From her sickbed, she called on followers to support their leader and promised that she would give him her all, even in her weakness.

Evita's autobiography, a first draft ghost-written by a Spanish journalist with Nazi sympathies, was announced for imminent publication. Perón disliked its vulgarity and political provocation. A second text, which smoothed some of Evita's revolutionary roughness, but kept the melodrama and the nonsense of her love for the masses, was prepared by government information officers. It robbed her of the ingenuousness that was her charm, and which most infuriated her enemies.

Early in November a bomb shattered the display window where the book, *My Mission in Life* (*La razón de mi vida*), had been stacked for the launch. Perón's enemies attributed it to a book reviewer, but the Justicialista party thought it no joke. The women's branch of the party and the trade unions organized pilgrimages of prayer for the defeat of Evita's enemies and the recovery of her health.

People called her a saint. She was their friend, the only real heroine and protector they had ever had. They prayed outside her house and outside the hospital. The depth of feeling came through the shallow distortions of despotism and dictatorship. The women's tears came from the heart.

On 19 November 1951 for the first time an edition of the newspaper *La Prensa* rolled off the presses under the management of the Newsvendors Union. The paper had suffered many attacks from Perón's government since the mid-1940s, when it had criticised the pro-Axis policies of the Argentine army. The building on Avenida de Mayo had been stoned, arson had been attempted, and raids by hired thugs had terrorised the staff. The Peróns, Juan and Eva, accused the paper of being the oligarchy's megaphone. The Newsvendors Union, under government orders, had presented the publisher with a set of conditions to close down branch offices and modify production routines that were detrimental to the union's right to newspaper distribution. The publisher rejected the demands and the union struck. Gunmen attacked *La Prensa* workers to force them out on strike. One employee was killed. The publisher shut down his paper and escaped to Uruguay. Sometimes, when speech is equated with death, there is no choice but silence, even if ignominious. The government began expropriation proceedings and finalized matters rapidly in controlled courts.

Señora Eva María Duarte de Perón died on Saturday, 26 July 1952. Really she did not die, but 'passed into immortality at 20.25.' The official communiqué was issued at 21.40 that evening and the text, repeated dozens, hundreds, of times in the following days, would be etched in the memory of a generation. '*The Subsecretaría de Informaciones de la Presidencia de la Nación* has the painful duty of informing the people of the Republic that Señora Eva Perón, Spiritual Chief of the Nation, passed into immortality at 20.25 o'clock.' She was thirty-three, or perhaps thirty-four. Rumour said she had tampered with her birth certificate to make herself born within wedlock, rather than 'on the wrong side of the blanket.'

By the time the announcement of her death was on the air, the Spanish embalmer, who had stood outside the dying woman's room on the first floor of the presidential residence in Olivos for two hours before she breathed her last, was injecting preservatives into the shrivelled body to prevent decomposition through lying in state and the funeral.

Outside the residence wailing filled the cold damp night air. The sound became a terrible moan of shock and pain. The wound lay deep in the bowels. The agonised noise transformed into loud prayers, urgent entreaties in which imploring words could be identified above the mumble as each beseeching syllable raced between the thousands of lit candles and rushed at the presidential residence in the hope that all might be changed. Evita's soul might still be recalled and entreated to return to the shrunken body on the first floor. People, 'the people, her people', asked that everything be the same as before last September. Their prayers travelled the full scope of fantasies; the women wanted Evita to come back to give them something more for the house, to visit them in their new shanty home to see how a husband had installed the doors and the windows they had received from the Eva Perón Foundation; the boys wanted bicycles, the girls wanted dolls, the old men wanted a pair of crutches, the young men wanted their love requited, even though they had been ashamed to admit it. And had she been alive she would have answered all their dreams, as benefactor, Mother Christmas, furtive lover. The crowd had been gathering and growing for weeks. Every man and woman, and many children, had spent days on their knees, in the cold damp weather of mid-winter, praying for the recovery of their angel. The last time they had seen her in public was early in June, when she had accompanied Perón in an open car to the ceremony of inauguration of his second term as President.

On Sunday night many of the women and children outside the Residence were trampled underfoot as the crowd stampeded to get a glimpse of the coffin when it was moved to the ministry of labour in the city. Nobody knew how many were injured or killed in the crush. It was unimportant compared with the magnitude of the tragedy of Evita's death.

On Tuesday, with embalming still in progress in sporadic bursts when the line of mourners could be temporarily stopped, the body was moved to the trade union headquarters. There it remained on show.

The winter weather made men and women look more pitiful and unhappy as they stood for hours, moving slowly to get their brief glimpse of the dead heroine. However quickly the police and security men ushered each mourner by, trying to prevent people from kissing the corpse as the saliva added to its decomposition, each person stood for many hours in the silent crowded street. To walk the length of the queue took an hour. Tired bodies, in wet clothes and plastered down hair, permed or brilliantined for the wake, smelled strongly in the damp city air. That was what struck most: the strong odour of mourning. Old bodies, exhausted bodies, unwashed bodies, surrounded by discarded food remnants, fruit peels, the oily wrappings of cold *tortillas*, babies' towel diapers abandoned after being soiled for many hours, lay at the curbside. Babies' bottoms raw with rashes were washed at stand-pipes and dried painfully with musty-smelling damp towels. The procession lasted four days.

Perón and his courtiers went on a homage spree. Male civil servants had to wear black ties and black armbands, women a black ribbon. Genuine mourners, party supporters and the plain timid who always conformed just in case, added to the sea of black.

Max René Hesse, the German doctor turned novelist who had shaken his community with nationalist stories nearly twenty years before, died in Buenos Aires in December, aged 67. It was bad luck to drop dead in the shadow of Eva Perón because no other death could be noticed that year. Hesse became a forgotten writer. His books secured him a paragraph in the directories of published works.

Controls grew more visible as Perón felt threatened by disorder. Exit visas were introduced to travel across the river to Uruguay in reprisal for the growing criticism in Montevideo newspapers, and because Uruguay offered safe haven to Argentine exiles. At every factory or workplace a bust of Evita had to be erected. And every Friday evening fresh flowers had to be laid at the foot of the bust. Stonemasons, statue and plaque makers and florists became the most profitable occupations in the growing economic hardship. Everybody was trying to get into some aspect of the business.

Everywhere the slogans were the same. Perón was Argentina and Argentina was nothing without Perón. At all official functions the Peronist March came immediately after the national anthem and before the national flag song.

Perón loved this. He never sang with the crowd, he never conducted, not even playfully, when people sang his March. But he was called The Conductor. He never came too close to his followers, he only embraced men, and a few women such as the Italian actress Gina Lollobrigida, which was a temptation difficult to resist. Too great a proximity with the masses gave him goose pimples.

On 15 April 1953 Perón's followers set fire to the Jockey Club headquarters, on the pedestrian Florida Street. That was where his enemies held out, he told the people. From the club, the old patrician oligarchy opposed the cause of the people.

The arsonists moved in after the trade union central had called a demonstration of support for Perón. They were called all the time, to give the leader the evidence of continued devotion even when the economic crisis was beginning to hurt the workers he needed, and as scandal and rumours of corruption had become the city's best and juiciest unpublished stories.

Two bombs exploded in the crowd in Plaza de Mayo. Five people were killed and one hundred injured. Communists were suspected. Perón encouraged the crowd to avenge the outrage.

Activists first set ablaze the Socialist Party offices, and burned the founder's library to ashes. Shouting 'Jews go back to Moscow!' the activists and their followers set fire to the Radical Party building, then struck on a better idea.

The group of arsonists ran to Florida Street, overpowered a watchman at the Jockey Club and tore through the building. Men with small axes went up the elegant stairs, smashing lamps, dragging down great curtains, slashing canvases in their frames and leaving the paintings and the splintered wood on the floor. They stole bottles from the wine cellar, snatched paperweights, ashtrays, small desk ornaments and one man took a fistful of stationery from an office. Another, in a suit and tie, carried off an old wooden coat-hanger on his shoulders. They left the books and the pictures behind.

The building was gutted by fire. Police did not answer calls for help. Firemen arrived when the flames were raging. When the water steamed on the hot masonry, the hoses were shot full of holes by unknown gunmen.

What kind of men burned oil paintings and precious first editions to harm political rivals? There were paintings by Goya and Velasquez, and a host of English and French watercolourists and travellers, and Argentine artists of the nineteenth century who were vital parts of the country's history. What people torched pictures and burned their own history?

Perón's presses boasted of the lesson taught to the enemies of the people.

Walter Hubbard Owen, Scot, poet, translator, died at the British Hospital on 24 September 1953, aged 67. By the time of his death he had spent nearly four years in hospital, wasting away quietly, patiently. He had published poems in that time. But he was a translator of South American epic poems. His dream was to render all the great authors, from colonial times to the end of the nineteenth century, into English. They were all labours of love, the printings supported by friends and by a former British ambassador.

There was no connection between the savagery and the arson of the autumn nights and the death of a minor poet in the spring. But somehow side by side both events mattered as an inexplicable synthesis of the country. The President's hordes had burned the cultural wealth and history, while the gentle poet lay dying, still working at translations which he hoped would explain that same wealth and history to the English-reading world. There was no more to it than that. Walter Owen was rapidly forgotten.

# Chapter 37

SATURDAY AFTERNOONS IN SPRING retained a charm that had not vanished with Inés's death. For many months following, and Douglas had trouble saying 'her death', he had avoided repeating anything they had done together in the house or among friends for fear of spoiling his memory of her and the occasion. Four years later he was beginning to come to terms with the idea that he could not mourn her indefinitely.

Slowly, but without being able to reach a decision to change, he realized that such behaviour was robbing the children of the pleasures of family life. He fretted. He was not making a good father. Ideas for games, or any entertainment, did not come to him easily. Inés always did that. He had trouble cuddling the children. They seemed to have lost their laughter. He longed to sweep them up and sit them on his shoulder and dance with them and then put them on the lower branches of the oak and watch them climb. But he did not do that.

The children played in the swing he had hung from one of the branches of the oak. They laughed as they pushed each other in turn. Their joy came to him as a relief, not a pleasure.

How should a man practice, not just feel, parental loving; how should he show love for his children when he had depended on their mother to lead him in every moment of family life? His incompetence caused him acute discomfort. Inés's absence ached. It actually hurt. There was no spot of pain, no lesion that he could identify. When it took hold of him it would begin with a constriction in the throat, then his shoulders would feel a strain, something pulled at different parts of him. The bones in his legs and the muscles in his thighs tightened, as if they were turning in opposite directions. The absence of Inés was a sore whose presence he could feel and even see like an open gash, but there was nothing to show or explain.

The beginning of the flu was the nearest he could think of, to compare what he felt. He took an aspirin.

Then the back of his eyes pulled, as if he wanted to cry. Oh, God, why wasn't she there with them! Wasn't there anything that could bring her back! Why had she gone? The children were so small. The questions hurt too, mostly because he knew they were useless. Once, when he had asked the questions aloud, to know what they sounded like, they seemed ridiculous. He had been alone, weeding in the garden. He hoped that the stupidity of their content and sound would force them to go away. They came back a few weeks later.

How he wished she could be there with them, sitting in the garden, enjoying what was best about Ranelagh, the calm, the green lawn which he had mowed that morning. The enemies within the garden set him on crusades. Tough weeds with prickly burrs spread like water on tiles. The large black ants were unstoppable. Both needed constant vigilance and elaborate plans of attack. He chuckled with pleasure when he heard the children in their room shriek after repressing giggles as he swore loudly and angrily in his battle of wits against the ants. Overnight, the ants would strip bare a new rose tree and carry every last bit of fresh young leaf along a track cut across the lawn. The next dawn he would put down dust on the ant path and search for their stores. On weekends the children would join him in the adventure of digging up the nest. The game was to make sure nobody got bitten by the ferocious ants. A bite was a point against. The one with the fewest bites was the winner. The 'ants' palace' would be destroyed with paraffin and fire. And for days after they would watch for renewed activity. This was called guard duty.

Through spring and summer he tried to make the garden a pleasure to sit in.

Now they had just finished a barbecue and sat under the oak. This exercise required the boy, who was ten, to climb the oak and make sure there were no caterpillars in the branches. They were fat juicy green ones which made a loud and huge squirch when crushed underfoot. When they had fed to fulfilment on the new leaves, they would drop from the branches and if they glanced off a bare arm or a face their hairy backs would leave a stinging rash.

The housekeeper sat in the deckchair next to him, her shoulders bare, reading a copy of *Argosy*, a short story magazine published in London and which he had subscribed to for years. That, with *Blackwoods* magazine, which he still took as his last link with Edinburgh.

The housekeeper stretched out and stroked his arm. He lit two cigarettes and passed her one. She watched her son climb quite high in the oak and called out a word of caution. It was automatic and without endearment. A child's fall would break the afternoon calm. Her son was two years older than his boy and showed off the greater prowess of his age. The two boys fought often and were brutal to each other. She and her son were jealous of his children. Her feelings came out in loud arguments and fits of rage, which he tried to take in his stride. He often fled the house and went to the station for a drink, or a few.

Douglas thought he was treating the three children fairly, but recognised that it might be impossible. He was vexed by her charges of conspiracy and ulterior motives when he was trying to establish equanimity. Even at the best of times, when all seemed calm, he feared she would suddenly suspect his reasons for a small gesture of friendship or generosity to all three children.

She had been with them over three years now and the neighbours, the people of Ranelagh whom he used to see a lot of with Inés, were a tiny bit apprehensive about how to deal with the relationship. She had taken a dislike to all of Inés's friends, accusing them of being ill-intentioned snoopers and meddlers. People no longer visited and Inés's younger brother, who had stayed in the village after helping build the school, did not call either.

One of Douglas's neighbours, a third generation Argentine who still kept English as a first language in his home, broached the subject of their frozen friendship one morning on the train into town. Douglas had a black eye, where she had hit him with a wooden spoon in one of her outbursts of rage because, she said, he had chatted with somebody she disliked and she was sure they had spoken ill of her.

'You might like to put things in order,' said the neighbour helpfully. 'Get rid of her.'

'I need somebody to stay with the children when I go out of town,' Douglas said.

'Perhaps she'll settle down if she's given certain security...' He did not say marriage, but that was what he meant. 'Keep the property in your name though.'

Douglas resented the intrusion but knew it was inevitable. She was one of the displaced people of the war, with a child to educate. She was hungry for a marriage that would give her the safety of a home. He wondered if she also wanted to have property of her own. That pleasure he would never give anybody. The house had been his and Inés's and it would go to his children and no others.

The sun was strong. He felt her hand stroke his arm again. She stood up and winked at him. Her son was in the lower branches of the tree and the other two were still in the swing. They usually played alone in the garden for hours and no supervision was needed.

'We'd like to go in for a siesta,' she announced.

'All right, Hen,' Douglas answered. He had always called her that, a vulgar familiarity retained from Edinburgh jargon. She had no other name.

They went into her room, which she shared with her son. He had never asked her into the bedroom he had shared with Inés, and where his children sometimes came to sleep in the spare bed.

They removed their clothes before they lay down. She was short and plump which showed in substantial buttocks, and she had rich round breasts. As he lay on top of her and she guided him in, he found himself thinking it was not much fun. They were both doing this for want of something better to do. It was a weekly routine, like letting off steam. Both needed that and might have missed it if it were not there. As he thrust in he thought of the last time with Eva. That was a memory to keep. He grunted at the recollection and she, underneath him, thought it was his pleasure with her. In the split second he had drifted and realized again where he was he thought this was useful, but he would hold no good memory of it.

Douglas had felt remorse from the first time it had happened, but did not have the strength to stop. One evening, when her son was spending the night with a school friend, Douglas had come back the worse for *ginebras* at the station bar. She did not complain, but massaged his neck and then for further comfort led him to her bed. As he drunkenly rolled onto her he was sober enough to know that he would always regret that night.

Now, he took part in their weekly love-making with no enthusiasm to make up for distaste at himself.

He was doing it for the safety of the children, he lied to himself. Often, when he was away, he was afraid for them. Her discipline ran to severe corporal punishment. A neighbour had reported the howls of the children on more than one occasion. Douglas fretted on his own, but did not challenge her. He tried to will the events away.

She was a good housekeeper. The children were clean, the house was spotless. She was an excellent cook. She embroidered, had tastefully painted Alpine motifs on new lampshades, her cakes were a joy to eye and tastebud. The linen cupboard had never been so well stocked and orderly. All this she had learned at a finishing school in London, where her Greek father had been a tea importer. Then she had been sent to Switzerland, where she had met her son's father. She had spent most of the war in Germany, near Stuttgart. In circumstances that were not clear, she had sailed for Buenos Aires after Germany's defeat by the allies.

On a sunny Saturday afternoon during their siesta routine, he suggested that they get married. It was hardly a proposal, not much more than a casually put idea. She accepted with a sense of relief. As the neighbour had said, it was what she needed at the moment.

Why do men feel a need to remarry? He asked himself. There was no love and not a large amount of affection, he said. He would now become a stepfather and she a stepmother. And the only reason each was agreeing to such a move was to secure the shelter of his house, in her case, and her continued housekeeping services and brief weekly intercourse, in his.

They were married in the autumn. Some friends from his office joined them for lunch. He chose a restaurant and a hotel nowhere near those he had occupied with Inés.

Domestic harmony lasted a couple of days longer than the week's honeymoon in the Córdoba hills.

There was a cold damp bite in the Buenos Aires weather in May and he quite looked forward to his six-monthly sales trip to Mendoza. The Andes foothills were dry, there would be some early snow and good crisp wine at the *bodegas* his clients would take him to.

The house was tense on the morning of his departure. The two children followed him everywhere until they could delay no further going to school. His son asked repeatedly how long he would be away, the girl suggested there might be a way of him taking them with him. Douglas asked them what they were afraid of but they did not reply. The trouble was he knew, but while they did not put their fears into words he felt excused from any decision on their behalf.

He left the house after they were on their way to school. His parting words to his wife were, 'Look after them, please.'

When he stepped out of the train at Plaza Constitución he realized that he had left his briefcase behind. If he went back to Ranelagh for it, he would never get into town again to catch the train at Retiro for Mendoza. And going on without it was pointless. He would reach Mendoza minus all his crop study reports and the analysis of spray volumes necessary to combat rot in imported French vines.

He sent a telegram to the client apologizing for the delay and promised to be there on the next train in three days time. Then he went to the office to explain the mishap and caught his usual evening train back to Ranelagh.

All the lights in the house were on as he let himself in. The first sound that met his ears was a shout from his son and the sobs of his daughter. He dropped his suitcase and ran into the sitting room. The girl, looking very small, was crumpled in a corner. A stream of blood trickled from her ear, her cheeks were puffed with crying and she looked badly bruised. His son stood in tears by the fireplace. His nose was bleeding. Douglas looked at the woman. She had a knife in one hand and the fire poker in her left. A lit cigarette dangled from her lips.

'You cow,' he shouted and went for the hand with the knife. As he stepped forward, pain streaked his chest, and he collapsed.

His brother-in-law, Ines's younger brother, was at his bedside when he woke, three days later.

Douglas took some time to focus on his stern-looking visitor and on the note he held in his hand. It read, 'Gone to uncle's.'

'They left that on the kitchen table yesterday morning. Both are safe, they came to our place last night, apparently after wandering in the streets all day. I went to fetch some clothes for them today. She would not let me in. So I kicked the door down.'

Douglas felt he was slipping back into unconsciousness and was rudely shaken.

'Wake up, you bastard,' his brother-in-law said. 'Listen. There's nothing wrong with you, except you're full of booze. Listen, very carefully. I'm taking out a court order to keep your kids. I don't want them, you know that. I've got three. But we're not going to watch them being beaten senseless by that bitch.

'She'll go to court to get the children back, to keep hold of you and the house, I suppose. No judge'll buy that but it will be too public. Get rid of her and I don't care how it's done. She goes, alive or dead. I'll even help you wash up if you have the guts to finish her.

'And then dry up. Otherwise, you're not seeing the kids.'

# Chapter 38

IN JUNE 1955, Perón defeated a rebellion in the navy. He had distrusted the entire force since 1945 and now the Church, the Holy Roman Catholic Apostolic church, established, supported the navy. The Church was angry at Perón's defiance of its authority. Conservative the Church was, but it had to repudiate the introduction of divorce and the expulsion of worker priests who had been heard to be critical in the shanties, and it was angry with Perón for trying to turn the nation's youth away from the Church and onto the Peronist party. In June 1955, roving thugs burned down half-a-dozen churches. The historic archives at the Jesuit Church of San Ignacio, built at the beginning of the eighteenth century with the financial assistance of English and German slave-traders, and where Father Guillermo Furlong had worked for so many years, were lost to the flames.

What kind of men burned down the church they were born into? What kind of men burn their religion's libraries and precious archives? The same as burned pictures of Goya and ancient first editions.

Perón denied responsibility for the arson. But the crews that ran through the streets carrying battering rams, crowbars and cans of fuel, shouted 'Viva Perón!' and death to priests. Two bishops were put on a plane accused of burning an Argentine flag. They flew out with no destination to go to. It was Perón's defence against the charges of arson. Perón was excommunicated by the Vatican – which in 1917 had welcomed Evita, on her first state visit anywhere, as a good customer of Rome.

Perón never said how many people were killed in the bombing of Plaza de Mayo and Government House by the naval rebels in June. His rivals were as debased as he was. Perón called for revenge. Five of 'them' would die for each fallen Peronist. His anger was frightening, and dangerous, and grotesque. His enemies were no better.

Before the rescuers could get to the casualties, and while the machinegun on Government House still chattered into the air, the boys from the technical college a few blocks away were searching the rubble for empty machinegun shells. In the college workshops they made coffee table cigarette lighters which sold very well.

After June, Perón ran downhill. Excommunication was a minor matter. Repentance, a few Hail Marys, a little genuflection and a small sum of money could solve his dispute with the Church. But he had a large number of naval officers in exile in Montevideo. The army, his beloved institution, had stood by him and beaten off the rebels. But the army was also split.

By July the army, even that section that had defeated the rebels, was not defending Perón. The generals had been protecting their privileges: free petrol in times of inflation, duty free imports in a heavily taxed market, good postings and predictable promotions, in a near-bankrupt economy. If the perks had to be defended, Perón had to go.

All over Latin America armies were on the move again. In Bolivia there had been revolution; in Brazil the president had committed suicide rather than surrender to air force rebels; in Guatemala there had been a US-backed invasion. Newspapers in Buenos Aires noted that an Argentine citizen with a society name from a respectable family, Ernesto Guevara Lynch de la Serna, had been trapped in Guatemala, but had managed to escape.

On Friday, 16 September 1955, the navy, with substantial sections of the army, rose against Perón.

Offices and banks closed in the middle of the afternoon and commuters hurried to terminals before all services were halted.

In a backwater like Ranelagh, 'revolution' was exciting, especially for the children. Schools closed early and indefinitely. All the children's mothers and stepmothers gathered in huge crowds at the two schools in the village to collect their offspring. And then, as if by agreement, all the women dragged their children to the shops. Each child was posted to a different queue, while their mothers discussed the crisis and what they were going to cook for tomorrow's supper. It was a terrible problem. The women shared it with deep understanding: one child would not eat salads, the other could not eat steak, the doctor had said the little girl had to eat more fruit but she would not.

All the fresh food in the shops was sold out on that Friday afternoon. And in every home dry pasta and canned food was hoarded for the duration. Pasta had always been synonymous with 'revolution', the military overthrow of an established government: pasta kept well. The military proclamations might have been a pasta shopping list – *fideos, macaroni, tallarines, ñoquis* – and, accompanied by military marches, would have conveyed the sense of emergency and of purpose far more clearly than the long and oft-repeated communiqués about national salvation. Never had Ranelagh eaten so much *pasta* as in the week starting Saturday, 17 September 1955.

There was an abundance of rumours too. Squadrons of Gloster Meteors flew high over Ranelagh and small propeller-driven planes flew low over Ranelagh. Truck-loads of troops passed through Ranelagh, though there was no reason to take a detour from the road between Buenos Aires and La Plata other than obscure strategic readiness. Only one truck stopped. The front axle broke as it swung into the village, at the end nearest the road between the two cities. It never left. Weeks later it was lifted onto an elevated, if low, concrete base and declared a monument to the memory of the 1955 Liberating Revolution.

The soldiers in the vehicle, conscripts all, were stranded in Ranelagh, under the command of a lance corporal, encamped at the corner of the breakdown.

The barman on that corner accepted their cash, pieces of uniform and promissory notes, as well as charity raised by begging in the village, to supply drinks and food. He employed one or two conscripts to sweep the floor and wash out the rooms used by his three daughters. The three women made a small fortune out of the men. The lance corporal pulled rank and demanded first choice, greedily requiring a turn with each of the women every night. Then the conscripts could follow and the screams and laughter would last until dawn. When the lance corporal was thin and wasted by his exertions, and by his greed, the women went to him where he lay in the truck's cabin. One day he was not there and only his army fatigues, worn very thin, were found on the driver's seat. The barman imposed order with an axe handle to prevent anarchy in his daughters' bedrooms. The conscripts were forgotten. Some months after their national service should have ended, their demob papers finally arrived in Ranelagh, redirected from their regiment.

Official radio stations were awash with communiqués as the government announced victory and severe punishment for the enemy, then the stations changed hands and another army group had won. The most scurrilous stories came from an Uruguayan radio station. Rumours throughout the rebellion were savoured. It was the truth that was unbelievable. The radio reported heroic battles. The truth was that officers were shouting at each other over the telephone. Many people regretted that the peak of the conflict took place during the weekend, which meant that cinemas which should have been open were not, and schools and offices would have been closed anyway.

Some shops reopened on Tuesday, when a ceasefire was announced, or as soon as the owners thought it was safe. There were no shortages. Every home was well stocked with pasta. On Thursday, most schools reopened.

Perón's rule was no more. He had fallen under the weight of his excesses. His indescribable vulgarity had brought him down. He had invited teenage girls to the presidential residence and had gloated over their small pubescent bodies. He had asked young females to put their hands in his pockets to fish for rewards, and they had accidentally fondled his genitals in the lucky dip. He gave the girls, and some boys, motor-scooters, and watched them ride around in the garden in tight shorts, ogling their buttocks. The Church denounced perversity in high office. It did not matter if it was true or not, these were the really good rumours that applied to dictators. Was any of it true? Nobody cared.

All the pictures of Perón and Evita were torn to shreds, the 78 rpm records with the music of the Peronist March were destroyed and there would be no more school essays about the Second Five Year Plan, or any need to learn by heart the chapters of the Justicialista Doctrine. Copies of Evita's *My Mission in Life* were burned.

What kind of people burn books?

Parents, nice people... teachers. But they said these were bad books and that they were good people.

After the fall, schools organised day trips to the presidential residence, parents took their children, and other parents went too, to see the contents of the house. They stared at the motor-scooters Perón had owned, his vast collection of baseball caps, the beautiful and hugely expensive dresses which Evita had bought from the best couturiers, and her jewels. The new military government threw open the doors to Perón's homes so that all could see the evil excesses of dictatorship. People went in hushed curiosity. There were no discussions, few exchanges of views about the accumulated possessions. There was no serious assessment of the despot's loot. People had lost the habit of arguing about political issues in public.

Argentina was going to be friends with the United States and Britain again, formally. This was noticeable in the streets. Members of the British and North American communities spoke English quite loudly, and they went around congratulating one another.

One of the symbols of the new relationship was the Royal Navy goodwill visit, in September 1957, of the aircraft carrier HMS *Warrior*, escorted by HMS *Lynx* and HMS *Mounts Bay*. In July 1958 Argentina's navy announced the purchase of *Warrior*, which became the ARA *Independencia*, and people wondered if the goodwill had just been a sales tour.

The United States took part in an air display over the airport with the most modern fighter planes. After years of off-and-on arms embargoes against Argentina, Washington really felt Buenos Aires could do with some new weapons.

## Chapter 39

IF LIFE'S STAGES had happy endings like Hollywood pictures, then that Christmas, Christmas 1962, was Douglas's happy ending. Here he was, at home in Ranelagh, with his two children. Together again. He had been ill, seriously, in hospital in the last year, heavy drinking, mostly. He had been in and out of treatment during much of the previous seven years. Now he was off the drink, almost, and feeling healthy, nearly. The hedge all round the garden had taken him the best part of two days to cut, for the children's arrival, but he had not felt exhausted after all the clipping.

His son had arrived three days before Christmas at the end of a no-hope job up-country with lots of money – more than a nineteen-year-old should have, Douglas thought – and his daughter, two years younger, had finished school and put an end to her long residence at her uncle's home.

They were together. Douglas skipped and danced and served dark malt beer because the doctor said it was low in alcohol and there was no harm in having a couple of bottles in the evening.

The house had been stripped of any signs of his second marriage. Douglas had burned everything that might remind him of his mistake after her lawyers had come for all her possessions. The hand-painted lamp-shades and the embroidered tablecloth she had given him as a present, even the pillow-slips with his initials embroidered by her had been destroyed. Everything now was almost as Inés had left it, the furniture, the books, the linen in the cupboard. Everything that had belonged to Inés before and during their marriage had come down from the attic and seemed put back into use.

On the mantelpiece, among a dozen Christmas cards, there was one from *Eva la polaca*. 'I must stop calling her that. Even in thought,' Douglas remonstrated. It was more than just a greetings card, a full letter, the first in years. But her information was correct, so she had kept in touch with somebody in Buenos Aires.

'Ten years!!! More!! Since I was last in Buenos Aires. Ten years, just think of all that time. I want to see you again. You must be terribly old (joke!) and I am only just coming out of my youth. But I am sure there is life in you yet. I want to see you again and I want to get away from here. How's Buenos Aires after the Peróns? Not much different, I am told. Just a new bunch going for the money, never mind the people. I sold the shops and bought gold. The people who know say it was a mistake, because the price is stable. But I have a feeling in my bones that some day soon I am going to be stinking rich. Hope I live to spend it all. And I think we should spend some of it together. What d'ya say, old man?'

The letter went on at some length, on three sides of a large, expensive Christmas card. She had never said where she learned her English. Douglas thought it might be with North Americans. She took her holidays in Miami; and said she still hated flying.

Douglas had sent her a telegram immediately:

'Awaiting you when you choose to visit: the sooner the better.'

This time it would be all right with Eva. Everything would turn out fine. And if nothing else happened, he at least would assure her that now he wanted them to be good friends forever. The very thought embarrassed him. He wondered if he could make love to her now, or if they would even try again. Eva's letter seemed to offer something in the future, but would they be able to try anything more than a sound of diffident middle-aged closeness.

His daughter was putting the last decorations on the Christmas tree and his son was shoving elegant Bond Street-wrapped parcels under the lower branches. There were a great many parcels, Douglas thought. Or maybe he was just out of the habit of seeing a tree in that corner. The tree was away from the fireplace, which was full of dry pine cones covered with tinsel, and against a tall mirror mounted on the wall. This made the decorated tree look much bigger than it really was. Douglas watched the two of them at work and hummed a little, and smiled, and then felt one eye water. But his left eye was smiling more decisively than the right was weeping. His face looked frozen in silent laughter. His daughter looked up at him and smiled back.

'This is going to be fun,' she said. 'I haven't felt like this in years. Will we do it Argentine or Scots, Dad?' She meant opening the presents. Local custom celebrated Christmas Eve and presents were opened at midnight. Or could they wait until Christmas morning and be 'English'.

They decided that they would do as they pleased; midnight if it caught their fancy, but after breakfast if they were busy with something else. Over the years there had always been some debate about this, with the added problem that Christmas Eve was his birthday. In the end, the decision arrived at was the same as it had been way back when Inés was alive. Today, they would mark his fifty-fifth birthday. Tomorrow they would celebrate Christmas with presents and a barbecue under the oak. There were half a dozen bottles of white wine chilling on two blocks of ice in the laundry basin.

The temperature rose above thirty degrees Centigrade with no sign of rain. After thirty-four years in Argentina Douglas still found it difficult to accept red-coated Santas and snow imitations in the sweltering heat. All three were in shorts and the minimum cover decently possible.

In the heat of the afternoon, Douglas went out into the garden and stood staring at the parched grass. The white wall of the back of the house reflected a fierce brightness and he squinted as he made himself busy looking for ants. He lit a cigarette and drew in the taste very slowly, enjoying the mixture of the hot air perfumed by summer flowers and the mild tobacco smoke. The *chicharras*, or *cigarras*, or should they be called *cicadas*, filled the heavy lethargy of the afternoon with their loud whine.

He wanted to ask his son if they might work together to buy a piece of land, to farm. Douglas still thought of growing fruit in Patagonia, but they could also plant tobacco in Uruguay, not far from Montevideo. His son had done well, and had some cash put away after only a year's work. There were good wages for reasonably educated young men prepared to work in public works in the provinces. If he could keep his savings and help on the small farm, they might get things going together. If his son decided against farming, he would still be able to draw on his savings while he looked for something else.

Douglas thought he would wait for Eva to visit Buenos Aires. If she was on her way to being 'stinking rich' she might help him. He wondered if she would like Ranelagh and if she would stay with them for a time. He had some money, from two recent redundancies, and that would do for a down payment. If Eva helped, his plan would work like a dream.

The money he had kept in US dollars most of the time, selling when the market was high and buying back at the smallest drop in the rate to the peso. It was the way everybody was making money these days. It was the only way to save.

Just after Perón's overthrow, Coopers had asked Douglas to leave. His domestic upheaval and frequent absences due to excess drinking had prompted a disguised dismissal with a substantial compensation for many years service. He had then found a menial job in a meat-packing *frigorífico*.

The job had been a safe one, while it lasted, even fun. Anglo, the packing plant on Buenos Aires's South Dock owned by Lord Vestey's Union International since 1927, was seen as a last resort, but a good refuge, by Anglo-Argentines. The community had always seen employment in the British Hospital accounts department, the *Buenos Aires Herald* sports desk and the auditors department at Anglo as the repository of failures in everything else. People who could speak English but who had gained few other qualifications at school or in life went there.

Although Anglo had a few outstanding managers, most 'English' employees were not pressed for any efficiency and were kept on the payroll whatever their sins. Boys, not girls, entered the Vestey group in South America after school, with the promise that they would be trained as managers, or they were abandoned to their frustrations along the way if they were not managerial material.

Douglas was employed as a tally clerk, with not much to do in any place except to tick off numbers on ruled sheets. He counted heads on the killing floor, or counted the bits that each animal had been reduced to in the canning department.

For the 'English' as well as for working-class Argentines, the *frigoríficos* were a way of life. For the 'English' it meant a certain respectability and a regular income, for the others it was the achievement of political power. Though foreign master and Peronist worker were in theory incompatible, they functioned well together.

Douglas had enjoyed the awful jokes that both sides made about each other. The workforce at the plant was part of the history of Argentine politics and each man felt strong, answerable only to his foreman. The men were a power base of local despots, provincial bullies and governors with presidential aspirations. Since the early nineteenth century the workers had often been recruited into private armies for public vengeance. Those employed on the killing floors were experts in the use of their knives, brilliant surgeons who had entered the literature and the art of the River Plate, ignorant of their role as sinister folk heroes. There were no qualms, no doubts about the sight of so much death every day. At the end of the working week, every man and woman on the plant took home a packet of meat, which was theirs by right, secured thanks to the negotiating powers of Juan Perón's henchmen in the meat-workers union. Blood filled their days, beef filled their bellies.

Mornings for Douglas were filled watching the herds as they walked up the ramp to their death. If the animals slowed in their walk, a live electric wire, tied to the end of a long cane, was used to prod them on their way.

Buenos Aires police had liked the idea and had adopted the *picana* for use against detainees as far back as the 1930s.

The cattle climbed the ramp in groups, classified by weight and quality: export, domestic market, which were high grade, and canning. The latter were the wretches recovered from drought country.

As the cattle reached the channel leading to the killing floor, six steers, or cows, or heifers, were parted from the following line by a gate that isolated them from the ramp. There was no going back. On a ledge above the batch of six stood a man with a small metal hammer at the end of a long handle. The man swung the handle with ease. As the hammer-head met each forehead with a dry thud the beast's legs crumpled and the body dropped onto the concrete flagstone. When all six in the parcel were unconscious, a trap was opened by the hammer-man and the animals, still alive, rolled out onto the killing floor. One man tied their hind legs and hung the beast upside down from a rail. Another man cut the throat and a flood of blood – future meat extract – ran into a drain for collection. Other men deftly skinned the warm body, others cut it open and removed what was classified from then on as offal.

Douglas stood in white spotless coat, counting the live beasts and then keeping tally of the component parts. By nine o'clock each morning, the bulk of the slaughter was over and he was due a break. Usually this was a walk around other sections, to take coffee with workmates, contract men who had made better careers and looked forward to promotion and home leave, or several glasses of cognac with those who had abandoned any hopes of good prospects.

Lunch consisted of a large juicy steak and salad in the subsidized canteen, perhaps followed by a siesta in one of the many well-hidden nooks. Some of the *ingleses* who were not subject to performance checks as were the native Argentine employees seldom looked into their offices from one week's end to the next. They preferred the company of their drinking chums and the long conversations about failures and dashed expectations which were blamed on a remote Lord Vestey. The owner was never seen, regarded as visiting royalty. Vestey was famously mean. 'He is so tight you could not get a razor between the cheeks of his arse.' That is what his peers said of him in the House of Lords.

The canning plant, and the meat extract section, the corned beef department, all had their stories about the cats that kept the factory mice-free. From time to time a greedy cat had leaped onto the conveyor belt loaded with meat travelling to the mincer, and with hardly a sound pussy went too.

Some afternoons could be spent in the officers' mess of a refrigerated cargo ship docked at the plant, usually a Blue Star Line ship, owned by Vestey. This was an important access to supplies of Scotch whisky, Gordon's gin and cigarettes, all at very good prices.

Friday evenings Douglas, as junior auditor, was sent on a search of the plant to make sure that no *ingleses* remained hidden in a drunken stupor in a remote shed or worse, frozen in cold storage. The South Dock bars had to be searched as well. When no friendly ships were in the hard drinkers, who had excused themselves from the plant on the grounds that the factory telephone service was awful and work was best conducted from the public call boxes in the bars off the premises, all had to be found. The barman always expected them, they were good for business. Red wine was served in Coca Cola bottles and the local Old Smuggler whisky was poured in tea cups.

Douglas did not touch a drink on Fridays to be able to drive a company van around the plant and to the bars outside, collecting the drunk and the unconscious and making sure they were shipped safely back to their wives before the gates closed for the weekend.

Britain cut down on its imports again, and Argentine plants and cattle breeders were once more accused, probably to service political interests in a Europe that was closing in on itself, of not checking the spread of foot-and-mouth disease. Anglo shed its less profitable employees. Douglas took a good redundancy and went home to Ranelagh. He bought dollars and felt safe.

And then his two children advised that they were coming home.

Sometimes he saw Inés in the garden, although he could not see her this afternoon. He saw her as she had been then, very pale and quite lovely, always wearing an awful black housecoat with flowers as she fussed about the children. Once at siesta, Douglas had playfully tugged at the top button of the shabby dress and accidentally ripped it off. She was naked under the housecoat. They had lain, trying to be very quiet, under the fir tree in the corner of the garden and fallen asleep on the thick bed of pine needles.

He worried that Ranelagh might not be home to the children now that they were together, after the atmosphere of holiday reunion wore off. The village might stop being the centre of all of life's events. It was difficult to get to because of the infrequent train service. Ranelagh was self-sufficient in much of its social life and leisure, but remote from the events of the big city. Now, life's great entertainments as well as a wealthier, stronger, smaller, but more active Anglo-Argentine community, with elegant clubs, big dances every Saturday, after rugby in winter, polo in spring, cricket in summer, after rowing or tennis, all happened in the northern suburbs. The theatre, the practices for St Andrew's Society Annual Caledonian Ball, a night at the Colón Opera House, often required staying over at a hotel in the city, to avoid missing the late trains.

Ranelagh was a place of fond and gentle times past. The Anglican Church had been central to many family lives. It began in Sunday school, where the children would recite a Lord's Prayer which they thought was correct, 'And lead us not to Temperley station'.

The children, apart from a few Irish, tried to stay clear of the Roman Catholic Church. Rome's religion was a place of tragedy and terribly scary. In Ranelagh the church had been built with donations from the Ayerza family in memory of their daughter's small son who had been kidnapped and murdered. But even as Protestants the children had to go there almost every week to play football with the boys from the Catholic school, there to be told that they were living in mortal sin which became a fry-up in hell if they scored against the priest's team. Father Antidio had entered the church in penance for his name, given him by his unmarried mother. He played excellent football and he was sometimes on the 'English' side when numbers were short. His breath was so foul he breathed through his mouth so as not to smell his own exhalation, which formed greasy clouds about him.

Weekends had been spent in the garden, winter or summer, with walks around the golf club on Sunday afternoons.

The picture of Ranelagh was of orange home-sewn canvas deck chairs flapping in the summer breeze. They represented a peaceful and safe existence, and little action.

Earth streets were beginning to disappear under suburban concrete that ended in straight edges met by trimmed grass borders. Those earth streets had once been the bane of the middle-class 'English' housewife – oh, and others too, of course, but their domestic problems hardly mattered. The streets were the cause of thick coats of dust that settled on sitting-room chintz in the dry summers, and of the bog that sucked cars down to their axles in the rainy winters. But those streets had also been safeguards against speeding cars and accidents; nobody drove too fast on earth roads. The streets had been the playground of children locked out of their homes at siesta time. The children forsook their cool porches and large gardens to roll in the warm soft surface of the roads until their skin changed colour to a milky cocoa and their throats cracked from the dust. Then they lay in the cool grass of the ditches among the thick scent of the mats of camomile plants, eventually to rise scratching, covered in bites from small red fleas that inhabited the miniature daisies. How they itched... and then they lay in the bath or showered until they were scolded for running dry the water tanks or were rubbed down painfully with alcohol by unsympathetic adults. Only once did any vehicle take one of those tracks at great velocity and that was the fire engine from a neighbouring town, using a short cut over the drought smoothed earth to fields ablaze near the enchanted stream, the *Arroyo Encantado*. The dust raised by the engine had hung in the air for two days, an elevated north to south swathe. The talk about the dust, and the first fire engine to hurry through Ranelagh without stopping to explain, had taken much longer to settle.

Horse-drawn carts sank into the winter mud. The bakery cart delivered the 'English-style' white bread, with short 'French' baguettes and 'Italian' loaves. Inés had stopped buying from the cart after she had found a dead mouse in one loaf. But that might have been forgiven. What turned her against home delivery of bread of any nationality had been two occasions when the cart had slipped into the ditch outside the house. From the sitting-room window she and her children had stared in fascination and terror as the enraged driver whipped the mule and mare. Such cruelty had Inés in shock. And the cart had only rolled free when the mule had been unharnessed and the mare was made to pull alone, without punishment.

Every street in Ranelagh held a memory of an English home... Reynolds, Moore, Macfarlane, Kirby, Gibson, Jackson and so on.

The home of some friends had represented the children's discovery that their parents made love, and used condoms, and that this was not the equipment of the maid's boyfriends. A man had been cleaning out the septic tank one afternoon. Floating on the surface of one bucket of muck brought up was a long, very long, white condom. The children had reported their discovery amid giggles which lasted for days. It had come to them as a shock that an active sexual life might be one of their parents' pastimes. And from then on there were always questions at table as to whether Douglas and Inés thought that 'Mr & Mrs So-and-so did it...?'

Every Sunday afternoon seemed still to be filled by Tchaikovsky's 'Serenade in C Major'. The sombre tune with impressions of distance ending in the sounds of great events was stuck in Douglas's mind. Either *Radio Nacional* had very few records, all 78 rpm obviously, or that one had simply stayed in the brain's scenery. Tchaikovsky's *Romeo and Juliet* was also lodged in the memory of every weekday evening after school, when the music was used for the curtain in the episodes of an endless radio series of *Tarzan of the Apes*. Tarzan spoke in Spanish. Jane was Juana and she too screamed her warnings of imminent danger in Spanish. The children wanted to write to Radio Splendid to invite Juana to their treehouse in the weeping willow in another corner of the garden. The treehouse was a refuge for conspiracy for the children, for passing on the latest naughty stories and for learning funny songs at which parents pretended to be scandalized: 'Hitler, had only got one ball/Himmler had two but very small...' or milder lyrics, which the girls brought home: 'Lady of Spain I adore you/Pull down your pants, I implore you...'

The smells, like the sounds, were among the closest memories. The builder's ever present odour of cement on his overalls and skin, mixed with *ginebra*, sweat and black tobacco; the school teachers' gentle perfume; parents' Virginia tobacco; all were stored away for occasional recollection with the sounds associated with times gone. Sometimes, at night, Douglas had listened to the music of the first teenage parties which his own children might have attended had they still been with him. The arrangements by Ray Coniff and the piano of Harold Mickey and later Bert Kaempfert's trumpet, could be heard in the stillness of the Ranelagh air.

There were always ('English') visitors at the garden parties which Inés gave. Inés's friends included women who called themselves 'Auntie...' when they spoke to the children. They had faces from photo albums and would paint damp kisses on young cheeks. With the nice people came a host of Douglas's work cronies, infiltrated into the guest list, breathing gin fumes that could have ignited dragons. Douglas had favoured the hard-drinking remittance men – those people without consequence who had been scattered about the empire, always wearing the mournful look of ageing dogs; their fate determined by being the weaker contenders in domestic contests. What sins had they committed? Or were they fugitives from the police? When questioned by the children, parents referred only to family difficulties. Mrs Macfarlane (Auntie Marion) added to the mystery when, in the distended atmosphere of a Sunday evening by the fire, she told her eldest daughter, 'They probably got a maid pregnant.' Getting maids pregnant and probably having to marry them if there was no escape was a pretty terrible social crime in the Anglo-Argentine folklore.

The remittance men always seemed different to other Britons. They led more private lives, received the newspapers from England more regularly, discussed the news content more knowledgeable, recalled their days at public schools or universities in a manner so coloured as to make the local parents' lives seem quite grey. These men had the children in thrall. But it soon became evident, even to the small people, that their guests had nothing in their lives except the past. The men, and sometimes those women with flower-pot ankles and black cotton dresses, were crashing bores after five minutes.

But when spoken to the children had to take their hands out of their pockets and call the men 'Uncle', rather than Mister. Remittance men were generally employed as teachers or in British companies in dead-end jobs as department heads, because they could not be put with the 'Argentine' staff, but could never be made managers. Their failure to achieve promotion was attributed to their past, but also to their present of heavy drinking or to their marriages to Argentine women. As non-English speakers their wives were not well received at morning coffees or jumble sales.

Douglas commiserated with all the hard-drinking drop-outs. Later he would quote Robert Burns, 'A man's a man for a' that', until his children associated the line with the exculpation of alcoholics.

One of the visitors to the garden parties in Ranelagh was a man of rank, well regarded in British community circles if only for his title, but often avoided as life's failures always were in a small group that boasted veneration for commercial success. It was not easy to explain what a baronet was, but Sir Anthony Myles Chomsley Dering was an eleventh baronet. Whenever he was named it was with the qualification that he was a sad case – a tale of heavy debts incurred on grand living by a profligate great grandfather, the eighth baronet; of family files given away by a father resigned to ruin; and of the eleventh baronet's departure from his regiment under a cloud of suspicion after the Second World War.

Tony Dering died in 1958, just before his 57th birthday, and had been remembered over lunch in Buenos Aires by his drinking chums, who sang 'For he's a jolly good fellow'. They had raised their pink gins to his memory, but had been more concerned with the imminent inauguration of the first president elected since the overthrow of General Perón.

Douglas became ill on New Year's Day. He was vomiting blood and his son called on neighbours to help get him to the British Hospital. He returned to Ranelagh within the week, with strict medical orders to avoid excess of any kind.

The house in the corner plot of land looked as it always had, Douglas thought on his return, but there was something different about it. Inés should have been there.

'We expect changes in places where death has marked a cut-off point, but there is no visible change other than that imagined,' he remarked, with no listener but himself. His daughter took his small suitcase into the house. He leaned against the wooden gate, to steady himself. He was feeling very weak.

By the cypress arch over the gate there were shrubs where he had buried the last of his dogs, run over by a van, a Scottish terrier which he had named Scottie during a shortage of originality. The long hedge around the property needed clipping. It always needed clipping. The grand American oak, under which so many garden parties had been held in Inés's days, spread in full leaf over much of the garden. The tall fir in the corner stretched high into the sky.

He walked onto the porch and sat down. How he loved that place. Years ago, he and Inés would sit there and chat until the small hours. Now, minus his wife, he gossiped with his two children until dawn crept up over the hedge.

Eva had cabled to say she had to delay her visit until April. Did he have any travel plans, she asked. Did he not? With his son and daughter he planned to go travelling.

They promised themselves tours around Argentina and then they had to go to Scotland. Douglas wanted to find the Scotland he had lost, and to try to discover the Argentina he had always sought. He told his children that the country's wealth, when he had arrived in 1928, had been unbelievable. 'As in a novel,' he would say, translating from the Spanish cliché. '*De novela*', he would repeat in Spanish. If only Britain had worked harder at keeping strong links, Argentina would still have been so British. Now, everything seemed lost. A demonstrator had thrown an egg at the Duke of Edinburgh during the official visit in March 1962. And that had followed a Foreign Office circular in November 1961 that receptions usually given on the occasion of Her Majesty's birthday would not be held in 1962, as a cost-cutting exercise. Britain was the laughing stock of the Latin American diplomatic circuit.

The world situation was debated and decided on in that porch. They would go to Cuba, where Fidel Castro had said agricultural consultants were needed to grow oranges on the Isle of Pines. 'Might as well make a name for myself knowing something useful; be important somewhere for a change... Be nice some day to be thought of as useful,' Douglas mused.

And they would also go to British Guiana, which nobody really remembered as part of South America and which was now led by a dentist called Cheddi Jagan.

Their conversation during those warm nights of summer 1963 meandered through an interminable catalogue of topics. It was agreed, for example, by the men, that the most beautiful shape in the world was the female breast and the most ingenious of human accessories were a man's testicles. 'Any higher up and they would be ground to paste in any close contact.' Douglas held out an open hand, imagining both.

Douglas died on 13 March 1963 at the British Hospital. For a week before his end he had vomited his life out at home. His vomit was in torrents of blood, which dried on every lamp switch, and on every door handle that his bloodied fingers had touched as he raced to reach the bath or the toilet bowl, there to deposit his liquid bowels, the darker more solid pieces being traces of his liver which had begun to die before him.

Suddenly, a life of adventure, inconformity and private tragedy was over.

He died one week short of the end of summer.

Very softly now, so as not to disturb the stillness, Douglas, *adios*; farewell, Ranelagh, goodbye Buenos Aires.

# Acknowledgements

Goodbye Buenos Aires was written in part in the winter of 1994, at Wolfson College, University of Cambridge, to whose President I am grateful. I am indebted to the Press Fellowship, Bill Kirkman and John Naughton.

I would like to express my gratitude for the gracious permission of Her Majesty The Queen for use of material at the Royal Archives, at Windsor.

There are so many people I want to thank. First, there is Joanne Graham-Yooll, my sister. I am grateful to Mrs Lavender McMillan for permission to quote from Derek Drabble's book *Passenger Ticket*; to Mrs Laura Huxley and the Hogarth Press for permission to consult *Beyond the Bay of Mexique*; to David Higham Associates for permission to use Philip Guedalla's *Argentine Tango*; to Alan Ross and *London Magazine* for use of the letters of Gordon Meyer; to Judy Evans for reference to George Mikes's *Tango: A Solo Across South America*; to the Lawrence Durrell Estate; the Christopher Isherwood Estate; and the Public Records Office at Kew. The staff at the Newspaper Library at Colindale were always very helpful.

Many people gave of their time and information. Among them are James Smart, for the story of the family clothiers; Arturo J. Pruden for notes on A.G. Pruden Cia.; James Wright, for the notes on Bazaar Wright S.A.; Dr Bartolomé Mitre and Nicolás Cócaro (1926-94), of *La Nación*; the managers at Lloyds Bank, Buenos Aires; William Shand (1903-97), Ana Ezcurra de Ardiles, Arthur Edbrooke, David Mackern; María Luisa Rivera Antonini at the Post Office in Buenos Aires, for notes on Antoine de Saint-Exupery.

A special thank you to Dr Rafael Manovil, for details about Lisandro de la Torre, and politics in the 1930s, and to Dr Rodolfo Terragno, for his political views. Thank you to Jorge Gunn; and to Nicholas Tozer, Michael Soltys and Betty Lombardo, at the *Buenos Aires Herald*; and to Roberto T Alemann, of the *Argentinisches Tageblatt*; to the late Norman W. Ferguson, in Mendoza; to Janet Dickinson, for memories of her father, Barney Dickinson, in San Martín de los Andes; to Nora Mackinnon, in Esquel; Natalie Goodhall, in Ushuaia; Harold Mickey, in Winston-Salem; and especially to Michael Haag and Mary Hadkinson, for the Argentine letters of Lawrence Durrell; to Charles A. Lockwood, in Punta del Este; Sir Robert Jackson BT, E.V. Vines and Val Isaacs, at the British Embassy, Montevideo; Mr H. Winston Willans, of the British-Uruguayan Chamber of Commerce, who found articles written by Douglas Graham-Yooll; to Professor Hans Wysling, and R. Hintermann, at the Thomas-Mann-Archiv, Zurich, for information on María Mann; to Jonathan Callund, of the *Sociedad Anglo-Chilena*, in Santiago; V.J. Bensusan, in Sao Paulo; Donald I. Griffis, at the *Peruvian Times*, in Lima, for information on the English-language press in Peru; and Philip D. Somerveil, for notes on the history of the English-language press in Chile; Nigel P. Parkinson, at the British Chamber of Commerce, in Mexico; Mrs Virginia Young, at the British and Commonwealth Society of Mexico.

In London, I would like to thank Peter Preston, then editor, and Campbell Page, Martin Woollacott and Richard Gott on the foreign desk at *The Guardian*, where I was employed for a few years (1977-1984). They helped me to understand the English, as explained in *Point of Arrival* (Pluto). David Twiston Davies, Frank Taylor, Peter Eastwood were helpful friends at *The Daily Telegraph*, where I spent some happy times (1971-1977). And I will never forget the support received from Jimmy Burns (of the *Financial Times*) and Kidge, with John Fernandes and María Laura Avignolo.

My gratitude to Mary Niven, at the British Architectural Library; Dr John Hemming, director, Royal Geographical Society; Jill Quaife, of the British Uruguayan Society in England; S.W. Johnson, for notes on the history of the Vestey companies; Robin Rumboll, honorary treasurer at the Jersey Wildlife Preservation trust; Brian McGrath, assistant to HRH the Duke of Edinburgh; Kirsten Kraglund, at the *Goethe Institut Library*; W. Abbey, of the Institute for German Studies, University of London; Brenda Cluer, archivist, Grampian Regional Council; Peter Grant, city librarian, Aberdeen; Mrs R.M. Hart, Aberdeen University Library; Nadene Hansen, company archivist at Harrods, Neil Burton, at the Greater London Council Historic Buildings Division; Dorothy E. Welch, at the South American Missionary Society library.

Thanks also to the Earl of Wemyss and March, for notes on Martín Güemes; the Rt Hon Jean Lady Polwarth, for information on R. B. Cunningham Graham; the late George Gibson, Barney Miller OBE, and Ralph Emery, at the Anglo-Argentine Society; Sir Vivian Fuchs; Nigel Nicholson, for details on Lionel Sackville West; Eduardo Crawley, Biba McLellan, Shirley Currie, Andrew della Casa, Jean Lacey, Lita Ruccio, Celia Szusterman, Olwen Fordham, Miss Helen Moeller, Judith Sheppard, Nigel Brown; Gerladine Petley and Nicholas Dolman, in 1982 on the foreign desk at *The Guardian*; David Joy, in 1982 at the (closed) British Embassy in Buenos Aires; Roberto Cox, of the *Buenos Aires Herald*; S.A. Bagley, Miss C. Sadler, Mrs F.L. Dawson, Reginald Wood, Nina and Moris Farhi and Hugh O'Shaughnessy; and thanks to John Lucas, at Shoestring Press, who published the first edition.

Finally, a very big thank you, for their patience, to Micaela Isabel Meyer Graham-Yooll, to Inés Graham-Yooll and Jonathan Bradbury, to Luis Graham-Yooll and Isabel Graham-Yooll and Simon Smith.

## About the Author

Andrew Graham-Yooll was born in Buenos Aires in 1944. He was the editor in chief of the English-language *Buenos Aires Herald* up to 2007. He formerly worked for the *Daily Telegraph* and the *Guardian*, in London, and was the editor of *Index on Censorship*. Among his many books are *A State of Fear*, *The Forgotten Colony: A History of the English-Speaking People in Argentina* and *Imperial Skirmishes*. His most recent book, *Who do you think you are?* is an essay on identity and was published in London in 2011.

# ELAND

61 Exmouth Market, London EC1R 4QL
Email: info@travelbooks.co.uk

Eland was started in 1982 to revive great travel books
that had fallen out of print. Although the list has diversified
into biography and fiction, it is united by a quest to define the
spirit of place. These are books for travellers, and for readers who aspire
to explore the world but who are also content to travel in their own
minds. Eland books open out our understanding of other cultures,
interpret the unknown and reveal different environments as well as
celebrating the humour and occasional horrors of travel. We take
immense trouble to select only the most readable books and therefore
many readers collect the entire series.

You will find a very brief description of our books on the
following pages. Extracts from each and every one of them can be
read on our website, at www.travelbooks.co.uk. If you would
like a free copy of our catalogue, please email
or write to us (details above).

# ELAND

'One of the very best travel lists' WILLIAM DALRYMPLE

**Memoirs of a Bengal Civilian**
JOHN BEAMES
*Sketches of nineteenth-century India*
*painted with the richness of Dickens*

**Jigsaw**
SYBILLE BEDFORD
*An intensely remembered autobiographical*
*novel about an inter-war childhood*

**A Visit to Don Otavio**
SYBILLE BEDFORD
*The hell of travel and the Eden of arrival*
*in post-war Mexico*

**Journey into the Mind's Eye**
LESLEY BLANCH
*An obsessive love affair with Russia and*
*one particular Russian*

**The Way of the World**
NICOLAS BOUVIER
*Two men in a car from Serbia to*
*Afghanistan.*

**The Devil Drives**
FAWN BRODIE
*Biography of Sir Richard Burton,*
*explorer, linguist and pornographer*

**Turkish Letters**
OGIER DE BUSBECQ
*Eyewitness history at its best:*
*Istanbul during the reign of Suleyman*
*the Magnificent*

**My Early Life**
WINSTON CHURCHILL
*From North-West Frontier to Boer War*
*by the age of twenty-five*

**Sicily: through writers' eyes**
ED. HORATIO CLARE
*Guidebooks for the mind: a selection*
*of the best travel writing on Sicily*

**A Square of Sky**
JANINA DAVID
*A Jewish childhood in the Warsaw*
*ghetto and hiding from the Nazis*

**Chantemesle**
ROBIN FEDDEN
*A lyrical evocation of childhood*
*in Normandy*

**Croatia: through writers' eyes**
ED. FRANKOPAN, GOODING & LAVINGTON
*Guidebooks for the mind: a selection*
*of the best travel writing on Croatia*

**Travels with Myself and Another**
MARTHA GELLHORN
*Five journeys from hell by a great*
*war correspondent*

**The Weather in Africa**
MARTHA GELLHORN
*Three novellas set amongst the*
*white settlers of East Africa*

**The Last Leopard**
DAVID GILMOUR
*The biography of Giuseppe di Lampedusa,*
*author of* The Leopard

**Walled Gardens**
ANNABEL GOFF
*An Anglo-Irish childhood*

**Africa Dances**
GEOFFREY GORER
*The magic of indigenous culture*
*and the banality of colonisation*

**Cinema Eden**
JUAN GOYTISOLO
*Essays from the Muslim*
*Mediterranean*

**A State of Fear**
ANDREW GRAHAM-YOOLL
*A journalist witnesses Argentina's*
*nightmare in the 1970s*

**Warriors**
GERALD HANLEY
*Life and death among the Somalis*

**Morocco That Was**
WALTER HARRIS
*All the cruelty, fascination and*
*humour of a pre-modern kingdom*